MASQUERADE

MASQUERADE
Treason, the Holocaust, and an Irish Impostor

Mark M. Hull *and* Vera Moynes

University of Oklahoma Press : Norman

Library of Congress Cataloging-in-Publication Data

Names: Hull, Mark M., 1962 – author. | Moynes, Vera, 1970 – author.
Title: Masquerade : treason, the Holocaust, and an Irish impostor / Mark M. Hull and Vera Moynes.
Description: Norman : University of Oklahoma Press, [2017] | Includes bibliographical references and index.
Identifiers: LCCN 2016036175 | ISBN 978-0-8061-5634-7 (hardcover : alk. paper) | ISBN 978-0-8061-5718-4 (pbk. : alk. paper)
Subjects: LCSH: O'Mara, Róisín. | Authors, Irish—Biography. | Irish—Germany—Biography. | Irish—Germany—History—20th century. | National socialism—Influence.
Classification: LCC DA965.O564 H85 2017 | DDC 305.8916/2043092 [B] —dc23
LC record available at https://lccn.loc.gov/2016036175

The paper in this book meets the guidelines for permanence and durability of the Committee on Production Guidelines for Book Longevity of the Council on Library Resources, Inc. ∞

Copyright © 2017 by the University of Oklahoma Press, Norman, Publishing Division of the University. Manufactured in the U.S.A.

All rights reserved. No part of this publication may be reproduced, stored in a retrieval system, or transmitted, in any form or by any means, electronic, mechanical, photocopying, recording, or otherwise—except as permitted under Section 107 or 108 of the United States Copyright Act—without the prior written permission of the University of Oklahoma Press. To request permission to reproduce selections from this book, write to Permissions, University of Oklahoma Press, 2800 Venture Drive, Norman, OK 73069, or email rights.oupress@ou.edu.

Contents

List of Illustrations vii
Acknowledgments ix

Introduction 3
1. Point of Origin 10
2. Little Girl Lost 13
3. Rosaleen Abroad 20
4. Der Krieg 37
5. Francis Stuart 41
6. Best Laid Plans 51
7. Life in the Heart of the Reich 58
8. Publishing in Berlin: *Irische Freiheitskämpfer* and a Government Memorandum 70
9. Radio Star 76
10. Collapse 92
11. Defense of the Realm 95
12. 1945 to 1977: The Theater, a Playschool, and a Museum in the West 102
13. Letters from Europe, 1977–1982, and *In Search of Irish Saints* 113
14. Accessory after the Fact 128
Conclusion 146

Contents

Notes   155
Bibliography   183
Index   195

Illustrations

Jean Muir at the time of her marriage to Ian Hamilton   60
Sir Ian and Lady Hamilton   61
The Hamilton Clan, 1938   62
Harry Knight and Lady Hamilton, early 1930s   63
Sir Ian Hamilton and Adolf Hitler   64
Hamilton and Hitler in Berchtesgaden   64
Hamilton and Hitler at lunch   65
Phyllis "Rosaleen" James as she appeared on MI5's
   "Renegades" list   66
The building that housed the Inishmaan museum   67
Rosaleen James looks on as Irish Government Minister
   Tom O'Donnell opens the Inishmaan museum   67
Cover of *Who Is She Outside? Róisín's Memoirs*   68
Cover of *At Home and Abroad, Memoirs 2*   69

Acknowledgments

It is almost impossible to list the many people who have so generously given their time and material to this project, but here's an attempt: Kate O'Brien and the staff of the Liddell Hart Centre for Military Archives at King's College London—they were invariably intelligent, knowledgeable, helpful, professional, and cheerful; Sir Ian Kershaw; Dr. John Koegel; Professor Eunan O'Halpin; Geoffrey Elborn; my old friend, Commandant (ret.) Victor Laing, formerly at the Irish Military Archives (Victor knows more about the secretive world of Irish history than anyone else); Dr. David O'Donoghue, a generous historian and friend; David Pryce-Jones; Michelle Goodman, City of Westminster Archives Centre; Dr. Deborah Lipstadt, Emory University; Dr. Richard Spence, University of Idaho; Dr. Phil Tomaselli; Dr. Roderich Jakobi; Dr. Penny Steinbach; Dr. William Kaut, Command and General Staff College, Fort Leavenworth; Dr. Nicholas Murray, Naval War College; Dr. Greg Hospodor; the ever-helpful people at the National Archives in Kew; my parents Don and Jane Hull, and, of course, Heidi Williams.

Vera is very grateful for the testimonials of Máire Phaidí Uí Mhaol Chonaire and Noirín Uí Ghoill, Aran Islands, Co. Galway; and Aonghus Ó hAonghusa, Dublin, regarding Ursula James's work in Galway and on the island of Inishmaan. For contacts, thanks to 'Scéal Aniar,' Raidió na Gaeltachta. Míle buíochas do Phádraig Ó Snodaigh, Coiscéim! Thanks also to library and archives staff and to colleagues, friends, and others who shared material or provided feedback: Joseph Canning, Cardinal Ó Fiaich Memorial Library and Archives; Monica Crump, James Hardiman Library, Galway; Andreas Dan, Deutsches Rundfunkarchiv,

Acknowledgments

Frankfurt am Main; Kevin Kiely; Lisa Dolan and colleagues, Irish Military Archives, Dublin; Joachim Fischer, University of Limerick; Éamonn Jordan, An Tor, Co. Donegal; Tom Kenny, Galway; Dr. Peter Kramml, Amtsleiter, Stadtarchiv Salzburg; Peadar Mac Fhlannchadha, Conradh na Gaeilge, Galway; Swenja Preuss, Fritz Rémond Theater im Zoo, Frankfurt am Main; and Ian Lee, Dublin. Thanks also to an Irish friend who advised against publication—I listened, but thought eventually the story was worth telling.

Note on Translations

Most of James's own writings central for this study—her memoirs, newspaper column, and correspondence—were written in Irish, as were most items reviewing her work in the press. All translations offered here are by the authors.

MASQUERADE

Introduction

Rosaleen James (Róisín Ní Mheara) is an enigma. To some, she is "one of the great heroes of Ireland,"[1] to others "a strikingly beautiful Irish colleen"[2] and "an apostle of Irish culture."[3] The story is of an Irish girl adopted and raised by one of the most prestigious families in England, who lived in Germany during the rise and fall of Hitler's National Socialist state but never ceased working for Ireland and the Irish. She survived to bear grim witness to the hidden truth behind the lies and misconceptions of the Second World War. In recent times, she has been the recipient of grants from the Irish government because of her extensive scholarly pursuits, and is a recognized expert on the medieval travels of Irish missionaries on the European continent, in addition to being a tireless champion of her native language, Irish. She has devoted her life to this and other scholarly causes.[4]

Some of that is true. Most of it is not.

In the creation of this myth, she went by many names: Phyllis Ursula James, Rosaleen James, Nora O'Mara, and—most recently—Róisín Ní Mheara. She was English, not Irish. She volunteered to work for National Socialist Germany and against Britain during a time of war. For the last seventy years of her life she progressively reinvented herself as Irish, and along the way fooled the genuine Irish who should have known better. Her political and personal "testament" of World War II justified the persecution of the Jews and pointed the finger of responsibility for carnage at the Allied nations. In her version, self-defense motivated the German attack on Poland; British interference prevented Hitler's peaceful and logical "solution" to the Jewish problem; Allied behind-the-scenes machinations destroyed Germany's fervent desire to live in peace with its neighbours; and Winston Churchill, not Adolf Hitler, was the true war criminal.

For the most part, James lived her life on the periphery of major events. To the small group of historians and researchers who know her name at all, she is remembered as an Irish national in wartime Berlin who worked with Hermann Görtz, a German military intelligence officer who parachuted into Ireland in 1940. She was also a sometime co-worker of John O'Reilly, the smooth-talking Irish potato-picker on the Channel Islands who persuaded the SS intelligence service into returning him to Éire.

Her name resurfaced in documents at the British National Archives. Hidden away in the file containing the British Security Service (MI5) debriefing of a German intelligence supervisor named Kurt Haller, the name Nora O'Mara appeared again, but this time there was something new: O'Mara was given as an alias, and the document revealed her actual name as Phyllis James. Further search of the MI5 records led to some interesting discoveries, the most important of which was that the investigative file on her no longer exists: it was ordered destroyed by someone in the British government.

Piecing together Rosaleen James's story must therefore proceed from other sources—family papers, statements of others who knew her in wartime Germany, mentions of her in the intelligence files of the United Kingdom, Ireland, and Germany—but the most critical reference points are her own words. What she did with them is extraordinary. In what can only be seen as a deliberate, decades-long plan, Rosaleen James undertook a total metamorphosis during and subsequent to World War II. Starting as an abandoned English child, she adopted a very complicated disguise as an Irish person. The process was not an entirely smooth transition. In the early stages, she benefited from being around people who could not distinguish, and perhaps did not care to distinguish, a genuine Irish person from someone claiming to be Irish. She fudged the inconvenient details in her background; she obviously read a great deal, put in many years of dedicated study, traveled extensively in Ireland, threw herself into Irish-centric causes, and became fluent in what can be a challenging second language, Irish Gaelic. So much of this would be admirable if done with another intent—learning about another culture, perhaps, or

Introduction

advancing scholarship—but it becomes something else when the objective is to assume the ethnic identity of the culture under study. To even begin comprehending the complex motives of Rosaleen James, it is necessary to examine the evidence.

The centerpiece of that examination is her autobiography, *Cé hÍ Seo Amuigh?* It is an interesting mix of first-hand account (with carefully selected vignettes, to be sure), philosophy, and social commentary. It was published exclusively in Irish. Had an English language version been available at the time, it would almost certainly have attracted more critical attention; perhaps that was the plan. It is not an easy book to categorize, but there are a few clear narrative themes. Perhaps the most problematic and deceptive aspect is the retrojected veneer of Irish identity. In instance after instance, the "we Irish" refrain not-so-subtly attempts to convince the unsuspecting reader that the author was and is one of them—an Irish person—and that her life events should properly be viewed through that filter. This is a false construct from start to finish.

Following its practice of awarding grants to works published in Irish Gaelic, the Irish government was caught flat-footed in 1993 when the spotlight of public attention was drawn to some of the book's more obvious pro-Nazi and anti-Semitic statements, of which there are a great many.[5] For just a brief moment, there was debate among the Irish-speaking community—without the larger world paying any attention at all—between those few who read and were shocked, those who read and were congratulatory, and those who read and did not react at all. How this happened—that any reviewer would choose to praise the skillful use of idiomatic Irish or allegiance to Irish nationalism and yet ignore her Holocaust denial—more than seventy years after evidence for the genocide became impossible to deny is an important part of this story and one which defies easy explanation.

As morally reprehensible as some of James's statements are, or even the degree to which they radically diverge from established historical facts, the cumulative impact is even greater. She lived through one of the most significant events of the modern era, and interacted, at least to some degree, with key people at important moments. However, when confronted by the almost unimaginable crimes committed under the Third Reich, she chose to identify with the perpetrators instead of the victims. And her viewpoint did not evolve over time as she became better informed; this was not a case where she subsequently adopted a repentant mind-set. She instead continued to spill forth doctrinaire National Socialist ideology for the next seven decades. The Nuremberg and Eichmann trials did not alter her warped sense of history; she has been entirely unaffected by rational evidence—even the mountain of evidence preserved by the Nazi war criminals themselves—or historical fact. Rosaleen James was neither the first nor the most significant British citizen to work for Hitler; neither is she the most prominent person to deny the Holocaust.[6] Her published work, however, is the first unabashedly pro-fascist work to receive, albeit indirectly, a government grant.

Holocaust denial, though, is only one element of a complicated web. Using the pseudonym Nora O'Mara, she made radio broadcasts for Hitler during the German invasion of Poland in 1939, and later took to the airwaves in service of a propaganda campaign aimed at Ireland, as part of the larger, concerted radio offensive against Germany's enemies and compliant neutrals.[7] She had direct contact with and assisted at least two German agents who parachuted into Ireland. Among the various agencies of German intelligence, she passed herself off as an Irish resource, despite the fact that her only prewar contact with the country consisted of a weeklong visit in 1937. As a British citizen voluntarily working to advance the enemy's cause in time of war, she stepped into a new arena: high treason. Others received the death penalty for similar offenses.

In addition to her curious attachment to Ireland, it is clear that James developed a strong identification with National Socialist Germany.[8] In short, she followed a continuing pattern of attraction to places, cultures, and ideas that were radically different from her own background, concealing what she was and gravitating to the most radical alternative she could find. Viewed in isolation, there is nothing inherently wrong or, perhaps, psychologically dangerous in this. However, she went much further. She demonstrated not just affection for or attraction to foreign places and people, but a conscious effort to put on a masquerade, to convince the world at large that she was that "other." Again, had this been the only issue, her behavior could be viewed as bizarre but not necessarily criminal or amoral. But she went further.

So many contradictions! Some of them can be traced to her childhood. Parented by elderly people who had their own emotional and psychological issues, James was exposed to an atmosphere of pro-German

Introduction

appeasement and partially educated in German boarding schools with a National Socialist curriculum. Despite being raised with every material advantage—or perhaps because of that—she rejected the values of her upbringing unless temporary retreat to them was necessary to maintain her desired identity. This dramatic high-wire act was not simple to maintain; Rosaleen James was both intelligent and articulate, but she nonetheless held and shared beliefs that were utterly reprehensible, which makes it all the more disturbing that literary figures, government officials, and beloved religious leaders have praised her.

From the start of this investigation, we earnestly wished to let Rosaleen James (more recently using the name Ní Mheara) clarify the points at issue beyond what she published in the autobiographical works *Cé hÍ Seo Amuigh?* (Who Is She Outside?) and *I gCéin is i gCóngar* (At Home and Abroad). Historical evidence is open to interpretation; it is often incomplete, more often ambiguous, and it is a simple matter to misunderstand or emphasize certain aspects without a sense of proportionality or fairness. We made initial contact through James's son, Dr. Roderich Jakobi, and were initially hopeful that James herself would speak to us in person or perhaps respond in writing to questions if an in-person interview was impossible or unwanted. She declined, with her son lastly citing her ill health. (James died in 2013.) We then asked if family members would be willing to assist in telling James's story (and thereby have the opportunity to address the record and interpretation). There was no reply at all. Absent further input in terms of testimony or interpretation from Rosaleen James or her family, the records alone must speak. We have tried to allow them speak in a way that serves the truth.

The translated title of her autobiography can be rendered in English as "Who is she outside?"[9] That question—who is this person, really—is what this work will attempt to answer. But after a lifetime of half-truths and shadows, of half-truths and outright deception, it is not a straight path. As this narrative will show, there are a great many secrets along the way.

A Note about Irish

As one might expect, given the topic, there are a few Irish Gaelic words in here. While the language origins are ancient, the modern Irish language is alive and well. The Irish language had suffered a huge blow during the Great Famine (mid-nineteenth century); by the twentieth century it was seldom the spoken medium of everyday life, other than in designated areas in the west and south of the island known as the Gaeltacht. A small handful of scholars (many of whom were German and Scandinavian) studied it, but English had become the preferred spoken language for most people in Ireland. However, to some, English retained a negative connotation as a hated vestige of a foreign conqueror and occupier.

The situation slowly began to change in the 1880s and 1890s with the Gaelic Revival movement. Coincident with the growth of Irish nationalism during the same period, the language itself became a de rigueur element of identity and cultural discovery, and soon thereafter a badge of membership distinguishing those who were true believers from those who were not. It further acted as a hidden-in-plain-sight secret means of communication for the initiated. Irish has a rich heritage going back to prehistory, and reviving the language was a powerful way of connecting to that cultural legacy.

With the establishment of the Irish Free State and later the Republic of Ireland, Irish became a required subject in primary and secondary school curricula, and it is still required today alongside the other official language, English.[10] The social, nationalist, cultural, and political implications of Irish are still quite strong. One clear indication of this occurs when people change their names from the Anglicized form to what they believe, rightly or wrongly, to be an Irish-Gaelic equivalent. To do so makes an unmistakable cultural and political statement, but often does so at the expense of comprehension by those outside the small circle of Ireland.[11]

To a native English speaker, Irish spelling often features consonant combinations and accent marks that are next to impossible to pronounce upon first seeing them. A different, more specific intent manifests when it comes to personal and family names. Typically, Irish nomenclature contains "Mac" or "O" prefixes, both of which denote ancestry; "Mac" is the modern Irish word for son. As an example, take the surname McVeigh, which is the Anglicized version. The Irish Gaelic version would be Mac an Bheatha (pron. "Mac-an-vaha"). Returning to the Irish Gaelic form of one's name, as James's friend Proinsias Mac an Bheatha did (only for his writings, not his civil servant post),[12] is the outward trapping of something

Introduction

much more significant: Irishness. The language here is a critical aspect of that identity. Opting to change a name's Anglicized form—the colonizers' form—back to a truer spelling says a lot about the person doing the changing: what they believe, and what they want others to understand about them. When a parent bestows the peculiarly Gaelic Christian name "Medb" (pron. "Maeve") on a child, the reason has nothing to do with allowing the bearer of this name to get along in the wider, non-Irish speaking world. Quite the contrary. It is instead a badge of belonging, and the fact that outsiders cannot readily pronounce it by sight conveys an insular advantage. James's continual adoption of more Irish-sounding surnames is done for the same reason—an attempt to belong and associate herself with the Irish—but is much less straightforward, as will be seen. Her notion of Irishness, real and imaginary, is central to this story, and there will be points along the path where language and identity intersect in unexpected ways.

1

Point of Origin

As with most people, Rosaleen James is certainly a product of her family, upbringing, and experiences. That overly broad statement seems simple enough, but in her case it is anything but. Her confusion and displacement began early and are directly tied to the peculiar circumstances of one of Britain's best known, most experienced military figures: General Sir Ian Standish Montieth Hamilton. His own journey, from lionized military hero to pro-German political pariah, cannot help but have had an effect on an already insecure young girl.

Ian Hamilton was born in 1853 to Colonel Christian and Corinna Hamilton. Christian Hamilton was the commander of the 92nd Regiment of Foot (later merged with the 75th Regiment of Foot to become the Gordon Highlanders), and Corinna was descended from a prominent lineage as the daughter of John Vereker, third Viscount Gort. Following an education at Cheam (Surrey) and Wellington College, Ian Hamilton attended the Royal Military Academy Sandhurst in 1870, finishing in 1871 in time to briefly join the Suffolk Regiment before being transferred to his father's old regiment in India, arriving just in time to take part in the Second Anglo-Afghan War. His unit was then assigned to the Cape Colony and participated in the First Boer War (1880–81), where he was wounded at the Battle of Majuba. In quick succession, Hamilton then took part in the Nile expedition (1884–85), and served in Burma (1886–87) and Bengal (1890–93), where he earned the Distinguished Service Order (DSO) and promotion to colonel. He followed this with more active service in India: Chitral Expedition (1895), deputy Quartermaster General (1895–98), and commander of the 3rd Brigade in the Tirah

Point of Origin

Campaign of 1897–98. In this era of great imperial expansion and "small wars," Hamilton acquired a breadth of experience in almost every corner of the globe.

In the midst of all this, Hamilton met and married Jean Muir, daughter of Sir John Muir, a successful Glasgow businessman. Jean was likewise intelligent and socially adept, and the couple seemed a perfect society match from the moment of their marriage in 1887.[1] The union produced no children, which might have initially been due to Hamilton's frequent absences and the rapid pace of his military career, although other possible reasons for this surfaced later.

Hamilton first catapulted into the national spotlight during the Second Anglo-Boer War (1899–1902). Moving from the post of acting adjutant general to the Natal Field Force, he became an active combat commander and fought in the Battle of Wagon Hill at Ladysmith and later distinguished himself at Diamond Hill. Hamilton was knighted in 1902, promoted to major-general, received the Knight Commander of the Order of the Bath, and became chief of staff to Field Marshal Lord Horatio Kitchener. Remaining in South Africa, he led his force from Bloemfontein to Pretoria, fighting ten major engagements with Boer forces.[2]

During the postwar period, Hamilton served as both military secretary at the War Office and later as quartermaster-general. Upon the outbreak of the Russo-Japanese War in 1904, he lobbied for the position of military observer with the Japanese army, where his analysis of this first major "modern" war was widely praised. In 1907 Hamilton was promoted to full general and named adjutant general, and was later chosen above all others to take the Mediterranean command, which soon led to the post of inspector-general of all oversea forces. His star was on the rise. After Kitchener and Field Marshal Lord Frederick Roberts, Hamilton was widely viewed as the most promising and knowledgeable senior officer in the British Army.

When global war erupted in August 1914, Hamilton assumed command of the Central Force, responsible for all aspects of home defense. He was briefly considered to relieve General Sir John French as commander of the British Expeditionary Force (BEF) in France. By early 1915, the combination of Hamilton's experience, personal bravery, intelligence, and charm all but ensured that he would be next in line for the most senior military post in Britain.[3] Gallipoli changed that.

Masquerade

After a lifetime of exceptional service, it is ironic that the Dardanelles campaign of 1915–16 should define Sir Ian Hamilton in history. Unexpected enemy defenses (mines and shore-based artillery) prevented the combined British-French fleet from controlling their two intermediate objectives, the Dardanelles and Bosporus, and reaching their ultimate prize: Istanbul. As commander of the Mediterranean Expeditionary Force, Hamilton was charged with implementing a tactical solution. His plan called for unopposed beach landings followed by a short, decisive land action to remove Turkish artillery protecting the strait, thereby allowing Allied forces to proceed once the minefields were cleared.

The Gallipoli operation was instead an unmitigated and highly public disaster, and Hamilton's conduct there—mostly due to repeated failures to supervise and correct his subordinates' inaction—effectively ended his military career. A few key decisions on the unforgiving Turkish coast turned Hamilton into the object of hushed whispers. He was recalled in 1916, awarded the Knight Grand Cross of St. Michael and St. George, and never again given an active assignment. He quietly retired in 1920. He soon became a founding member of the British Legion, and devoted his time and considerable intellectual energies to writing and speaking. Now approaching age 70, he also had two children to raise, a project he resisted from its inception.

2

Little Girl Lost

It is appropriate that, like so much in her own narrative, the true story of Rosaleen James's origins is contradictory and uncertain.

In James's telling, she was a war orphan, born in 1918. Her father, an Irishman in the British Army, had been killed in Flanders, and her ill mother was unable to take proper care of her.[1] Phyllis Holman, her godmother, thereupon took her to the London home of Sir Ian and Lady Hamilton, where Holman had been invited to sing at a reception for the British Legion. (Sir Ian was then the president of the organization.) Lady Hamilton was overwhelmed by the child's "huge, sad Irish eyes" and sympathetic to her circumstances. She decided to foster the infant, who eventually came to be adopted by Sir Ian and Lady Hamilton.[2]

That version is not true. Both James's pedigree and the eventual adoption process, if it happened at all, were anything but straightforward. Her father's identity and ethnicity present the first problem. James's birth certificate states that she was born on 2 July 1918 at 4 St. Paul's Avenue, London. Her birth name was Phyllis Ursula James, with her mother listed as Nora James, "a ladies maid (domestic) of 131 Gloucester Terrace, Hyde Park W." The father's name is conspicuously absent.[3]

Rather than being a singer or friend of the family, Phyllis Holman was the matron of an orphanage located at 3 Hyde Park Square.[4] According to Lady Hamilton's diary, Nora James had a baby out of wedlock, and Holman offered the child to Lady Hamilton to foster, with the goal of eventual adoption. The diary goes on to say that the biological father had been injured in a train bombing, had suffered brain damage, and was committed to a mental asylum.[5] He was never named. Lady Hamilton first saw the child on 13 July, eleven days after the child's birth—not, as in James's telling, at the reception for the British Legion (which was not founded until 1921).[6] In the interval, according to Lady Hamilton, the child had already been christened as Phyllis Ursula, after Phyllis Holman, but owing to her sentimental attachment to Roger Casement and Irish Home Rule, Lady Hamilton determined to call the child "Rosaleen," after the James Mangan poem "Dark Rosaleen."[7]

There is also a more disturbing version. In a consular report to the MI5 report dated 7 May 1945, Rosaleen James is "said to be the natural daughter of Sir Ian Hamilton and to have been adopted by the late Lady Hamilton."[8] The birth certificate address given for Nora James is 131 Gloucester Terrace, Hyde Park West, just a short stroll from the Hamilton home at 1 Hyde Park Gardens.[9] During the late nineteenth and early twentieth centuries, it was common practice to omit the father's name on a birth certificate in cases of domestic situations where the servant mother's employer was the biological father.[10] In the absence of James's file, it is impossible to know much for certain other than that her later version was untrue and she knew it.

For Lady Hamilton, 1918 was already an auspicious year in terms of her family situation. The precise nature of her marital relationship with Sir Ian is difficult to categorize. As early as 1904 she had written, "More and more clearly do I see that the feeling of love is something quite apart from brutal sexual passion which is the sacrilege and desecration of love."[11] This comment is echoed by other similar statements, and evidently at least one aspect of Sir Ian and Lady Hamilton's relationship was missing. Despite that—or perhaps because of that—Lady Hamilton wanted a child of her own without any physical complications. Sir Ian was less enthusiastic ["Ian is a mystery, I thought he wanted a child, but since I summoned up my courage to tell him I wanted it so much it seems to have created an impassable barrier between us."][12] Weirdly, Jean admitted to herself that "neither Edie [a friend of hers] or I much like babies."[13] It might be more accurate to say that Jean strongly desired a child in the abstract, but the reality of one proved to be more than she was able to fully comprehend. By 1918, Jean was 57, set in her ways, in a comfortable but not intimate relationship with a difficult older husband, and with attitudes that were in many ways out of sync with the times in which she lived. Her modestly pleasant looks had long since faded, and it was obvious that there was more time behind than ahead.

Little Girl Lost

Sir Ian Hamilton's attitude toward the new family member is even more difficult to discern, but it seems clear, at least from Lady Hamilton's diary and the later letters between the Hamiltons and Rosaleen, that he was largely indifferent.[14] In the wake of Gallipoli, his world was taken up by endless round of social engagements, writing, and strengthening ties among former servicemen. The idea of a growing family, particularly at his age, was not an attractive prospect.

In June 1918 and before Rosaleen's arrival, Jean had realized her dream of nonbiological motherhood without Sir Ian's participation. A sixteen-month-old boy was found abandoned at the door of the Paddington Crèche with only a note reading, "Harry." He went unclaimed for three months, at which time Jean, who was the honorary president of the Crèche, agreed to foster him. One of the Hamilton servants, Annie Woodger, was charged with nursing and feeding Harry, who soon settled into his new life. The child promptly named Sir Ian—who would have nothing to do with him initially—as "Boye," even as Rosaleen and Harry would always refer to Lady Hamilton as "Guardie" [guardian].[15]

To the Hamiltons, however, the fact of having fostered children was a different thing altogether from raising them.[16] For the first two years of her life, Rosaleen lived apart from the Hamiltons at Hill Martin, cared for by a Nurse White. Lady Hamilton visited occasionally and received reports, but took no active part in raising the children. Only in September 1920 did Rosaleen, now two, join the family at the Hamilton home, Lullenden.[17] Lady Hamilton remarked, "She is a rather sad little girl but very sweet when she smiles."[18]

The curious nature of Lady Hamilton's diary entries reveals a continuing emotional mismatch. She talks about both children as one would pets, but seems perplexed and hurt when the children's behavior deviates from her narrow expectations. On the occasion of Rosaleen's fourth birthday in 1922, the child was smiling and delighted by presents—as anyone but Lady Hamilton would find natural: "I saw this excitement was not for me . . . which cut me to the heart and I felt dreary . . . one wants their spontaneous love and delight."[19] She returned often to the trough of self-pity, and frequently interpreted normal child behavior as an affront. This is especially odd considering the subject of her musings is a four-year-old: "I hope they (Harry and Rosaleen) won't grow up like the generation of vipers I read about in the books of to-day."[20] When Lady Hamilton took the still four-year-old Rosaleen to a children's theater to see the play *Red*

Riding Hood, she observed that "it is a pity there are so few plays which are not frightening for children. I am so keen they should not suffer from nerves at night as I did when a child and sometimes still."[21]

Early on, there was a genuine fright about Harry. A woman approached the matron at the Paddington Crèche, asking where he was. Harry's surname was Stone, they learned. Lady Hamilton was panicked, and in such a way as to suggest that her "adoption" or fostering was structured in a less than legal manner. Now two years after his arrival, Lady Hamilton wrote, "I have written a long letter to Mr. Duncane, my lawyer to ask how I can get Harry made a ward in Chancery, and also how I can change his name and get him registered. I feel dreadfully worried and anxious about the child and think I shall leave him here till I can secure the position in some way."[22]

There may have been more going on here. Many years later, after Jean Hamilton's death, Ian Hamilton wrote to his solicitors that "Miss James was in Germany earning her living with the permission of her guardian, Lady Hamilton, when war broke out."[23] Sir Ian was a precise user of words, and he refers to Lady Hamilton as Rosaleen's "guardian," not her adoptive mother, and he only mentions the legal relationship in connection to Lady Hamilton, not himself. If the child had been formally adopted, there would be no need for a guardianship; however, a guardianship would be less difficult to obtain and might make more sense if, in accord with the postwar MI5 report, there was a blood relationship between Sir Ian and Rosaleen. In any case, there is no indication that James was adopted by the Hamiltons, now or later.

Rosaleen gave herself the nickname "Fodie." In 1925, she was sent to Miss Griffiths' School and only returned home during the Christmas holidays, which were typically happy affairs. Lady Hamilton, though, still couldn't bridge the gap in generations or overcome her self-pitying temperament:

> I feel like a fish out of water here. I feel terrified by the complete neglect and indifference of the young . . . I seem to have lost my influence over Harry and Fodie now—I don't think they love me anymore—they are getting drawn into the current, and becoming children of this age, and often fear they will accentuate, and not alleviate the loneliness of my old age. I am too old for them, and

don't find the joy I thought I would find in seeing them happy and giving them pleasure.[24]

Rosaleen's own memories of her early childhood are highly suspect and drawn with an Irish-centric viewpoint some seventy years after the event with the aim of crafting an Irish pedigree. She recalled once seeing one of Sir Ian's books, complete with unflattering caricatures. A nanny is supposed to have told her they were "German bastards! Demons! . . . you could find nothing worse except for the Irish." From that moment on, she later claimed to have identified with the Germans, who were so prejudicially linked with her own imagined Irish ancestry.[25]

In the same vein, James relates how one of the Hamiltons' maids, named Comiskey, first initiated her into Irish ways. She describes how she must have somehow instinctively felt the maid's truly Gaelic nobility. When Comiskey later left for another post and was expecting a child, Rosaleen, in an intentionally comic passage, says she rather precociously advised her to give the baby a truly Irish name and a Gaelic Catholic upbringing.[26] It is worth noting that the name Comiskey does not appear in Lady Hamilton's diaries when she was speaking about the household staff; it is referenced only in James' Irish-centric narrative.

The family blamed this nurse for Rosaleen's fervent wish to become a Catholic, developed, so James maintains, after a visit to St. Oliver Plunkett's martyrdom site in Tyburn, London. They flatly refused her conversion, but much later Rosaleen described herself as a fifteen-year-old paying clandestine early morning visits to a Catholic church in Doune, when on holidays in Deanston, and at the same time observing her new aunt Nadejda Muir, a Bulgarian, practicing her faith.[27] She never clarified when her eventual conversion to Catholicism took place; it quite possibly happened during or immediately after the war when her Irish identity was being assembled.

In any case, Rosaleen's childhood was not an isolate; she was raised in conformity with the formula dictated for every upper class child in her era, with all the advantages and pitfalls that situation contained.

Parents and nannies in virtually every old-fashioned English house of this kind set apart their children and charges as though in fear of contamination from the common touch. The intention was to inculcate a proper sense of duty, to teach that rank did indeed make them not quite as others. What happened instead was a horrible prolongation of adolescence; a stunting of healthy instincts, a spellbinding out of which adults might never emerge. Lacking contact with everyone except similarly placed captives, children of the upper classes in the twentieth century grew up lonely, whimsical, therefore ripe for wild conversions.[28]

While her book *Cé hÍ Seo Amuigh?* contains many questionable recollections, in one of the more telling sections James discusses her childhood memories of visiting Lady Hamilton's family, the Muirs. Leaving aside a nonsensical section about how Lady Hamilton was forced to agree that Rosaleen was barred from any rights of inheritance, James goes on to talk about the family surname. Because—she claims—she did not know her original surname, she decided in 1969, with the help of Seán Ó Dochartaigh (an Irish linguist, director of the Galway vocational educational committee), to adopt a supposedly Irish version of Muir as her own; the resultant Ní Mheara is incorrect, as she states herself.[29] However, it was as early as 1940 when James started using the first of many pseudonyms, "Nora O'Mara."[30] The choice of "Nora" is unlikely to be accidental: it was her birth mother's name, suggesting that at the very least she knew her mother's non-Irish identity. She also lied about not knowing her surname: "James" was on every one of her official documents until she stopped using it in the 1940s.

In 1932, Rosaleen evidently attended a boarding/finishing school in Munich, Germany, run by the brother-in-law of the former German Minister to England, Prince Karl Max Lichnowsky. Her account of this is sketchy, and only mentions that Lord Howard de Walden's daughter was her travelling companion.

If there was a single most important expectation of well-bred young women, it was the "coming out" ball and formal debut in society. It was the beginning of a series of expectations, the end-product of which would be a suitable marriage and pedigreed children. Despite the overwhelming social emphasis on these key events, Rosaleen does not seem to have participated, which is in itself highly curious. The sole mention is one line in her autobiography where she says that she deliberately ostracized herself from polite society by failing to curtsey for the king, an event of such singular rudeness that, if it really happened, would have been the leading item on every London society page. "It seemed to me that my days of welcome in England were past for me, at any rate. I took the leap of the blind."[31] Something, some combination of circumstances, obviously happened to cause her to deviate so far from the planned course. Given James's tendency to be less than forthright, her explanation is both absurd and incomplete.

There is another point. Despite the plethora of society news, diaries from the period, and later reminiscences of those who took part in the social events, not a single person mentioned Rosaleen James.[32] The Mitford sisters in particular were in the same social stratum, and were voluminous correspondents. Yet no one reported James's presence during the entire period of the late 1920s and 1930s. Why? Was she never there, or was she simply overlooked amidst a collection of young men and women who were more popular? The sons and daughters of the other families would have known about her plebeian biological background—at least in so far as she or the Hamiltons told anyone the truth—and this could not help but compromise her reception and prospects in patrician society. It might also explain her willingness to react so strongly against this same family, class, and country, and instead follow the path that, at least on the surface, was the diametrical opposite of those who had rejected her. It did not matter whether that rejection was real or imagined.

In any event, Fodie's time with the troubled Hamiltons was coming to an end. By 1935 she was infatuated with the idea of becoming an actress, and the narrow confines of England could not hold her. Particularly after making this decision, her relationship with Lady Hamilton ebbed and flowed, and Jean was quick to label Rosaleen's behavior as ungrateful: "It is cruel to have brought her up, lavished everything on her, love, protection, care, money and after years of life together, to be cold strangers to one another, living together, separated by walls of ice . . . Fodie intends, I can see, to make no ties, no contacts here which would hamper her wings of freedom."[33] Plans were made to stay with a Frau Gerbalke in Berlin, and on 10 October 1935, the seventeen-year-old Fodie departed. She would return several times between 1935 and the outbreak of war, but metamorphosis and adventure were ahead, and nothing would ever be quite the same again inside the Hamilton family.[34]

3

Rosaleen Abroad

Writing for *Harpers* in 1941, American journalist Dorothy Thompson, who worked in Germany during the 1930s, made a prescient assessment of the type of person who was likely to fall under the sway of Hitler and Nazism. She described National Socialism as a "disease of generation," and concluded that it

> appeals to a certain type of mind. It is also, to an immense extent, the disease of a generation—the generation which was either young or unborn at the end of the last war. This is as true of Englishmen, Frenchmen, and Americans as of Germans. It is the disease of the so-called "lost generation."
>
> Sometimes I think there are direct biological factors at work—a type of education, feeding, and physical training which has produced a new kind of human being with an imbalance in his nature. He has been fed vitamins and filled with energies that are beyond the capacity of his intellect to discipline. He has been treated to forms of education which have released him from inhibitions. His body is vigorous. His mind is childish. His soul has been almost completely neglected. . . .
>
> Kind, good, happy, gentlemanly, secure people never go Nazi. They may be the gentle philosopher whose name is in the Blue Book, or Bill from City College to whom democracy gave a chance to design airplanes—you'll never make Nazis out of them. But the frustrated and humiliated intellectual, the rich and scared speculator, the spoiled son, the labor tyrant, the fellow who has achieved

success by smelling out the wind of success—they would all go Nazi in a crisis.[1]

When Rosaleen James arrived in Germany, all the necessary elements described by Thompson were in place. James evidently intended to enroll in a formal acting study program, but this plan must have gone off course. Only a few weeks after James's departure, Sir Ian wrote to her:

> I am moved to deliver myself of an opinion—not so much because I expect it to convince as because it is up to me to be able in the hereafter to say to my own conscience, "I did warn her." Apparently, you have shied at the original idea of entering through the ranks and working your way up. Instead, you want to buy your commission as an officer right away; an hour's work with an actress and a great deal of looking at cinemas—that appears to be the programme. Unfortunately, the very last way to get things is to look at them . . . do definite things together with the rank and file and do them so energetically and cheerfully that you attract the attention of some boss or another; not by your sex appeal or your purse but by your character and personality."[2]

Despite having made arrangements to stay with Frau Gerbalke, by December 1935 unspecified problems had developed and Rosaleen moved in with a Frau Nostitz.[3] It is unclear to what degree she was formally studying acting, but less than a month later a mutual friend wrote to Lady Hamilton that "Fodie is not what you think or hope—I feel you must open your eyes to it. Perhaps one day she will really be a great actress, which I believe—but she is an awful responsibility for anyone to shoulder."[4]

The Rosaleen–Lady Hamilton relationship remained difficult. "I feel it's foolish to allow myself to be annoyed or allow her words to bother me but just can't help feeling hurt when I realise from what Norah says that Fodie has discussed me with her and evidently told her that she can't get on with me. . . . I feel very, very sad, for Fodie is exactly the child I longed for . . . apparently because I have been able to do so much for her and people have told her she ought to be grateful, she resents it bitterly."[5]

There is a marked difference, too, in the way the Hamiltons related to their two wards. Voluminous correspondence still exists between Sir Ian,

Lady Hamilton, and Harry Knight. He wrote chatty letters from Wellington College in the 1930s, and the Hamiltons did everything possible to speed his acceptance into the Scots Guards in 1933. In one particular exchange between Colonel Warner (Scots Guards) and Sir Ian, there is a mention of the legal arrangements that concerned both children: "I shall be please to accept *Lady Hamilton's adopted son*—Harold Knight—as a candidate for the Regiment."[6] In a responsive letter from Lady Hamilton to Colonel Warner, she again speaks of "my adopted boy Harold Knight"—not "our" adopted boy. She continues, "You will not think all that about his parentage being unknown very satisfactory but he was a lovely baby and I took him gratefully on trust and he has never disappointed me."[7] To judge from the correspondence alone, their relationship with Rosaleen was a disappointment.

A pressing tax issue reveals Rosaleen's activities during this period, much to Sir Ian's evident consternation. Owing to the Hamiltons' relatively high income, revenue regulations directed that a rebate/tax credit per child was available but would only continue if the child was continuing his or her education at a "recognized educational establishment." Accordingly, Sir Ian wrote to Rosaleen to ask for the necessary proof: "It merely amounts to this: that we shall lose a good lump sum of money if you cannot make out a case for yourself and for us to the effect that you are studying seriously."[8] She did not take the news well. "Why am I being pounced upon suddenly for this? . . . Ask them why suddenly this blasted idea has cropped up in their heads, and if they intend to demand such details of the pastimes of all young girls on the continent." Her study schedule was more informal, it seems: "I pay for lessons, at no regular times or prices, and with no regular teachers, try to earn odd jobs at film studios—it is such a whirlwind of energetic days and weeks." She enclosed a receipt for 52 Reichsmarks that she received for unspecified work at the Berlitz School in Berlin.[9] In early spring, despite the differences of opinion over Rosaleen's educational development, the Hamiltons (including Harry) met her in Italy and enjoyed a happy vacation. By October, she reported that she was acting in the play *Jeanne d'Arc*, although she did not give any specifics.[10] In discussing the superiority of the Reich-sponsored leisure organization, Kraft durch Freude (Strength through Joy), she noted that "Little chance there was now for Karl Marx and his disciple Rosa Luxemburg to carry on massaging the workers!"[11]

Rosaleen Abroad

Rosaleen's postwar descriptions of events in this prewar period present almost insurmountable difficulties; it is almost impossible to determine how much is fact and how much fantasy, or a mix of the two. Events she could not plausibly have witnessed are described in such a way as to appear that she had, and always in service to larger social or political points she was making. In the narrative chronology of this early visit to Germany that she wrote decades later, James goes on at length about her innate understanding of German character, which she contrasts to the character of her most pernicious enemy: Great Britain as personified by Winston Churchill. The irony, of course, is that she is British herself.

> The threat that was put down to Hitler, that the Jews also ought to pay for their share of the damage, and that they could not hope to emerge unscathed from a war they had secretly started, pales by comparison with the words of rage and fury from [Robert] Vansittart [Permanent Under-Secretary for Foreign Affairs and opponent of Nazi Germany], forever saying the Allies were "to rid the earth of this diabolic German race of gangsters and cannibals" (his own words!).[12]

To authenticate this, Rosaleen talks about being a witness, while on a Hamilton family outing to Monte Carlo, where Churchill and Vansittart walked and discussed how best to deconstruct Germany by means most foul: "It was not in Ireland alone that famine was one of England's policies, indeed not!"[13] The idea of this is, of course, ludicrous: Winston Churchill and Vansittart plotting a malicious, Machiavellian starvation scheme against Germany, and taking into their confidence the sixteen-year-old Rosaleen James. Her repetitive agenda is clear: Britain is bad, therefore Germany is good, and Ireland and Germany have common cause because they are the innocent victims of bad Britain.[14]

Rosaleen James is not the only upper-class Englishwoman to have been snake-charmed by Hitler. Indeed, James's conversion almost pales in comparison to that of the Mitford sisters, particularly Unity (d. 1948) and Diana (d. 2003). As two of the six daughters of Lord Redesdale, they existed in much the same social circle as James, but their connections were of a slight grade higher than the Hamiltons, and their parents from a younger generation. Indeed, the Redesdale and Hamilton London residences overlooked the same section of Hyde Park.[15] Unity was also a profoundly unstable anti-Semite. There are several important similarities between the Mitford sisters and James, but one is most relevant: the psychological need to reject class and country and to identify with people, places, and things that were the diametric opposite. Shocking the establishment was an end in itself. Like James, Diana and Unity found fulfilment in National Socialist Germany.[16] However, James eventually took collaboration to a place where even the Mitford sisters dared not go.

Unity certainly knew the Hamiltons, and presumably Rosaleen, well. Rosemary Peto wrote:

> Before I came out, I used to meet her [Unity] again quite often at Sir Ian and Lady Hamilton's. They had a house in Hyde Park Gardens and gave enormous luncheon parties for twenty or thirty people, mixing politicians, publishers, painters, distinguished elderly men and some young. The young men when I had finished my row there with Bobo [Unity's nickname] were Jim Lees-Milne and Lajos Lederer. We'd finished lunch and were coming down from the place where we had coffee. Bobo was wearing a swastika in her buttonhole. The Nazis had just done something particularly horrible, and I said, It's shocking that you are wearing that. She answered, If you had any sense you'd be wearing it too. Once she boasted that it was such fun to have supper with [Julius] Streicher, as he'd have the Jews in after the meal, they'd be brought up from the cellar and be made to eat grass to entertain the guests. She was like a blank wall, with this thick obtuse quality.[17]

Discussing a meeting with Unity, who was also staying with an impoverished noble family during a finishing school year in Germany, Rosaleen notes, "She was a girl that went under the wheel with her dream, but she was not to be pitied. We see an awful lot of people that turn their sheets to the wind. Is not the way of the man sitting on a fence the most pitiful?"[18]

James told a story from this time which she claims she heard directly from a Cork girl, Helen Daly ("the only other Irish among us"), who shared her finishing school odyssey. In James's version, Lady Sydney Redesdale (Unity and Diana's mother) was practically stalking Hitler,

Rosaleen Abroad

trying desperately to catch his attention, finally arranging to be in one of Hitler's favorite Munich cafés during a time Hitler often had lunch. Daly was there as Lady Redesdale's translator, just in case. Hitler arrived, and Lady Redesdale bleated, "My dear Führer, I just have to let you know, all England adores you!" Hitler disregarded the woman, and amused, turned his attention to Helen Daly. Fascinated that she was Irish, he said (according to James), "I am highly interested in the history of your brave race. . . . from what I know, it is a wonderful story! I am sorry I haven't got a very clear idea of it!"[19]

That never happened. Rosaleen James borrowed this episode, minus the ridiculous Irish addendum, from a fairly well-known episode at the Osteria Bavaria restaurant in Munich, but in the original version (minus James's enhancement), it involved Unity Mitford, not her mother, and "only-Irish-among-us" Helen Daly was not present.[20]

Whereas Rosaleen never claims to have met Hitler, the Mitford sisters were more fortunate. Both sisters attended several Nazi party rallies as official guests, Diana married British Union of Fascists leader Sir Oswald Mosley with Hitler as a witness, and Unity, whose psychological health was ever in question, became a regular in Hitler's intimate circle.

Events moved swiftly. In January 1937, Rosaleen, now inexplicably in Vienna, announced her engagement to a forty-two-year-old Austrian sculptor named Karl Eidlitz. Eidlitz was apparently dying, and according to Lady Hamilton's diary, "she [Rosaleen] told me really and truly that she had given up all thought of the stage and wanted to marry her sculptor whom she assures me I would very much like—and that he had plenty of money to support her."[21] Eidlitz did not make it into James's memoirs. Perhaps out of concern for Rosaleen's impulsive, puzzling behavior, Lady Hamilton hurried to Vienna; the trip was not a success. All the signs were there of the strained relationship between them, and it was evident to Lady Hamilton that they had little left in common. There is no further mention of Rosaleen's pending marriage to Eidlitz. In her letters describing the trip, Lady Hamilton noted in passing that Rosaleen had an incredible facility with languages, to include Hungarian—among the most difficult to learn. This knowledge of Hungarian has evidentiary value much later in the Rosaleen James story.

In July 1937, the Hamiltons paid Rosaleen's passage back home for a short vacation. During this time, starting on 20 July 1937, Rosaleen took a one-week trip to Ireland, the only such trip she made until after the Second World War. It obviously made a tremendous impression. Since Rosaleen had no existing contact with that island, familial or otherwise, Lady Hamilton was puzzled by her attitudinal change after returning to England: "She talked all the time about the sorrows of Ireland and the cruelty and wickedness of England to her. She presently has a passionate belief in all the lurid Irish tales against England. She is especially bitter about the "Black and Tans"—it makes me sad to hear her."[22] This, then—for whatever psychological reason—is the starting point for an Irish masquerade that lasted more than seventy years.

But there is another version. In her autobiography, Rosaleen makes mention of an earlier trip to Ireland. She dates this as September 1934, when she would have been sixteen. While sailing from the United Kingdom to Brittany on board Howard de Walden's yacht, "the sea became very rough, and we had to find a harbour. This is when a sudden fit took hold of me, and without telling anybody, I went to Holyhead [the British port most frequently used for Ireland]."[23] From there, the descriptions become increasingly romanticized: "Could it be true? Good God? Was it me setting foot on this pier [in Ireland, after a spontaneous sea voyage], in the coolness of day-break, or was it a dream?"[24] This quickly transitions to a pro-Irish, anti-English vignette where she remembers a pamphlet describing the British shooting 1916 rebels of "my father's generation," which in turn convinces her that Dublin's Parnell Square was the "best place for an exile that had come home to spend her first night."[25]

The poverty she witnesses in the lodgings is "Dickensian," but compassion spurs her on, and she recalls tearful joy at being awakened by Irish children and, on a trip to St. Audeons in Dublin, being reluctant to give her name to the priest because she did not know the Irish form of it. The priest helped her write out her baptismal names in Irish (although "Phyllis James" does not have a smooth Irish equivalent), and she kept the paper for years afterward. Rosaleen went on to Limerick (to see the Treaty Stone), was saddened at the deterioration of nearby Bunratty Castle, and heard of the British Black and Tan atrocities from a local woman.[26] She does not say by what means she returned to Holyhead and thence home.

It is just possible that this happened the way she relates it sixty years later, but there are a number of problems with this story. Lady Hamilton was a painstaking diarist and correspondent, recording the minutiae of almost every day of her married life, particularly when the events discussed concerned Sir Ian, Harry, or Rosaleen. There is not a word in her letters or diary about Rosaleen taking an Irish excursion in 1934, and it would be almost unthinkable for a pedigreed sixteen-year-old to wander across the Irish Sea unsupervised, spend several days in Ireland, and then mysteriously return. A much more plausible scenario is that Rosaleen's short 1937 visit was the only one before the war. In Lady Hamilton's description of Rosaleen's trip in 1937, she mentions what seems to be the identical Black and Tan conversation incident.

After Rosaleen's return to Germany, she auditioned at the Universum Film-Aktien Gesellschaft (UFA Studios) and seemed confident that she would transition from the stage to movies. She did not. Instead, Rosaleen moved to Vienna again, and—at least according to her letters home—enrolled in a film acting school.[27] She wrote back to Lady Hamilton that "this may last a year but it depends on how quickly I get on." Vienna, when Rosaleen James returned there, held a Jewish population of approximately 200,000—some 28 percent of Austria's Jews—and they were prominent in the arts and cultural and business life of this thriving city. She could not have helped working alongside them in whatever theater projects she became involved with.

It was a time of change in Austria and elsewhere in Europe: Hitler was moving south. By early 1938, German diplomatic and military resources were in place to facilitate something specifically forbidden by the Versailles Treaty: the political union of Germany and Austria. This first international crisis of 1938 set off alarms all over the continent, finally bringing Édouard Daladier and Neville Chamberlain to Munich, caps in hand, to negotiate with Hitler and hopefully to avoid another general European war. Their efforts succeeded insofar as war did not erupt, but the bloodless victory raised Hitler's estimation of his own abilities and demonstrated that the British and French would go to any lengths to prevent a military confrontation. Under their new masters, Austrian Jews had little choice: flee if they could or begin the slow process of civic degradation that eventually ended at the gates of Auschwitz.[28]

To Rosaleen James, German union with Austria (*Anschluss*) was an event to be admired. Speaking about the wave of anti-Semitic violence in the wake of the Anschluss, she notes that local authorities had to request help from Berlin: "The SS . . . came down in order to put things in the city to order. They had to protect the Jews from evil, aiding them in emigrating in a proper and befitting way."[29] Written fifty years after the events in question, the moral obscenity of that statement seems to have escaped her. She writes admiringly of watching Hitler's arrival in Vienna on 14 March: "It was with the eyes of the architect that he appraised the building (the opera house), as if put into a trance of his own."[30] To her, "The German race thought at this moment of reunion they were able to overcome the world and the devil, and to establish their own right. But as it happened, they only succeeded in awakening envy."[31] Unity Mitford was in Vienna at the same time and likewise reacted with pleasure at Hitler's appearance on the balcony of the Hotel Imperial.[32]

Other contemporary witnesses do not remember the events in the same way. In 1938 Gitta Sereny was almost the exact age as Rosaleen James, and had likewise come to Vienna to study acting, but unlike James was a native Austro-Hungarian, and with a more solid grasp of the reality playing out around her:

> By now, we knew of course that there were three categories of people who were in real danger: Jews, communists, and Austrian patriots. For the rest, life could go on more or less as usual, although foreign embassies sent small pins in the national colours to their citizens, urging us to wear them.... In the weeks that followed, people began to disappear: one of my teachers, a small man of incredible kindness to fumbling young drama students, killed himself by jumping out of a fourth-floor window; two others left for the United States.... We no longer went to theatres for rehearsals or performances. All of us came and went in groups, orderly, quiet, and in many cases, suspicious of each other.[33]

November 1938 brought *Kristallnacht* (night of broken glass) to Vienna's Jews. Officially an unplanned public outcry after the shooting of a German diplomat in Paris by a disgruntled Jew, it was in fact part of a concerted plan conceived by Hitler and Goebbels to terrorize every Jew in German territory, an active measure to facilitate the legalized racial and social pressure enacted by the Nürnberg Laws in 1935. All across the Reich, organized mobs of SA men (*Sturmabteilung*, or Storm Troopers) burned and looted synagogues and Jewish-owned shops, beat up and even killed Jews, sent hundreds to concentration camps, and terrified the rest.

In 1938, SS Captain Adolf Eichmann (later the Reich's most zealous "deportation expert"), working closely with the Inspector of Security Police and SD in Vienna, Brigadier General Walter Stahlecker (later commander of a mobile killing unit, Einsatzgruppe A), established a Central Office for Jewish Emigration in Vienna. By May 17, 1939, nearly half of Austria's entire Jewish population had emigrated, leaving only approximately 121,000 Jews in Austria (all but 8,000 in Vienna). Though the pace of emigration slowed to a trickle with the increasing threat of war and its outbreak in September 1939, another 28,000 Jews were able to leave Austria between May 1939 and the middle of 1942.[34]

For the Jews in Vienna's theater community, the Anschluss results were immediate and permanent. Reacting to what has been described as an attitude of "anti-Semitic excess," many who had fled from persecution in Germany after 1933 were obliged to flee for a second time, or face an even worse alternative. Rosaleen James was unsympathetic: "The Jews of Vienna started getting worried at this time [before the Anschluss]. In my mind, it would be an exaggeration to say the people had any more than a false respect for that all-powerful minority. They had a say on the cultural life of the city, and a strong grip on the media. On top of that, they also owned the opulent ugly yet splendid houses which the distressed poor so badly needed. They prospered over the people's plight, and many had a life of plenty among the poor. . . ."[35]

In another chilling description she writes: "As regards the city of Vienna, this powerful minority now had to pay for the dissatisfaction of the people. That is how, on occasion the citizens took their spite out on the Jews on the spur of a moment, and those Jews who went into hiding rather than take a seat on a train usually did not succeed well."[36] No, they did not succeed well at all. During World War II at least 65,000 of Austria's Jewish population were murdered, many of them former residents of Vienna.[37] Today, a somber monument in Vienna's *Judenplatz* commemorates the Austrian Jewish victims of Hitler, and stands in stark contradiction to Rosaleen James's version of events.

Despite the official policy of "racial cleansing" (*rassische Säuberung*), a handful of Jews classified as "half-Jews" or "ancestral Jews" under sections of the Nürnberg Laws governing racial determination were allowed to remain in the Burgtheater temporarily. The authority for this came from the Reichstheaterkammer (Reich Theater Chamber [RTK]) or Theaterabteilung (Theater Department), created in September 1933 as an adjunct of the larger Reichskulturkammer (Reich Cultural Chamber), itself an important part of the Ministry of Propaganda and Public Enlightenment (RMVP), during the first year of National Socialist ascendency in Germany.[38] As but one part of the multi-headed organization that controlled all German arts, the Theaterabteilung was the professional organization for theater artists, but its chief purpose was to ensure ideological conformity rather than a voice for its members.

The RTK was subdivided into sections controlling stage, dance, performers, and others, having absorbed the functions of the traditional stage guilds and what had been the premier theater organization, the Deutscher Bühnenverein. While membership in the RTK was not synonymous with Nazi Party membership, and many of the performers were enrolled out of necessity for professional reasons, the purpose and character of the organization was clear even in the decree from Hitler that created the Propaganda Ministry: to direct the "spiritual indoctrination" of the German nation.[39] Control of the message put forward by theater performances was a powerful tool in establishing and maintaining that influence. The fact that it was, by law, impossible to work in the theater without being a member of the RTK proved helpful. The Theaterabteilung also had the responsibility to investigate charges of political deviance and to maintain the integrity of National Socialist cultural standards in all its productions. After the Anschluss, all provisions of German law were extended to former Austrian territory.[40] All existing members and applying candidates had to show proof of Aryan ancestry, the *Ariernachweis*.

The Ariernachweis requirement affected Rosaleen James as well. She had been a member of the Bund der Österreichischen Bühnenkünstler (Association of Austrian Stage Artists), which had no such genealogical requirement, but now had to prove her Aryan pedigree. There were two possible types of proof: the lesser and greater Aryan ancestry certificates. Even the lesser would be a problem for James. There were several options:

(1) presenting the birth or baptism certificates for the candidate and their parents and grandparents; (2) presenting an *Ahnenpaß* (ancestor's passport); or (3) a certified genealogical table (*Ahnentafel*).[41] With her parentage in doubt, James wrote back to Sir Ian asking for her baptismal certificate: "Could you get hold of my christening certificate and send it to me. I must have it to prove that I have no Jewish blood—to prove that my parents were not descended from Jews. This is essential."[42] Evidently she fudged the truth about her murky background on the Reichstheaterkammer application because she was granted membership number 74188 as of May 1938.[43]

For Sir Ian Hamilton, too, the German union with Austria was a time of personal and political affirmation. Even before Hitler came to power in 1933, his politics had been moving in the direction of Berlin. In 1928, Hamilton became a founding member of the Anglo-German Association, an organization with the avowed aim of promoting better understanding between the former enemies in the Great War and, on the German side, to promote pro-German attitudes in England. The complex behind-the-scenes politics involved in the A-G Association drew in the somewhat politically naïve Hamilton like a moth to a flame. While not substantively pro-Nazi, his distinctly pro-German attitude led him down a poisonous path.

The Association was an entirely German idea, aimed at making the most of business contacts and using those to change British popular opinion at a politically influential level about Germany's position vis-à-vis the territorial limitations in the Versailles Treaty. With Lord Reading elected as the British half of the joint British–German presidency, Sir Ian was—significantly—the vice president of the Association. Addressing a dinner audience in 1929, Hamilton made his position clear: it was in Britain's best interests to come to "good terms with her German cousin. Seeing both countries had envious rivals who would try their best to keep them apart, the sooner England came out in to the open as the friend of Germany, the better."[44] It is important to note that his expression of Germanophilia occurred before Hitler's rise to power, and certainly reflects an amalgam of military, fraternal, and social attitudes that were prevalent up and down the social ladder after the carnage of World War I. Many hoped that understanding between former enemies was the surest way to avoid future conflict. However, Hamilton went further.

Masquerade

The Anglo-German Association ran aground after January 1933, with the National Socialist electoral victory. The Nazi boycott of Jewish shops on 1 April made headlines all over the world and had a dampening effect on British enthusiasm for the New Germany; it made clear to many that Hitler's anti-Semitic ravings were more than empty rhetoric. Lord Reading (a Jew) resigned his presidency of the Association in protest. Worried about the effect of further resignations, which would "be a positive slap in the face for Germany and very much to be deprecated," Hamilton advised that it would be "unwise at present to offer our membership to any Jewish gentleman." To effectively remove any doubt that his affinity for Germany was apolitical, Hamilton wrote in November that he was an "admirer of the great Adolph [*sic*] Hitler and have done my best to support him through some difficult times."[45] The Association's German branch dissolved (it was later replaced by a more virulent Nazi version), and the British affiliate limped along until 1935, with the Jewish issue rapidly separating the doctrinaire anti-Semites from those otherwise inclined. Thoroughly vexed by this, Hamilton wrote that he did not "feel it is patriotic or right of his countrymen to let the whole question of internationalism be clouded over by this one aspect of Germany's present condition," and that the Jews and their sympathizers "would prefer to smash up the whole concern" as opposed to allowing it to continue without them.[46] Unable to solve the central issue, the Association dissolved itself in April 1935.

Hamilton, though, was clearly committed to maintaining ties between Britain and Germany. In September 1935, Hitler issued the Nürnberg Laws, which, among other restrictions, prohibited Jews from owning land, practicing the legal profession, serving in the military, and participating in the public arts (including the theater), with more incremental persecution to come. Even before the Association folded, Hamilton had discussed participation in a new group with more overt political objectives: the Anglo-German Fellowship. His contact was Richard Meinertzhagen, a former British army intelligence officer and noted ornithologist—as well as a plagiarist, serial liar, and possible wife murderer.[47]

Sir Ian coupled his growing ties with the Anglo-German Fellowship with his role as the face and voice of the British Legion, which already numbered close to half a million members. The Legion's political views, to the extent that they spoke with one voice, are difficult to characterize, but they became increasingly more pliable to German interests as the

1930s continued. Hamilton was not alone in his belief. Lord Rothermere, owner of the *Daily Mail*, more profusely supported Hitler, was more overtly anti-Semitic, and was even less able to temper his inclinations with a modicum of reality. Two of Hamilton's closest friends, Phillip Kerr (Lord Lothian) and Charles Vane-Tempest-Stewart (Lord Londonderry) were, to the degree it was even possible to be so, even more sympathetic to National Socialist Germany. Hitler met both of them.

To enhance these growing ties, Sir Ian led a British Legion delegation to Germany in 1934 to participate in a ceremony in which he received the captured drums of the Gordon Highlanders from the ailing President Paul von Hindenburg.[48] Part of this impulse likely came from the positive memories of his time in Saxony as a young man, part from a sincere desire to effect peace between former soldiers as an example of what could be done between nations, and part from naïve wishful thinking. The Anglo-German Fellowship had a German counterpart, the *Deutsch-Englische Gesellschaft*, which came under the control of the German Foreign Office. It was later directed by Joachim von Ribbentrop, who advanced from German ambassador to England to become the German foreign minister, and eventually to executed war criminal after the Nuremberg Trials. While the A-G Fellowship was aimed at the upper segments of British society and had a strong commercial appeal, Ribbentrop's German version was more clearly directed at political and intelligence objectives: to foster a positive image of Germany, which could then be used in whatever manner most beneficial to Adolf Hitler.[49] Doing his part for Anglo-German harmony, as he saw it, Hamilton publically expressed his approval when Germany reoccupied the Rhineland in 1936, in clear violation of the Versailles Treaty.

By 1937, Hamilton became even more involved. Writing an editorial for the *Manchester Guardian* in March, he criticized talk of British rearmament and what he perceived as an anti-German tilt in British foreign policy. "We are arming in favour of Russian and France, and against our blood relations, the Germans." This apparently pleased the Germans, so much so that SS-Gruppenführer Reinhard sent a letter to Sir Ian, inviting him to the Nazi Party rally in Nürnberg in September 1937; Hamilton declined owing to a previous commitment.

The key moment came almost a year later when Hamilton led yet another British Legion delegation to Germany in August 1938. What happened next was momentous: he was invited to Berchtesgaden—where Hitler awaited him at the mountain house on Obersalzberg. The two World War I veterans met, talked, and were photographed. Hamilton was delighted. Hitler clearly understood the importance of treating his British visitor with consideration; in addition to providing Hamilton with pajamas and a toothbrush, he ordered his personal JU-52 aircraft to take Sir Ian back to London in style. Writing of his impromptu adventure in a short piece in the *Sunday Referee*, Hamilton concluded that Hitler was the genuine voice of reason in Europe. "They are much more active for peace than we are here."[50] Continuing this theme in a *Daily Mail* interview, Hamilton said that "You can be sure the Herr Hitler has the deepest appreciation of what war could mean in terror and disaster for Europe, and that the German people sincerely desire peace."[51] In this, Hamilton's misplaced naïveté was soon evident. Sir Ian Kershaw's conclusion to all this is that "Hamilton was a pillar of the British Establishment, certainly no Nazi despite his expressed approval of much that Hitler and his regime stood for, and undoubtedly well-meaning if guileless in his efforts to bring about friendship between Britain and Germany. He succeeded, however, only in making himself, and the organization he represented—the British Legion—vehicles of Nazi propaganda."[52]

Reaching its low point at the Munich Agreement between Chamberlain, Daladier, and Hitler, the complex tapestry of the British appeasement movement is connected to Rosaleen James's formative attitudes. The Hamiltons' (and, by extension, Rosaleen James's) sense of self existed in a world where social standing was everything. As Ian Kershaw observed, the patterns of upper class society necessitated regular appearances, and in such places of "harmless amusement, contacts could be made, connections established, relationships built up, gossip exchanged, and minor plots hatched."[53] As was to be expected from someone of her class, Lady Hamilton's diary makes it clear that she delighted in the endless rounds of reciprocal obligations necessary to maintain a prominent place in British society. Others in this same rarefied strata of society—the Rothermeres, the Londonderrys, the Lothians, and many more in the appeasement camp—were of like mind with the Hamiltons, believing that friendship with Hitler's Germany was the only logical way forward. Although none of the key players would have discussed political ideas with the then fifteen- or sixteen-year-old Rosaleen, it would have been impossible for her not to have assimilated the prevailing attitudes in this clique which favored National Socialist Germany.

Though she had no actual involvement in the serious conversations between adult contemporaries, Rosaleen James's own postwar narrative goes to great pains to say otherwise. She devotes considerable space to the deteriorating relationship between Hamilton and Churchill, and as usual places her revisionist Irish-centric spin on the events. In her version, Hitler begged Hamilton to intervene with Churchill to stop the dangerous arms buildup that threatened European peace. Germany and Britain must—she says Hamilton told her Hitler said—find common cause against their common enemy, Soviet Russia: "There is no hope that we ourselves could put a halt to that global spread or could stand without any defence or help to preserve the nations from the barbaric threat of the East, full of weapons as it is. God with us, we need to stand together!"[54] She reports that Churchill was unimpressed.[55]

James's attitude toward Churchill was—at least from the view of sixty years after the fact—unwavering in its hostility. It may be that she never met him at all, and even if she did, their last possible encounter would have been when James was fourteen or fifteen. Nevertheless, in the space of two pages in her memoirs, she describes Churchill as a "bloodthirsty goat," and as *Seán Buí*—"yellow John"—a derogatory name for the British. He was habitually untruthful, she writes, in comparison to Sir Ian, and had a "capricious mind forever fuelled by drink." In her memoirs, she interrupted this character assessment to add another retroactive aside about Ireland: "But above everything else, what was in store for Ireland on this gambler's chessboard of pawns?"[56] James's Churchill is responsible for much more—for the start of World War II itself: "his [Churchill's] reaction [in refusing to listen to Hitler's message] was a clear sign that he had a fast intention of putting Germany to war, if he could. He was not yet at the height of his powers, but was working away diligently. . . . Churchill was driving towards war well knowing what he was doing."[57]

Hitler certainly thought likewise. Fresh from his diplomatic triumph of uniting with Austria in 1938, the Führer next turned his attention to the Sudetenland, inside the borders of neighboring Czechoslovakia. The portion of the Czech state closest to Germany held some three million people who self-identified as ethnic Germans, now living in a state that was unsympathetic to their position. Soon after the start of the crisis in

April 1938, the British government made efforts to study the problem and mediate between the various sides, eventually concluding that no perfectly satisfactory solution was possible: Ethnic Germans in Czechoslovakia wanted independence or to join the Reich, the Czechs wanted to retain the areas ceded to them under the Versailles Treaty (and maintain the bulk of their fixed border defenses in the Sudetenland against Germany), and Hitler had taken it upon himself to espouse the Sudeten cause as his own as part of his overall aim for German hegemony in Europe. With existing treaties between Czechoslovakia and France and Britain, and Czech president Edvard Beneš promising to resist any German attempt to intervene, it looked to most people in Europe that a general war was inevitable at any moment.

In a sincere effort to broker a peace, British Prime Minister Neville Chamberlain met with Hitler at Berchtesgaden and Bad Godesberg, and later on 29 September, Hitler, Édouard Daladier of France, Benito Mussolini, and Chamberlain met at Munich. "Peace for our time," came on 1 October 1938 when German forces occupied the Sudetenland and annexed the disputed territory into the Third Reich. In a letter to a Dr. Goebel in Germany on 29 September, Hamilton makes his position clear: "I have ventured to make an appeal myself as an admirer of the Führer and his Army." He then goes on to say that he suggested using the British Legion to occupy the Sudeten territories until such time as Germany was ready to assume control.[58] One can only imagine Hamilton's impact on Hitler's assessment of British character and resolve. In any event, the time for appeasement had passed, and others were waiting in the wings. Unlike Sir Ian Hamilton and Rosaleen James, they—Churchill most prominent among them—saw Hitler as the incarnation of evil.

However, even Hamilton's faith had limits. Hitler's occupation of the remainder of the Czech state on 15 March 1939 was too much, and an obvious violation of the Munich agreement where Germany pledged to respect the redrawn Czech borders. At last, perhaps only just realizing that his belief and trust had been horribly misplaced, Hamilton wrote that "the 'sane atmosphere in Anglo-German relations' has turned into thunder and lightning."[59] For once, Hamilton was correct.

Adolf Hitler was about to unleash a terrible storm.

4

Der Krieg

It is difficult to verify any of what James said she did in 1939; much of her version is mixed with fantasy Irish revisionism. In the period approaching the war, she was apparently still in Vienna. At one point, she described a train trip to Berlin, where—she says—Germans were fascinated by all things Irish, and German libraries were well-stocked with Irish books until "Churchill's bombs destroyed them."[1] Although it almost certainly never happened, she later wrote that she sent a letter to the Reichskulturkammer in May 1939, expressing the opinion that England would once again falsely promise Ireland reunification to gain support and simultaneously "besmirch the country [i.e., Germany] that had been so sympathetic to Ireland." It would be—she claims she wrote—her task to stop any such lies in the making. She does not explain why one would address such a letter to an administrative body that controlled such activities as public art and theaters, where the recipients would be, at the very least, puzzled; the cause of Irish reunification was not one of their responsibilities.

In connection to the Reichskulturkammer, she says that in 1939 she returned to Berlin from Paris with a letter from "my old general" (Hamilton) stating she was descended from Irish people only, and was surprised that without much fuss and delay the Reichskulturkammer yielded and accepted her, so that in the spring of 1939 she was made a full member of this body. Curiously, wartime German documents, including her own answers on an official questionnaire, contain no declaration of Irishness.[2] In yet another memory-versus-fact issue, the German documents list her membership in the Reichstheaterkammer from 1938, not 1939.

James claims that she was soon contacted by an official—she does not reveal by whom or from which office—who was delighted when she promised to give her loyal service to the cause of Irish neutrality. He asked her to contact him in Berlin, where she soon went "to play a principal role" in a stage production. While in transit, she says she passed through Bohemia (part of German territory since its occupation of Czechoslovakia in March 1939) and saw German troops near the Polish frontier. If only in her skewed recollections, it was clear to her at the time that Germany was only defending itself:

> While we Irish were only neutral observers as WWII began, we don't forget one unassailable truth: Germany did not decide on military action until Poland partially mobilized its army in March 1939. It was a silly decision that would draw a like reaction from the Germans. There was no other solution for the struggle between them and for the reasonable proposal made by Germany. It received an offer of war in reply.[3]

Her frequent use of the phrase "we Irish" (*sinne mar Éireannaigh*) in her autobiography is meant to create the impression that in 1939 she was a self-aware Irish national. James saw Germany's next moves as motivated by self-defense:

> As for Poland, Germany advised again and again on a moderate policy to settle the question about the border, but that country's government, under the influence of England, refused to discuss a solution with its neighbour. As an answer, and in opposition to it, they mobilised their forces and in early 1939 began in earnest their ugly campaign of persecuting the 2 million and more Germans resident inside its bloated borders. Germany had to keep the way east open, in case England declared war.[4]

German forces crossed the Polish frontier early in the morning of 1 September 1939, not in self-defense, but as the first stage in a continental war of aggression. Britain's declaration of war on 3 September presented several obvious problems for its citizens living in the German Reich. Both governments followed, for the moment, the diplomatic protocols, and allowed (or demanded, in the case of Germany) foreign citizens who wished to do so to leave. Rosaleen James elected to stay. As a British national, she crossed a personal demarcation line at that moment between her odd, prewar sympathy for National Socialist Germany and the first steps on the path toward treason.

On this same day, 3 September 1939, James's ideological twin, Unity Mitford, shot herself in Munich's Englischer Garten, apparently overcome at the failure of England and Germany to reach an understanding short of war. She only succeeded in inflicting a nonfatal head wound, although she later made a second, rather strange suicide attempt by swallowing the gold Nazi Party badge that Hitler had given her.[5]

In one particular section from her autobiography, James goes on at length to make the case that Germany's actions were solely motivated by altruistic defense of an ethnic German minority, but that British behind-the-scenes machinations perverted their good intentions. "They [the Germans] went right ahead and with a blind hope that what they made was just a small step to do away with certain injustices doled out to them in 1918, necessary for a lasting peace," adding "but the English was a foxy sort of person and skilled in all tricks." She describes Hitler as attacking problems in a direct way, reaching one solution after another, overcoming all obstacles "without shedding but one drop of blood," but that the British ensnared him. "It is hard to excel the fox in matters of smartness, as we Irish know only too well."[6]

She likewise praises German intervention on behalf of ethnic Germans by citing the example of the "Bloody Sunday" incident at Bromberg (Bydgoszcz) also on 3 September 1939. A number of German inhabitants—responsible estimates range from 100 to 400—were killed by Poles following an episode during which retreating Polish troops were fired upon. The German Propaganda Ministry made maximum use of the incident as proof of Hitler's claims. In his radio and press coverage of the incident, Reich propaganda chief Dr. Josef Goebbels failed to mention that German forces, mostly SS, subsequently conducted reprisal actions that resulted in 20,000 Bromberg Poles being executed by firing squads or sent to their deaths in concentration camps.[7] James, following the Nazi party line, reported that 6,000 to 7,000 Germans had been murdered in Bromberg before the German army could reach them.[8] This pattern is discernible in much of her writing: what she cites as historical evidence is often based on fringe and conspiracy theories, inevitably in lockstep with the propaganda manufactured by the Nazis themselves.

Upon reaching Berlin on 1 September 1939, James later claimed that the official she had met in Vienna asked her to go immediately to the Rundfunkhaus (broadcasting center) because her acting and linguistic skills were needed. Balanced against contemporary records, it is difficult to verify. She had attended an acting seminar in Vienna, but had not yet performed in anything of substance. She seemed to have a facility with languages, although this was not rare in central Europe. She said that she was asked to broadcast on the radio in French and English, pretending to be a Warsaw station, but the Germans were actually operating a "black" propaganda service to confuse the Polish population until such time as the military phase was complete.[9] James claimed to work as both on-air talent and the impromptu editorial team, owing to a lack of competent oversight. There is no supporting evidence for her debut role in German radio propaganda to be found in the German Rundfunkarchiv, and this vignette appears to be another of her fictions.[10]

James wrote that the head of the broadcasting department, an SS officer named Dr. Türmer, invited her along to Danzig when the German radio effort closed on 20 September, but that she refused. Türmer, she says, questioned her possession of a British (instead of an Irish) passport. She informed him—at least according to her memoirs—that this was the passport given to all Irish citizens when she was born[11]—an interesting statement since she was at no time an Irish citizen.

Without explanation, James's autobiographical narrative then skips ahead at least four months from the end of the Polish campaign to several months into 1940. Existing German records do not show any activity of James's, on stage or otherwise, in this time period, so it is impossible to determine what she did, or in whose service. For some reason, though, she was not arrested or detained, despite being an enemy alien in the Reich.

5

Francis Stuart

By the early spring of 1940, Rosaleen James was back in Berlin. She was pregnant—the father was said to be a Ukrainian whom she met at the Vienna broadcasting studio; she could not continue with stage work in that condition and was without any means of support.[1] She was sleeping in the sitting room of an apartment owned by two elderly Russian ladies but was not allowed to return there until they had gone to bed.[2] According to an MI5 report, someone who knew her from the Reichstheaterkammer mentioned her situation (and presumably her English background) to Hauptmann Friedrich Marwede, an officer with Abwehr (German military intelligence). Marwede dispatched another Abwehr officer, Dr. Kurt Haller, to interview her; Germany's strategic situation had changed, and even marginal resources were needed for the war effort.

The blitzkrieg that overcame Poland in slightly over a month turned westward in 1940. Holland and Belgium were invaded, and a strong German panzer force gutted the French defenses with a surprise attack from the Ardennes. Fall Gelb (Case Yellow, the name for the initial campaign in France), for all of its improbable operational success, failed to achieve its strategic objective: after the fall of France, Great Britain did not come to terms with Hitler. When it became clear that Britain under Churchill was quite unlike Britain under Chamberlain, Germany had little choice if it was to win the war. Other than the gradual tightening of pressure on Britain via U-boat attacks on logistical supplies, and a less-than-effective attempt at strategic bombardment, invasion was the only practical means of forcing the British to surrender.

The chief difficulty—and there were many subordinate difficulties—was that no one in the German hierarchy had previously asked the "what if" question: what if Great Britain fails to capitulate when France is defeated? After the French surrender at Compiegne, German planners were caught unprepared. They had no idea of how to deal with the problem, let alone an accurate assessment of the resources needed to subdue the British. Blitzkrieg, for all its wonder, had fallen short.

German military intelligence likewise dropped the strategic ball. Instead of having a ready list of agent networks to call upon in the event of conflict with Britain and an established pipeline feeding essential data back to the German high command, the Abwehr had practically nothing of value: no in-place agents, no communications network, no detailed knowledge of the British defense plans, and only a hazy understanding of the enemy's industrial capacity. Only after Hitler issued the warning order for Operation Sea Lion in July 1940 did the Abwehr wake up to the realization that they needed expertise about Britain and the British—fast. As it happened, the Germans knew of a British woman who was nearby, who claimed to have the right contacts, was ideologically sympathetic, and in desperate financial straits.

Dr. Haller spoke excellent English and was assigned to Abwehr II, the section devoted to sabotage and contact with discontented nationality groups. In that capacity, he dealt with a number of English-speaking factions, including the Irish and Welsh nationalists. Like everyone else who encountered Rosaleen James in Germany, Haller was at a loss to understand her pedigree; she maintained she was Irish but also English. Clearly there were some interesting elements here that could be leveraged by German intelligence given the right operational circumstances, particularly with the pressure on Abwehr to produce results in preparation for a continued conflict with Great Britain. Haller recommended to his superiors at Abwehr II that James be kept on the payroll at the rate of 400 Reichsmarks a month, with the idea of perhaps using her as a courier to still-neutral Ireland, where she claimed to have ties. Haller also advised James to give him her British passport and offered to get her a *Fremdenpass* (passport for non-Germans) listing her as "stateless." She agreed, handed over her passport, and Haller was successful in getting police surveillance on her stopped.[3] He eventually realized that his initial assessment was hasty and concluded that James was not suitable as an agent. James, Haller said to his interrogators, "although not actually volunteering for any mission, seemed not disinclined to go, and constantly tried to prove to [Haller] her strong Irish nationalist and pro-German sentiments, but he thought her views were merely opportunist in order to make the most of this unexpected source of income."[4] In other words, she was in it for the fast buck.

Rosaleen James's version is quite different. She later told MI5 that her first contact with Abwehr occurred in September 1940, and then only because someone had asked about her missing passport. Two men, one of whom she identified as Haller, arrived and offered her the foreigner's passport in the meantime. "He then suggested that I should accompany the German troops to England, to point out to them people and places, mentioning Churchill and his country house, and other people I know who they would want to find. I laughed it off. . . ."[5] She further told the MI5 officer,

> I saw Haller again about two months later by appointment in a restaurant. He then asked me to go England to get into touch with the Welsh Nationalists in London. They had been getting into touch with the Germans, he said. I said at once I wouldn't do any work against England. Haller was annoyed and suggested I was only posing to be Irish. I was independent with Haller because . . . of my father the Germans would not dare to put me into a concentration camp.[6]

James did not explain what she meant by this, to which father she referred, or why the Germans would be hesitant to incarcerate her because of that. She was certainly only posing as Irish. November–December 1940 would seem an odd time for Abwehr II to send an agent to England. The Luftwaffe had been defeated in the skies over Britain, Operation Sea Lion had been cancelled in September, and German planners then busied themselves with the pending invasion of the Soviet Union. Although using James as a pathfinder is an unlikely scenario, German military intelligence officials did maintain the "Irish option" well past the point where it made any operational sense.

While still trying to decide how to best make use of James's qualifications, Haller put her in contact with several people—Franz Fromme,

Hermann Görtz, and eventually Francis Stuart. Franz Fromme—or "Professor," as he liked to be called—is a strange character even in a cast of strange characters.[7] He had been affiliated with German intelligence going back to World War I, and in the interwar period studied languages. Fromme visited Ireland in 1932 (and again in 1937) to research his pro-nationalist book, *Irlands Kampf um die Freiheit* (Ireland's Struggle for Freedom), and by the start of the war, he was, out of necessity, regarded by Abwehr as one of their few Irish "experts." The degree of his expertise is open to question, but it meant that he was the contact man for anything remotely having to do with Ireland. No record of Fromme's impression of Rosaleen James survives, although she obviously regarded him with affection: "That old professor was a wonderful person. A small man, loose-limbed and agile, his eyes sparkling with a force of humor behind the frameless glasses. . . . Because of his profound ethnological studies, a deep empathy and interest had been awakened in him for peoples under oppression."[8] Fromme was also given to dancing impromptu jigs and mazurkas on tabletops.[9]

Fromme, in turn, introduced Rosaleen to another German who was preparing to go off on an Abwehr II mission of his own: Hermann Görtz. James incorrectly describes him as a lieutenant-colonel in 1940; his rank was only that of a Luftwaffe reserve lieutenant.[10] Originally from the north German coastal city of Lübeck, Görtz served as both an infantry officer and then as a pilot/observer on the Eastern front during World War I. He was wounded and awarded the Iron Cross (2nd Class) as well as the pilot qualification badge. With his prewar training in law, Görtz struggled to make a living in the 1920s, accumulating debts, and at one point finding himself on the losing end of a libel suit filed by his former partner's wife. After so much sustained failure, Adolf Hitler's rise to power in 1933 offered Hermann Görtz a faint glimmer of hope. He applied for admission into the new Luftwaffe, but was rejected when officials discovered he had lied on his application. In desperation, Görtz turned to another organization, the Abwehr. With his excellent command of English and his aviation background, he offered to travel to England and obtain crucial information on the Royal Air Force. Amazingly, the Abwehr agreed—and in some ways Görtz was the perfect deniable agent. If he was caught, he was a civilian acting on his own: there were no official ties back to German military intelligence.

Görtz, accompanied by his nineteen-year-old mistress, Marianne Emig, proceeded to England, spied on RAF bases, and then was foolish enough to leave much of the compromising evidence of his espionage in a rented room while he and his mistress briefly returned to Germany.[11] The officers of Britain's domestic intelligence service, MI5, did not believe he would be gullible enough to be lured back. They were wrong.

Görtz was apprehended the moment he stepped off the boat at Harwich, tried in the Old Bailey (the Central Criminal Court of England and Wales) on charges of espionage, and convicted in 1935; he served a sentence of three years. Returning to Germany in 1939, Görtz knew better than to expect a hero's welcome, given the international ridicule he garnered during the trial. Future active service with the Luftwaffe was out of the question, but there still might be one option: work again for the Abwehr. It is impossible to fully understand why Görtz was chosen for field work—he was fifty years old and a failure as a spy, and he already showed indications of the acute psychological problems that surfaced later in his life. On the other hand, the Abwehr did not possess a pool of highly trained, highly qualified agents for a mission to England or Ireland. Görtz at least spoke English, had military experience (albeit of a dated variety), was educated, and had been to both Ireland (as a tourist in 1927) and England (prisoner from 1935 to 1939). Görtz wasn't James Bond, but he was available. Abwehr II decided to send him to neutral Ireland in an effort to coordinate and direct the Irish Republican Army's (IRA's) efforts against England in a way that would have operational benefit to Germany.[12] It was a decision they would all come to regret.

During the mission preparation phase, it made sense to find a native English speaker with whom Görtz could practice his English. Franz Fromme knew the perfect candidate: Rosaleen James. Although it is now impossible to date with precision, at some point between being in Vienna in 1938 and arriving in Berlin in March 1940, Rosaleen James first assumed a necessary element in her Irish identity kit: the surname of O'Mara. Her family in England continued to send her money addressed to Rosaleen James, but for the rest of her time in Germany, she exclusively used the O'Mara pseudonym.[13] To the Abwehr at this uncertain stage of the war, any Irish resource was welcome, even if turned out that the resource was not Irish at all.

Görtz and James met at least several times, although it is difficult to determine from her recollections the exact nature of the relationship. She reports Fromme being with them on one occasion, dancing another of his tabletop jigs to the discomfort of Leutnant Görtz.[14] In what becomes her familiar refrain, contrasting innocent Germany with the predatory intentions of her neighbors, James adds:

> He [Görtz] was a tragic individual, but a strong and resourceful person. One great weakness in him is the occasion of failure for the strongest of us; namely not to be able to see the good beyond evil. Görtz's race typically lacks discernment. They push firmly onward for the sake of their aim, but are blind to the tricks life can play. Both things were true for them, that they'd suspect people who were no danger for them, and to recognize the enemy too late. I saw how often this most intelligent and powerful race in Europe would walk as if on clouds, into the snares set by their envious neighbours.[15]

Given her limited contact with mission details, James's postwar memories seem to have been influenced more by what she read or wanted to believe than by the facts. While she is generally correct about the overall outline of Görtz's mission to Ireland, there are several curious errors. She describes him not as "an agent in the sabotage unit of the counterintelligence department, the Abwehr II" but instead as "an official of high rank of that department, doing duty with [Admiral Wilhelm] Canaris."[16] There are errors aplenty here. Görtz was assigned to Abwehr II, and although sabotage was indeed part of their tasks, Abwehr III was responsible for counterintelligence. Görtz was a low-level and barely trained tactical asset, certainly not an official of high rank in the Abwehr or anywhere else. During his many years in captivity in Ireland (1941–47), Görtz constantly exaggerated his military record and job description to the point where Irish Military Intelligence officers found it comical. It seems more likely that James's recollections are based more on this than on independent memories.[17]

Görtz landed by parachute in Ireland on 4 May 1940. He accomplished none of his mission objectives. While he had several close calls with Irish police and security forces, he managed to make contact with the IRA, discovered the IRA was more inept than the Germans imagined, and almost immediately started sending messages back to Germany, begging to return home. Given Ireland's delicate political balance—maintaining outward neutrality between two warring nations—Görtz was useful to have around, up to a point. If Germany won, Irish inaction toward the German spy might go a long way toward sweetening Hitler's view and in redressing Irish grievances against a defeated Britain. Once the prospect of Operation Sea Lion receded in late 1940, and certainly after the German invasion of Russia in June 1941, Görtz became a liability in a world where Allied victory seemed more likely. He was arrested in November 1941 and spent the next years imprisoned in Custume Barracks, Athlone, where his paranoid delusions grew increasingly fantastic. Faced with the prospect of returning to Germany after the war, he committed suicide in 1947.

In what is probably the most psychologically prescient statement ever written about Rosaleen James, Irish writer Francis Stuart observed, "The girl's delight in what she believed was the discomfiture of her own people, or at least her mother's, came . . . because of the hurts and slights, real or imagined, she had suffered as a child and adolescent."[18] Stuart was in a position to know; he lived with James for the better part of a year in wartime Berlin. Stuart's own odyssey to that time and place was no less remarkable. The son of Irish parents who had immigrated to Australia, Stuart returned to Ireland with his mother after his father's suicide. He rapidly gained fame as one of the exciting new voices in Irish poetry, and by 1920 had met and married Iseult Gonne, troubled daughter of formidable revolutionary Maude Gonne. The marriage did not prosper, and by the late 1930s Stuart was looking for an exit. Using the connections provided by his wife's family, Stuart traveled to Germany in 1938. The visit was arranged by Helmut Clissmann (representative in Ireland for the Deutscher Akademischer Austauschdienst [German Academic Exchange Service] and later an officer in German military intelligence). Stuart returned home to Ireland briefly before leaving again for Germany in 1939, carrying with him a secret message from the IRA to their would-be Abwehr sponsors. Although he later discussed returning to Ireland as a German agent, Stuart was largely apolitical and spent much of his time in an academic appointment at Berlin University and as the unofficial resident Irishman in Berlin.

In this capacity, Stuart first met Rosaleen James. Dr. Kurt Haller introduced Stuart and Hermann Görtz during the preparation phase for the latter's mission in the spring of 1940; Stuart could provide important details about Ireland that were otherwise unknown to the Abwehr. He went so far as to offer his own home, Laragh Castle, as an emergency refuge to the German agent.[19] Görtz's pre-mission support clique was fairly small, and it was inevitable, perhaps intentional, that James and Francis Stuart would meet.

Although Stuart did not write an autobiography, he dealt with Rosaleen James in two of his many works. The first of these, published in 1948, was *Pillar of Cloud*. In 1971, Stuart published what is generally regarded as his finest novel, *Black List, Section H*, a barely fictionalized narrative of his wartime experiences in Berlin. The protagonist, "H" (Stuart's given name was Henry) is approached by "Dr. Zimmerman" (Dr. Kurt Haller) and asked if he would be willing to write radio talks to be broadcast back to England; this paralleled exactly what Stuart began doing in 1940. In the book, Zimmermann wants to introduce H to "an Irish woman, or so she says." That woman, called Susan Loyson in the book, is Rosaleen James. Stuart describes the Loyson character as a "sick-looking girl" and speculates that "she looked, he thought, as though she might have been the daughter of a Spanish croupier, and Italian jockey . . . or the owner of a back-street hotel in, say, Cyprus or Malta."[20] What Stuart was getting at was that, wherever Rosaleen James came from, she looked intriguing and far from respectable.

In the novel, H and Susan Loyson meet again later in H's apartment, where H attempts to discover more about Loyson's Irishness:

"Your family must be worrying about you."

"All the family I've got is a grandfather in London. My mother's dead, and as for my father, I don't even know for sure who he was."

This or something like it, he sensed was true, and it partly accounted for her air of a lost child equally ready to melt or turn vicious.

"Zimmermann said you were Irish."

"I had to give them a good reason for my wanting to stay on here."

"Ah!"

"You see, I'm going to have a baby."

She glanced at him with a half-hostile, half-suppliant look. She couldn't have known she was going to be faced with a real Irishman when she'd told the Germans her story, and he wondered a little about what she'd just said (later she explained that her grandfather had taken his daughter with him on the first British diplomatic mission to Russia after the Revolution). She struck him as someone constantly having to defend herself as best she could against various kinds of authority.[21]

As Stuart discussed with author Kevin Kiely, the differences between the novel and the reality were slight: James was the adopted daughter of Sir Ian Hamilton, knew nothing about her biological father, and had been abandoned by her Ukrainian lover.[22] James discussed her time with Stuart in *Cé hÍ Seo Amuigh?* but her version was noticeably different. Putting on the mantle of an Irish expatriate, James says that at their first meeting she recognized a kindred spirit in Francis Stuart: "We were in the same boat, a little out of context, but here we were for good or for bad, and we would take up the fight for Caitlín Ní hUallacháin[23] if we could do her service, as did a lot of Irish artists over the ages, according to their abilities."[24] Whether due to their shared passion for Irish freedom or from some other motive, James and Stuart almost immediately began a physical affair, and she soon moved into his apartment on Nikolsburger Platz in Berlin's Wilmersdorf district.[25] She omits any discussion of their intimate relationship, instead moving quickly along to describing a joint secret operation whereby Stuart and James—following Haller's instructions—would move to a new location and operate a safe house for the Abwehr's Irish assets. The new apartment was the top floor of a building in a middle class neighborhood, with Stuart and James pretending to be brother and sister. Their first guest was IRA legend Frank Ryan.[26]

Ryan had been in difficult circumstances since 1938. Prior to that, he had been on the extreme left wing of the IRA and had formed the splinter Republican Congress within IRA ranks, directed at the working class and small farmers. Ryan and his allies were marginalized by the IRA leadership, and in disgust with the direction of politics at home, he left for Spain in 1937 to serve in the XV Brigade on behalf of the antifascist Spanish Republic. Ryan was wounded at the Battle of Jarama in 1937, recuperated back in Ireland, returned to Spain, and was captured during the Nationalist's Argonne Offensive in 1938. Initially sentenced to death for murder, his sentence was commuted to 30 years. Already half-deaf, Ryan had begun serving his time at Burgos prison when his dismal situation came to the attention of several notables: Leopold Kerney, Irish Minister to Spain; Helmut Clissmann (formerly of the German Academic Exchange Service, now with the Abwehr's Brandenburg Regiment); and Admiral Wilhelm Canaris, friend of Francisco Franco and head of the Abwehr. In a deal brokered among the various players—and with at least the silent assent of Irish Taoiseach Eamon de Valera—Abwehr agents arrived at Burgos to stage Ryan's false "escape" from Spanish custody and into German hands.

6

Best Laid Plans

After a brief stop in Paris, Frank Ryan was rushed to Berlin. His health was precarious and he was severely underweight, but the Abwehr's primary interest in him soon became clear: Ryan was to depart for Ireland immediately. During his captivity in Spain, many things had changed that brought German plans for Irish assets into play. Following the successful conclusion of the French campaign, Hitler issued a warning order to begin feasibility studies for the next operational target: Great Britain.[1] This and the subsequent directives of 16 July 1940 formed the basis of Operation Sea Lion. The various staff sections of the German military began their studies, assembled and evaluated information, and tried to hammer all this into a resourced and coherent series of objectives that might have a chance of success. Intelligence assessments drive the staff planning process, and it was evident that hard intelligence from and about England was essential, as was the need for a covert force capable of conducting pinpoint sabotage operations in support of the main invasion.

Unternehmen Hummer (Operation Lobster) was the Abwehr's ambitious and clearly ad hoc plan to fulfill this requirement. Teams of agents would be dispatched by various means—parachute and boat, among others—to various identified points and tasked with assessing the state of Britain's defenses and then communicating that information back to Germany. Despite a ready reserve of tough, highly trained, linguistically exceptional commando soldiers in the Abwehr's Brandenburg Regiment, the Abwehr instead chose to send largely inept, poorly trained, and geographically challenged personnel to conduct their intelligence-gathering missions. Many had difficulty speaking basic English, let alone passing themselves off without notice in a country already expecting invasion and primed for fifth-column espionage. Without exception, all of the subpar agents were apprehended.

Two dozen of these personnel were sent to England, and a small contingent went to Ireland as part of a secondary operation. The Ireland-bound troupe included a circus strongman (Ernst Weber-Drohl), a previously jailed spy (Hermann Görtz), an Indian exotic animal salesman (Henry Obed), and two enlisted soldiers (Dieter Gärtner and Herbert Tributh) from what had been German Southwest Africa, neither of whom had been in Ireland before or spoke unaccented, fluent English. By almost any reckoning, none of the agents had the slightest possibility of success, and most were apprehended within hours of landing in a country where outsiders are easy to identify. In what might have been a qualitative step up from the other missions, an opportunity presented itself in the spring of 1940 that might have at least offered the chance to put a German-friendly Irish national back in Ireland. That opportunity came in the form of Seán Russell.

Russell had been the prewar chief of the Irish Republican Army (IRA), but had run afoul of some senior members after the general failure of the 1939 bombing campaign against England; this resulted in a comprehensive security crackdown on both sides of the Irish Sea.[2] Russell voluntarily resigned his post and departed for America, ostensibly to raise money.[3] His American adventure saw few results, and in 1940, Russell—who was on both the British and American lists as a terrorist—was arrested and released on bail. He desperately wanted to return to Ireland. Normal passage was impossible because of his high-profile fugitive status, but German agent Carl Rekowski was able to list Russell as a crewman on the transatlantic ship *George Washington*, headed for Genoa, Italy. The Germans were not motivated by altruistic kindness; the price of transit was Russell's agreement to work for the Germans in exchange for their facilitating his return to Ireland. Authorization came directly from Admiral Wilhelm Canaris, the anti-Nazi officer in charge of the Abwehr. At that precise moment, a turf war was developing between the Abwehr and key officials at the Foreign Office, particularly Dr. Edmund Veesenmayer, who would shortly assume control of German operations dealing with Ireland.

Franz Fromme, Rosaleen James's jig-dancing friend from Berlin, acted as go-between. Russell finally arrived at Genoa on 1 May 1940 and was immediately taken to Berlin, with Fromme as his chaperone and translator. In fact, Russell arrived just as Hermann Görtz was departing. Russell and Haller made a desperate attempt to reach Kassel in time so that Görtz would at least have the advantage of being briefed by a genuine Irish person with the necessary political connections, but they missed Görtz by a matter of minutes. Russell's key task, though, had nothing to do with Hermann Görtz. Russell was instead focused on his own political/military mission back to his native country, and he began sabotage training at the Abwehr II facility in Berlin.

The Abwehr and Foreign Office insisted that Russell would have definite objectives in Ireland as well as the hazily defined "effective possibilities against English objectives." There are no specific details in either the mission files or in postwar interrogations as to what those Irish and English objectives were. Russell was directed to make contact with the IRA; the rest is a matter of conjecture. He was not going alone; his original companion was to have been Breton nationalist Paul Moyse, who had last been involved in an Irish-themed operation when he delivered a radio code word to IRA bomber Jim O'Donovan in 1939. In any event, Moyse was dropped from the mission when another, more valuable asset became available on 15 July: Frank Ryan.

Unternehmen Taube (Operation Dove), the Ryan–Russell mission to Ireland, ended badly. By the time Ryan arrived in Berlin on 4 August 1940, Russell's mission was just days away. Ryan later claimed, unconvincingly, that he never learned the mission agenda before departure, but in any case he was not trained for whatever mission that might be. Although Ryan certainly had a German-directed mission of his own, the existing records do not specify its nature. German submarine U-65 departed from Wilhelmshaven on 8 August, headed for Galway. Almost immediately, Russell began to complain of stomach pains, which grew increasingly more severe. Russell died while on board, some 100 miles away from his destination, from what was probably a burst gastric ulcer. He was buried at sea, and Frank Ryan elected to return with U-65 to occupied France. Despite overwhelming evidence to the contrary, Rosaleen James maintained in her autobiography that Russell was somehow poisoned, likely on orders from Admiral Canaris.[4]

Absent another mission suited to him, and also for lack of suitable Irish company in wartime Berlin, Ryan was afterward sent to live with Francis Stuart, which necessarily put him into direct contact with Rosaleen James. James's daughter, Nadejda, was born on 16 July 1940.[5] With Hermann Görtz then busy in Ireland, Rosaleen's source of income had evaporated, except for whatever money was paid to her by the Abwehr. Stuart arranged a position for her as his secretary at the Drahtloser Dienst (Wireless Service) where he polished English translations of German material for broadcast.[6] Although she continued to live with Stuart, the nature of their relationship changed. In *Black List*, the character inspired by Rosaleen starts becoming even more untruthful, and secretly begins seeing a Breton who is her child's father. If the stress of taking care of a newborn was not enough, her already rocky relationship with Stuart was made more acute by Ryan's arrival. James and Ryan did not get along. She describes him as behaving "like a spoiled child, much to our embarrassment." Ryan suffered from partial deafness and was therefore "suspicious of those around him," finding fault with those—meaning James—who tried to care for him.[7] Perhaps more importantly, Ryan would have known immediately that James was not what she claimed to be.

At least according to his own postwar version, Stuart did not get on much better with Ryan, although the two of them were in constant contact. As Stuart later recounted to historian David O'Donoghue:

> Ryan was in a very ambiguous position; started off fighting for the International Brigade and ending up as an advisor to the SS Colonel Veesenmayer, a Jew exterminator. I never liked Ryan, we didn't really get on. . . . As long as the Germans were planning an invasion of England, Ryan was treated like a VIP. . . . He got diplomat's rations and facilities, and he used to share them with us. He was a generous person but very, very touchy.[8]

Ryan's actions in Germany from 1940 to 1944 were not of any great consequence and did little to enhance his postwar reputation. Stuart, too, despite his outwardly apolitical ethos, flirted with collaboration in a way that was more serious than the mostly innocuous talks he gave on the radio. Both Ryan and Stuart crossed the line into collaboration. On at least one occasion, Rosaleen James joined them in this endeavor.[9]

Best Laid Plans

The German idea of recruiting British military personnel to fight against their own country had a precedent. In the second year of the First World War (1915), German Military Intelligence (IIIb) and the German Foreign Office (Auswärtiges Amt) conspired with dissident Irish nationalists, in the person of Sir Roger Casement, to engineer a favorable end to the war in Europe by promoting Irish rebellion behind Allied lines. Casement's ill-considered theory was that both Germany and the Irish nationalists in Sinn Féin (the leading Irish revolutionary group founded in 1905) would find a ready reserve of Irish nationalist manpower from among captured British prisoners of war. Right-thinking Irish, they reasoned, would have an existing animus toward Britain. For this purpose, captured personnel thought suitable for indoctrination and with politically amenable ideologies were concentrated in a special camp near Limburg, where it was anticipated that better conditions and pleas from Casement would be sufficient to encourage volunteers. The plan failed. Mostly jeered at by the captive soldiers, and even physically attacked by a soldier from the Royal Munster Fusiliers, Casement managed to scrape together only two volunteers (Robert Monteith and Daniel Bailey) out of fifty-odd members of the "Irish Brigade" for a covert return trip to Ireland in April 1916. They were captured just in time to see the Easter Rising go off half-cocked. The rebels garbled the co-ordination plan for the landing of German arms and ammunition; the freighter *Aud*, unable to raise any rebels on land, was scuttled after being intercepted by a Royal Navy patrol.[10]

German intelligence in World War I also attempted to use an Irishman as an espionage agent: Corporal Robert Dowling, who served in the Connaught Rangers. The Germans landed him by U-boat off County Clare, but this attempt, too, was destined for failure. Dowling was captured almost immediately and narrowly escaped the hangman's noose for his treachery.[11] Overall, Germany's experience with recruiting enemy prisoners for operational missions should have taught them that British (or Irish) subjects were not the most promising candidates. Despite this, and following further experimentation along these lines early in the Second World War, Germany still clung to the belief that this tenuous notion had merit—if not for operational purposes, then at least for propaganda value.

With the outbreak of World War II and the availability of British prisoners following the French campaign, the Abwehr and the German

Foreign Office took another look at using English POWs for covert operations. By early 1940, the former IRA chief of staff, Seán Russell—waiting to return to Ireland and then under the protection of SS-Brigadeführer (Major General) and Foreign Ministry Irish expert Dr. Edmund Veesenmayer—suggested recruiting ethnic Irish from among the captured British soldiers and forming them into an "Irish Legion," purposefully attempting to resurrect Casement's folly from almost twenty-five years earlier.[12] At the direction of the Foreign Office, and with the oversight of Abwehr II, a special camp was established near the village of Friesack: Stalag XX A (301).

The numbers of prisoners at this camp varied, but ranged from 100 to 160 at any one time. Prisoners were placed under the command of their own officers that the Germans considered reliable, with the majority of the men having been captured while serving in the British Army.[13] However, with rather strict regulations governing the service of foreign nationals in the German Army (usually restricted to *Reichsdeutsch* or *Volksdeutsch*), the Abwehr and Foreign Office intended to use Friesack to recruit Irish nationals for espionage missions rather than for conventional military service. Their aim was to capitalize on the propaganda value that might be derived from an "Irish Legion."[14]

In mid-1941, Rosaleen James, Frank Ryan, and Francis Stuart—accompanied by Kurt Haller and Helmut Clissmann—visited the camp at Friesack and participated in the plan to recruit Irish prisoners.[15] The theory was that Stuart and Ryan would be better able to determine whether the Irish prisoners were trustworthy, and both Stuart and Ryan operated under an implicit debt to their German hosts. While they could at least make the argument that their Irish nationality precluded a charge of treason for this conduct, James had no such defense.[16] She mentions this incident only briefly in her autobiography, framing it as another example of the Germans' noble motives: "It was a German characteristic to enter into things like that with a childlike trust or hope."[17] Despite claims that he was disillusioned afterward, Ryan later met with one of the few recruited prisoners in Berlin, telling him "anything he [the British collaborator] could do to help the Germans would be alright."[18]

After expending considerable time and resources on this pipe dream of a mission, the Abwehr failed again. As an example, officer recruitment among the prisoners was a problem: of the original eight selected, three were mistakenly picked because the Germans did not understand their responses; two were doctors who wanted better rations than they received at their home stalags; and one was a (non-Irish) journalist who saw the possibility of a good story while in the initial screening camp at Stalag III B.[19] Only nine enlisted men eventually came forward for duty. Of these nine, two had previous criminal convictions in Ireland, one was later confined to an asylum, and another Irish volunteer, formerly of the 1st Battalion/East Lancashire Regiment, was later incarcerated by the Germans on a rape charge.[20]

The Germans finally extracted a few collaborators, but only on a very temporary basis. The Abwehr selected Sergeant John Codd (Royal Welsh Fusiliers), and he successfully completed several training R/T (radio/telegraph) courses while various missions were considered and then abandoned. Codd and another recruit, Frank Stringer, were scheduled to participate in Unternehmen Gastwirt (Operation Innkeeper), which was designed to establish a radio link with Germany from London, but this too was cancelled.[21] Codd was soon arrested by the Gestapo for fraternizing with German women, though he was later released and joined the rival SS intelligence service, the Sicherheitsdienst (SD).[22] The other members of this erstwhile band of brothers were soon arrested and jailed after one of them confessed his intention to turn himself into the British police upon landing.[23] By 1943, the bitter pill of experience caused the Abwehr to cease recruiting potential agents from among British and Irish prisoners.

Ryan's utility to the Abwehr had likewise come to an end. Although he was briefly mentioned in connection with other fanciful return-to-Ireland scenarios, in one of them to be accompanied by Francis Stuart, his last years were spent in declining health. He was admitted to the sanatorium at Dresden-Loschwitz and died there on 10 June 1944.[24] Germany had run out of meaningful IRA resources and was left with only pitiful substitutes—Rosaleen James among them—should Ireland again come back into operational calculations.

7

Life in the Heart of the Reich

Jean Hamilton died on 23 February 1941, leaving a codicil in her will revoking an earlier bequest to Rosaleen, effectively disinheriting her. Rosaleen's share of Jean's estate was redirected to Harry Knight. The reason for this is not explained in the Hamilton papers, but with Captain Knight's own death in June 1941 in Egypt, the entirety of the estate reverted to Sir Ian.[1] It is clear from correspondence between attorneys that no one in England had a precise idea of Rosaleen's whereabouts or situation: "We understand that she married a Russian and we suppose she thereupon became a Russian subject."[2] Although Rosaleen later claimed that she only heard about Lady Hamilton's death a year afterward, this is untrue. Writing to Nadejda Muir (her aunt by marriage)—interestingly, not to Sir Ian—on 21 May 1941, Rosaleen asks about specific items located in the Hamilton home, apparently unaware she had been disinherited: "Should there be things in the will concerning me, or even my child, I give you complete authority to act in my name." Her concern, though, seems more directed at items with a sentimental attachment, not money. She asked about a photo album of childhood snapshots, a doll, a photo of herself at age three, and a good photograph of Lady Hamilton. She further asks that one of the Hamilton servants, Annie, get £20 from a post office account and use the money to buy wreaths for Lady Hamilton's grave.[3]

Monthly payments to Rosaleen under the existing trust continued, albeit by a very circuitous route. Until the United States entered the war against Germany in December 1941, Sir Kay Muir sent money to the Foreign Office, which in turn forwarded the amount of £15 to the U.S.

Consul in Berlin. Rosaleen's current address was unknown—apparently by design—but American authorities delivered that amount to Augsburgerstraße 24, her last known whereabouts.[4] Earlier in the year, Hamilton had written to his solicitors, "Miss James was in Germany earning her living with the permission of her guardian, Lady Hamilton, when war broke out. Since then she has not, presumably, been able to get home and is now living, as far as I know although she never writes to me, in Berlin."[5]

By this point, Rosaleen's involvement with Francis Stuart had reached a crescendo. In Stuart's version in *Black List*, the Susan Loyson character (inspired by Rosaleen James) became reacquainted sexually with her child's father, and turned secretive and withdrawn. Stuart's attention had already shifted from James to a woman who worked as a translator in the Rundfunkhaus, Gertrud Meissner, and as that relationship deepened, the existing one between Stuart and Rosaleen James weakened accordingly.[6] Stuart's biographer writes that James attempted to continue an acting career with the help of their mutual acquaintance, Brigitte Horney.[7] This was apparently unsuccessful; James did not appear in any German wartime films, and there is no record of her appearing on stage.

In what was more of fantasy than a likely scenario, Stuart and James briefly discussed fleeing Germany for Soviet Russia. Stuart was always somewhat left-leaning (as indeed was the IRA), but this scheme became more focused when they met Harro and Libertas Schulze-Boysen. Probably unknown to Stuart and James, the Schulze-Boysens were part of a Soviet-controlled spy network called the Rote Kapelle.[8] (They were arrested, tried for treason, and executed in 1942.) As the acquaintance of a notable *Landesverräter* (traitor), Stuart (but not James) was interviewed by the Gestapo but was never taken into custody.[9] After the German invasion of the Soviet Union on 22 June 1941, any fanciful plans Stuart and James had to shift to Russia were no longer feasible.

Decades later, and almost certainly referencing the Schulze-Boysens and the Rote Kapelle, James wrote that "Communist infiltration was underway even right at the center of German authority." Considering James's later statements about Communism (i.e., her reference to "accursed Bolsheviks," and her statement, "Was it not Germany's own business to put a stop to the barbarians as it was wont to do before?"), the idea of her flirting with a move to Stalin's Russia is ironic.[10] She likewise labels Frank Ryan as a Communist convicted for a life sentence.[11]

Jean Muir at the time of her marriage to Ian Hamilton. Portrait by John Singer Sargent, 1896. Courtesy National Portrait Gallery, London.

Sir Ian and Lady Hamilton, Lennoxlove, Scotland, 1938. Courtesy Liddell Hart Centre for Military Archives, King's College, London.

The Hamilton Clan, 1938. *Front row, seated, left to right*: Harry Knight, Lady Hamilton. *Back row, standing, center*: Sir Ian Hamilton. *Back row, far right*: Rosaleen James. The rest are relatives from the Montcrieffe family. Courtesy Liddell Hart Centre for Military Archives, King's College, London.

Harry Knight and Lady Hamilton, early 1930s. Courtesy Liddell Hart Centre for Military Archives, King's College, London.

Sir Ian Hamilton and Adolf Hitler, Berchtesgaden, 1938. Courtesy Liddell Hart Centre for Military Archives, King's College, London.

Hamilton and Hitler in Berchtesgaden, 1938. Courtesy Liddell Hart Centre for Military Archives, King's College London.

Hamilton and Hitler at lunch. Courtesy Liddell Hart Centre for Military Archives, King's College London.

Phyllis "Rosaleen" James as she appeared on MI5's "Renegades" list. The photo was taken near the end of the war. From the collection of Mark M. Hull.

The building that housed the Inishmaan museum from 1973 to 1974. Courtesy Vera Moynes, 2010.

Rosaleen James looks on as Irish Government Minister Tom O'Donnell formally opens the Inishmaan museum, 2 August 1973. Courtesy *Connacht Tribune*, Galway, 10 August 1973, 46.

Cover of *Who Is She Outside? Róisín's Memoirs*, 1991. Courtesy Coiscéim, Dublin.

Cover of *At Home and Abroad, Memoirs 2*, 2006. Courtesy Armagh Diocesan Historical Society, Armagh.

8

Publishing in Berlin
Irische Freiheitskämpfer *and a Government Memorandum*

Through Francis Stuart, James achieved a marvellous thing for a young, nonacademic foreigner: she published an essay in a collection dedicated to Irish freedom fighters. The achievement is the more remarkable at a time when paper was scarce and German publishers cut down on titles and circulation. The publication brought James together with Ruth Weiland, a German academic and translator and editor of the volume, whose acquaintance with James ended only after the war, under circumstances worth exploring here. Two years after this publication—or so James claims in *Cé hÍ Seo Amuigh?*—Stuart passed a job of research on to her for another, more ambitious essay or book that came within a hair's breadth of publication and fell victim to a British bomb.

Sometime in 1940, Francis Stuart introduced James to Weiland, whom he had first met in the spring of 1939.[1] Weiland had begun to translate Stuart's work into German after he took up his academic post in Berlin, and she had also published a German translation of Maud Gonne's *Servant to the Queen*. As James misremembered it fifty years after the event, Weiland next intended to bring out Stuart's new novel; however, it was likely Stuart's analytical piece on Roger Casement, which he was working on at this time, that Weiland intended to publish (*Der Fall Casement—Das Leben Sir Roger Casements und der Verleumdungsfeldzug des Secret Service*, 1940).[2] James describes how she herself was intimately involved with the writing process of that "novel" for a time. Despite James's protestations that she had no typing skills, Stuart furnished her with a borrowed typewriter and gave her dictation. James soon gave this up, and makes much of her indifference toward the female students that took her place.[3]

Weiland's acquaintance, however, became more important to James: under the name "Nora O'Mara" she contributed a fifteen-page essay to *Irische Freiheitskämpfer*, a volume edited by Weiland and with an introduction by Stuart. The publication was a collection of biographical sketches of Irish "freedom fighters"—taking the term in the widest sense, as Stuart explains, by including pieces about the noncombatants Charles Stewart Parnell and Douglas Hyde.[4]

The purpose of this publication was to present to the German public the last few "milestones" of Ireland's pursuit of its independence. Weiland herself might be the author of the blurb (there is no preface by her):

> Die Geschichte Irlands ist die mit Blut und Tränen geschriebene Passion eines tapferen Volkes, das Jahrhunderte hindurch einen ununterbrochenen, erbitterten Kampf um Freiheit und Unabhängigkeit seines von England unterjochten Landes geführt hat. Es ist aber auch ein Heldenlied von Männern die neben ihren Beruf als Gelehrte, Dichter und Bauern ihr Leben lang Kämpfer waren, und von Frauen, die Kinder, Heim und alles freudig ihrem bedrängten Vaterland zum Opfer brachten.

> [Ireland's history is the passion play of a courageous people who for centuries has been leading a constant and bitter struggle for its country's freedom and independence, while suffering from English oppression. But it is also the heroic epic of men who—besides their work as scholars, poets and famers—were also fighters, and of women who joyously sacrificed children, a home, and everything for their set-upon fatherland.]

The men and the woman whose lives are treated by the essays are "Irish leaders who gave themselves in hundredfold for the freedom of Éire, a bardic island wrapped in myth."[5] Beyond using the word *Heldenlied* (epic saga), a word immediately associable with the Siegfrieds, Kriemhilds, Dietrichs, and Gudruns deployed by Nazi mythologizers, the editor does not intrude any further in linking Irish nationalistic efforts with

Germany. The reader is left to draw his or her own conclusions about these subtle suggestions of fraternity.

Stuart identifies Ireland's history as defined by

> jener kleinen Gruppe, die durch die Jahrhunderte hindurch das Ideal der irischen Freiheit lebendig erhalten hat. . . . Irlands Geschichte ist ungleich der anderer Länder, sie ist die Geschichte eines Landes, das beständig im Kriege lag.

> [that small group who has kept the ideal of Irish freedom alive through the centuries. . . . Ireland's history is unlike that of other countries; it is the history of a country continuously at war.][6]

The essays cover the lives of Charles Stewart Parnell, Douglas Hyde, Roger Casement, Maud Gonne MacBride, Pádraig Pearse, and Eamon de Valera. The decision to exclude freedom fighter par excellence Michael Collins was a matter of course: the book belongs within the wider context of a German state siding with a nation that had been the victim of English imperialism, not with a nation seeking to come to a political and peaceful arrangement with its neighbor.

The choice of James as a contributor had to have been a fruit of her connections with Stuart and Franz Fromme, since she had no previous journalistic or academic work to her name, and no personal claim on the subject of her essay: the politician, educator and writer Pádraig Pearse. Three other contributors either had a real connection to their subjects, or else they pretended they did: Franz Fromme, one of the German Abwehr's experts on Ireland, wrote about Roger Casement, whom he claimed to have taken care of during World War I;[7] Weiland herself wrote of Maud Gonne McBride, with whom she had been in correspondence while translating and publishing her autobiography;[8] and Stuart—most tangibly, one could say—wrote of Eamon de Valera.[9] Another contributor, Ludwig Mühlhausen, was also very likely acquainted with his subject: Douglas Hyde. As head of Celtic Studies at the Berlin University, Mühlhausen had spent a prolonged period of time in Ireland in 1937, collecting folk tales in the Gaeltacht and doing research in Dublin.[10] And lastly, Vincent Coyle wrote—at the furthest remove of all contributors—about Charles Stewart Parnell; Coyle seems to have been a Dubliner turned German industrialist.[11] As such, the contributors were a motley crew indeed, and in many instances (Fromme, Coyle, O'Mara [James]) reflect the lack in Germany of professional Irish historians or journalists more suited to the task. When James in her memoir talks of "several professors of Celtic studies" contributing to the book, she perhaps mistakenly added Hans Hartmann, who a year later became co-responsible, with Mühlhausen, for the *Irlandreferat* of the German–Irish broadcasting effort. Maybe she wished to lend the publication more gravitas. However, she endeavored to make little of the publication in her memoirs, alluding to it again later with diffidence, and incorrectly, as "that book about the [Easter] Rising which I had contributed to."[12]

James's own piece, then, a biographical sketch of Pádraig Pearse, is a ringing endorsement of Pearse's life and death: "He died so that we may live" (er starb, damit wir leben können).[13] By pseudonym she poses as an Irish-born writer, by expression she identifies herself with the nation, and the choice of subject was apt, given Pearse's complex political and linguistic manifesto: much of her anti-British vitriol and her postwar hopes for the Irish language are paralleled in Pearse's writings. The Irish language was what set her apart from Francis Stuart, whose Anglo-Irish dream she could not share, herself being one of the "extremists" who were absorbed by the Irish language revival.[14] Apart from whatever Irish she had learned during her one or two brief journeys to Ireland before the war, James was taking up Irish language lessons with an Irish national at the time, a certain Liam Mullally, who will feature here again.[15]

James had free rein to celebrate Pearse's selfless patriotism and his vision for the language. The piece begins with the rousing statement that "Irish blood was once again victorious over English blood. Pádraig Henry Pearse, son of an English father and an Irish mother, born in Dublin, felt more Irish than Ossian himself."[16] She describes a talented and well-respected writer, teacher, and orator, an idealist and a shy person, who became a successful entrepreneur (as founder of St. Enda's school), and whose plans for the Rising, however precise, were not bolstered by any military experience. She recounts matter-of-factly the events in the fight for the Dublin General Post Office during the 1916 rebellion and the subsequent surrender, and she finds that the English, in seeking to make examples, merely created martyrs. Pearse's mission, James judges eventually, was fulfilled in his death: "Ireland has canonized another son."[17]

Using Pearse as the vehicle, the anonymity of her pseudonym allowed James free rein to pose as Irish and champion the revolutionary and nationalistic cause without the danger of exposing herself as the English woman she really was. It likewise previews her narrative trajectory in the years following World War II.

It is difficult to say what research James may have done for this essay. By 1940, Pearse had already been the subject of three biographies, one of them in French, one in Irish; and his writings had been collectively published by Talbot Press in 1932. The Berliner Universität (today Humboldt Universität), which James may have had access to through her friend Fromme and maybe also her co-contributor Mühlhausen, can boast that it survived both the Nazi auto-da-fé and the severe bombings of Berlin, suffering very little damage.[18] Its catalogue does not include any of these works, but it is likely that Stuart or other Irish expatriates owned Pearse's writings, or even the biographies by Louis Le Roux or Séamus Ó Searcaigh, so that James could quote Pearse's words from his famous oratory at O'Donovan Rossa's graveside in 1915: "Life springs from death; and from the graves of patriot men and women spring living nations."[19] Her only other recourse to historical quotation in her essay is her citation from Pearse's last manifesto of 28 April 1916, and a reference to George Bernard Shaw's protest, printed in an English paper, against the executions.

Despite this rather prestigious achievement—that is, for a young woman without much in the way of advanced education or experience, and with spurious connections to the nation whose interests she defended—James has little that is good to say of Weiland, her publisher. It is worth enlarging on this. On their last encounter just after the War, James describes Weiland as a "pánaí mná scothaosta den mheánaicme" (a plump middle-aged woman of middle-class background)[20] who had been translating English works until the market for those translations dried up owing to the war. Weiland then, according to James, turned to Anglo-Irish authors, banking her hopes on the great wave of interest in Ireland. An opportunist, in James's eyes, Weiland had her eye solely on business and did not act out of sympathy for the Irish cause.

Added to the real achievement of publishing this chapter, James also claimed that she was given a second commission to write. The opportunity came about two years after *Irische Freiheitskämpfer* and was ostensibly for the government: this plan was eventually thwarted by an Allied bomb, so she said, making it nearly impossible to check up on her implausible account. In her telling, a German state publisher asked Francis Stuart, sometime after the German declaration of war on Russia, to write an account of the English occupation of Ireland and their misrule, which might be used as a guide for German policy for Poland.[21] Because he was busy with his novel at the time,[22] Stuart deflected this work onto James.

James's approach to this fanciful commission was heavy with her usual romantic view of the Germans and their judgment as to what was best for the Poles. She was characteristically full of praise for the circumspect Germans who tried to do their best for their "neighbors"—that is, the newly colonized Poles:

> Here are the Germans for you, again! They would try to get to grips with any problem as soon as it appeared on the horizon! The question of returning fallow lands in France to cultivation, and the getting to grips with racial enmity in the east, did not matter, and could be left to one side for a while. They could not for anything restrain themselves, or deny the old missionary spirit. You see the Germans, what with their own lives upside down around them, taking up with visionary designs like this which concerned the uncertain future that lay before them![23]

This political book was to be a study of how one should *not* do things in the occupied Polish lands. It would have been an extraordinary choice for German policy makers to employ an English woman with a spurious Irish background and no academic kudos for counsel on the future of their Polish conquests.

For James, it was very engaging to study the failings of the colonization of Ireland, though not many of the relevant books were available to her. "Still, as a testimony for all that happened afterwards, it is quite a matter of regret for me that a bomb destroyed the publishing house in question with my manuscript gone in the conflagration before it was published."[24] If her claim bore a kernel of truth, it would be fascinating to see how she gave account of English imperialism and its most regrettable impact on Ireland.

9

Radio Star

Although the physical and emotional relationship between Francis Stuart and Rosaleen James ended in 1941, they continued to see each other, and Stuart arranged for James's next position with what was called the Irland-Redaktion: the Irish service of Germany's radio propaganda network. James's financial situation was desperate, but her autobiographical memories portray her initial meeting at the Rundfunkhaus as one of relief—on the German director's part: "When I came to help him it was an obvious relief." She describes the Irland-Redaktion director, Dr. Hans Hartmann, as a Celtic scholar who was unqualified for his post and who therefore allowed her free rein when it came to writing, production, and broadcasting.[1] That is untrue, and James's version is contrary to existing records and the memories of everyone else who worked there. James says that her work for German radio was done for but one purpose: to combat the "lying stories that were broadcast by England, no doubt seeking to lure the Irish into a fight without good cause."[2]

Even considering the idiosyncratic nature of Germany's wartime radio propaganda effort, the Irish service was an anomaly. A few prewar advisors (Germans who had visited Ireland) suggested that there were many Irish who could be swayed to Germany's viewpoint, or at least content to support the Irish government's neutrality. Hartmann's idea, though, was to direct the programming at even more of a niche market, but one where the German message might find an even better reception: the smaller Irish-speaking segment of Ireland's population. Before studying the Irish language became mandatory in 1928, only a small percentage of the citizenry was sufficiently fluent, and of those who were fluent, most lived and worked in the Gaeltacht (primarily Irish-speaking regions). It was no coincidence that this same population was considered to be the bedrock of Irish nationalism, which the Germans considered a potential reservoir of anti-British sentiment.

Sending anti-British words and ideas in the direction of an audience already primed to hate England made perfect sense to German planners on a number of levels. This theory's success hinged on the answers to several questions. Was there a sufficiently large Irish-speaking audience with radio sets? What was the desired outcome, assuming the subtle propaganda message got through? Could the British successfully jam or counter radio programming beamed at the target Irish audience? Who should properly direct the effort: Ministry for Propaganda, Foreign Office, Abwehr, or another agency? The key jurisdictional issue was never solved. Although Hitler eventually decided that the Foreign Office (Auswärtiges Amt or AA) was responsible for overseas broadcasting, radio propaganda still remained under the control of Goebbels' Propaganda Ministry (Reichsministerium für Volksaufklärung und Propaganda, or RMVP)—a typical Nazi bureaucratic solution of having overlapping, mutually exclusive agencies charged with identical responsibilities despite their very different political agendas.

At war's outbreak, 166,275 Irish homes had radio licenses—approximately one person in every seventeen. Most of the sets were in Dublin, while the target Irish-speaking areas in Connaught and Donegal had few.[3] Perhaps in recognition of this painful reality, the Irish service broadcasts evolved from an all Irish format to a bilingual Irish–English one, with English having the largest airtime share. Even with that, other German programming aimed at the British home market (and also heard in Ireland) was usually more interesting and informative, and more popular.

Dr. Hartmann, the creative force behind the Irish service, prevailed in developing a propaganda message that emphasized Irish neutrality. Attempting to create an Irish ally by means of radio broadcasts was nonsensical, and given the degree of familial and economic exchange between Ireland and Britain, such a scheme had no chance of success. Attempting to further subvert that relationship would provide England with a motive to block the already tenuous radio link between Berlin and Ireland. As it happened, while the RMVP was initially charged with producing an Irish service broadcast, they soon lost interest in the project, and the AA assumed responsibility in late 1941. The AA and RMVP were both often prone to mistakes, but the AA was typically the more restrained of the two; placing the Irish service under the AA aegis helped ensure that less of the virulent anti-Semitic material was broadcast.

As a practical matter, it was impossible for anyone at the Foreign Office or the RMVP to find out if their expenditure on Irish-centric propaganda had any effect whatsoever. Although in a comprehensive series of evaluations, Irish military intelligence concluded that the impact of all of Germany's Irish language efforts was entirely benign.

When James joined the radio team, she must have marvelled at the sheer range of personalities who made up the Irland-Redaktion.

> *Dr. Hans Hartman*: A professor and Celtic scholar, he had made many pre-war visits to Ireland and lived there for two years.
>
> *Liam Mullally*: Of Irish/English parentage, he was an exceptional linguist who left Ireland in 1939 to teach at the Berlitz school in Berlin. Briefly considered for employment in German intelligence, he was ultimately rejected.
>
> *James Blair*: A British journalist who had an Irish mother, he had worked for the Irish radio service since 1941. Fired from the Irland-Redaktion in 1942, he later broadcast for the German InterRadio service in Austria.[4]
>
> *Susan Hilton*: A British/Irish survivor of a sunken ship, an alcoholic, and intelligent, she could write scripts but was gradually consumed by depression.

Because of a severe shortage of authentic Irish, the Irland-Redaktion was obliged to take the closest alternatives to actual Irish it could get. Although the majority of wartime broadcasts were done from the larger facility at the Reichs-Rundfunkhaus on Adolf-Hitler-Platz, Irish programming originated from the smaller venue at the Deutscher Kurzwellensender (German Shortwave Transmitter) at Kaiserdamm 77 in Berlin-Charlottenburg.

Rosaleen James characterized the Rundfunkhaus as place infested by an internal threat: "There were many German Jews working undisturbed there as actors. The impotence of the Germans here was obvious; because they never distinguished between friends and enemies the place little by little became a sort of headquarters of spies."[5] Her link between Jews and spies is never specified; neither does she give the names of any of the "many Jews" she claims worked at the heart of Germany's propaganda empire. Some of her more detailed language is reserved for two foreign broadcasters at the Rundfunkhaus whom she included as being among those who "were without any connection to politics who were caught up in the big maelstrom of the war": William "Lord Haw-Haw" Joyce and Mildred "Axis Sally" Gillars.

There are some intriguing parallels between Gillars and Rosaleen James. Starting out with the goal of becoming a theatrical actress, Gillars was singularly unsuccessful and eventually drifted to Europe, where she worked as a dressmaker and sometime fashion model, finally teaching English at the Berlitz School in Berlin during the same time James worked there on a part-time basis.[6] Her work as a broadcaster on the Reichs-Rundfunk-Gesellschaft began in 1940, but her true stardom dates from America's entry in the war in 1941. To American soldiers from 1942 to 1945, Mildred Gillars was the voice of the enemy, Axis Sally.[7] Her weekly "Midge at the Mike," "Home Sweet Home Hour," and "G.I.'s Letterbox" programs specialized in mocking satire designed to weaken Allied morale, and implied that wives and girlfriends of soldiers were serially unfaithful.[8] These broadcasts also targeted the families of wounded and captured Americans, all mixed with a healthy dose of anti-Semitism. Her particular brand of invective never varied in content or tone.

> Well, you seem to think you've got a grudge against Germany? You prefer perhaps the Jews? You'd like to crony around with them. You prefer Communism. You prefer Bolshevism. Well . . . that's no America for me, I must say, and I'd rather die for Germany than live for one hundred years on milk and honey in the Jewish America of today.[9]

Her beliefs never wavered, even when the cause was lost. "The war for me was one against England and the Jews," she said after her arrest.[10] Gillars was a true believer.

In her memoir, James's admiration of Gillars is palpable. She describes Gillars as "a very handsome woman," and "neither an intellectual, nor a highly political woman, or a great activist, but she was mature, honest and full of fun." James's approval for the tone of Gillars's radio persona is likewise evident; she speaks of Gillars's forthright stand against the United States and its part in the "shameful and useless" war. Gillars, she maintained, was committed to the idea of putting "her compatriot soldiers back on the right path, led astray as they were by perverse influences." Gillars loyally worked for Nazi radio until the week after Hitler's suicide. American authorities were less than grateful for her efforts to raise consciousness among their troops.

William Joyce, whose passion and personality Rosaleen James found appealing, was in a different category altogether. Joyce was born in 1906 to an Irish Catholic father in Brooklyn, New York, and the family moved back to Galway, Ireland, a short time later. Unlike James, Joyce was never comfortable with an Irish identity, and actively sided with the Protestant cause and the Black and Tans during the War of Independence (1919–21). Fearing reprisal, the family again moved, this time to England, where William attended school and became attracted to the fascist policies then being advocated by Sir Oswald Mosley and his British Union of Fascists (BUF). Joyce rose rapidly in the ranks, eventually becoming director of propaganda and the Deputy Leader of the party. Despite the meteoric growth in British fascist circles, Joyce grew disillusioned with his fellow believers, thinking that Mosley was too timid and not carrying the movement to its logical extreme. In particular, Joyce subscribed to the anti-Jewish, anti-foreign philosophies of the extreme right wing of an already extremely right-wing political movement. He was expelled from the BUF in 1937 and founded his own marginal party, the National Socialist League, which was modelled even more closely after Hitler's German National Socialist party than was its predecessor. Under the normal course of events, Joyce would have been interned—like Sir Oswald Mosley—under Defence Regulations 18B as a potential wartime threat to state security. He and his wife, Margaret, circumvented that fate by using fake British passports and leaving for Germany in 1939. Both the passport and his British citizenship (which he formally renounced in 1940, becoming a naturalized German citizen) became the key issues that decided his fate.

Rosaleen James remembers first meeting Joyce at the radio station, where he made a drawing of her daughter. In her retouched postwar memories, James claimed to have immediately recognized him as Irish, but Joyce bristled at this. "It was not often that a Gael abroad would deny his blood," she observed.[11] As with Gillars, her respect for Joyce as the mocking British voice for Hitler's Germany was strong: "His vision was a thorough reform of the world and if you disagree with it he still deserves our respect. William Joyce stood by that course. When that course was run, he died courageously." Her singular view of the man stands in stark contrast with the surviving audio recordings. Joyce's nasally tone was highly suited to the mocking, sneering, and degrading commentary he provided for nearly four years, all of which was designed to damage Allied morale. Joyce was not a mere tool of the regime; his writings before, during, and after the war show him as a dedicated acolyte of National Socialism. His last broadcast, made in the final days of Berlin's fall, ended with the phrase "Heil Hitler and farewell." There were salient common elements between Joyce, Gillars, and Rosaleen James: all worked for the German radio propaganda service aimed at the Allies; all volunteered to serve Nazi Germany; each manifested the core beliefs of Nazism and anti-Semitism. Even Joyce's last writings were filled with it: "I defy the Jews who caused this last war, and I defy the power of darkness which they represent. I warn the British people against the crushing imperialism of the Soviet Union." Rosaleen James held similar beliefs, only she nurtured them for far longer than did Lord Haw-Haw.

Of her fellow employees at the Irish section, James reserved her most critical comments for an authentic Irishman, John Francis O'Reilly, who likewise had some interesting observations about James. O'Reilly's adventure in Germany was just that: a grand experience. Born in Kilkee, County Clare, his father was a member of the Royal Irish Constabulary who had taken part in arresting Sir Roger Casement in 1916 when Casement unwisely decided to initiate a rebellion in British-controlled Ireland. John O'Reilly went through a number of false starts: Irish customs service trainee, priesthood, hotel receptionist, and finally a seasonal potato picker on the island of Jersey, where he remained, despite the threat of German occupation. When the Channel Islands fell to Hitler, O'Reilly quickly adjusted to his new circumstances and acted as a go-between for the German garrison commandant and the remaining Irish workers. After successfully persuading the occupation authorities to send him to work in Germany (provided he recruited other Irish to go along), he abruptly volunteered to work at the Irland-Redaktion under Dr. Hartmann.

O'Reilly, although intelligent, was an exceptionally poor subordinate, a trait probably reflected in his inability to work at any one place for more than a short time. He questioned Hartmann's programming choices, refused to read news items he considered boring, and criticized the music played as having no Irish basis. Despite that, he had one redeeming feature: he was almost the only authentic Irish person working in the Irish section of German radio. The propaganda work, though, couldn't hold his interest, and he decided to approach the Abwehr, volunteer for a mission back to Ireland, and thus return home courtesy of the German intelligence service. Throughout 1942 and early 1943, he was considered for a number of possible insertion schemes: via sea cutter to the Irish west coast, as a refugee via Portugal, or by parachute drop. Designated "Agent Rush," he trained with the naval section of the Abwehr at Bremen. To enhance the likelihood of his being sent home, O'Reilly exaggerated his underworld connections, causing the Germans to describe him as "an enthusiastic Irish patriot [who] has been active since his boyhood with the IRA movement. He maintains that he has close connections with other friends in the IRA movement. He is modest in his way of life and reserved. He makes an excellent and trustworthy impression."[12] In point of fact, none of that was true.

Eventually, Dr. Edmund Veesenmayer of the Foreign Office heard of the scheme to send O'Reilly home; he immediately recognized the operation's impractical nature and raised this issue with Abwehr chief Admiral Canaris. Kurt Haller performed an independent assessment of O'Reilly and, more accurately than the previous vetting, described O'Reilly as a "pig-headed opportunist." The mission was scuttled. With no other immediate prospects, O'Reilly's only option was to return to work at the Irland-Redaktion, where his talents barely outweighed his defects. At this point, however, Rosaleen James reenters the picture.

O'Reilly certainly met her during the course of his first stint as radio personality and renewed the acquaintance once he was dropped by the Abwehr. On the surface, O'Reilly's social connections were better than James's; he was welcome at the Irish embassy and frequently interacted with the Irish consul, William Warnock. In his postwar serialized memoirs, O'Reilly described a conversation he had with Rosaleen James in which she claimed that Seán Russell had been poisoned, and then she unexpectedly offered to help O'Reilly return to Ireland. Shortly afterward, he received a call from SS-Obersturmführer Geisler of the Sicherheitsdienst (SD), the SS intelligence service. In those same memoirs, O'Reilly gave a more detailed description of James, whom he nicknamed "Deidre:"

> [James] was slightly built but not strikingly so, with very little color in her cheeks. Her hair was long, jet black, and parted severely in the middle. Although she appeared to have some Irish background I never learned what is was or whether she had Irish parentage. Despite her good looks and her enigmatic personality there was very little of the glamorous Mata Hari about "Deidre." What puzzled me about her was that she appeared to maintain equally friendly contacts with the various espionage groups of the Wehrmacht, the Admiralty, and the SS. Their intelligence departments usually maintained completely separate identities. They exchanged neither agents nor information, though their activities frequently overlapped. Yet here was "Deidre," attached to every group, but tied to none.[13]

This generally tallies with what O'Reilly told his Irish interrogators in 1944:

> O'Reilly first met O'Mara in December 1941 in the canteen attached to the broadcasting station. She heard him talking English, so came over and introduced herself, and said she was on the morning programmes. She spoke English like an educated Irishwoman, but never disclosed her connection with Ireland. She claims her parents were English and that she is the adopted daughter of Sir Ian Hamilton but has no papers to establish her claim. She is supposed to be married to a Russian nobleman, present whereabouts unknown, and has a three-year-old child, but still uses the name O'Mara in her correspondence. O'Reilly claims to have been on intimate terms with O'Mara, describes her as small and Irish looking with unusual blue eyes and a peculiar walk as if she had at one time injured her back. Good-looking, but with rather an unwashed appearance. Speaks French and German, the latter rather ungrammatically. Had at one time been a music hall artist and has connections with Poland.[14]

James's memory of O'Reilly is curiously different. Accurately recounting the essentials of his journey from Ireland to Germany, James admitted that she discussed his situation with a "Gerhard Pyper," whom she identifies as "director of the South America division of the German radio organization,"[15] and that after an introductory meeting, O'Reilly was offered radio training and a return-by-parachute to Ireland.

She writes:

> This is how it happened that one day I walked out of the Rundfunkhaus with this playboy from County Clare. We went around a few blocks, staying in that residential quarter, and rang a bell on the garden gate of the well-appointed Villa that bore the street number Gerhard Pyper had given to me. He had promised me that he himself would be there to welcome us, and so he was. He introduced us to a young officer who wore a military uniform the type of which I do not remember now—since I trusted Gerhard's plans, I did not pay much attention to him. Our host explained to us that there was need for a contact man who was to be parachuted to Ireland in order to place a radio set there. Might that business suit our man?—Doubtlessly he was technically trained for recording implements and for installing a transmitter. It was clear to me that the thought stimulated him, the type of work itself [did so too], and that he was interested in the adventure and not lazy either. He gave us to understand that he knew every inch of the Burren and that it would be easy for him to land there and to hide a radio set there. So it was decided therefore to accept him on Gerhard Pyper's and my own recommendation, so that he would be trained as a radio operator immediately.
>
> "If you will hear me out," I said to the lad when we were out of anybody's earshot, walking back to the *Rundfunkhaus*, "when you reach your home in Ireland, don't bother with all that they ask you to do! Don't we know both—something they cannot admit themselves—that the German nation has lost its game! It will be best for you to bury the equipment they'll give you, straight away, without mentioning anything to anybody for as long as the war will last—or maybe forever!"
>
> "Don't doubt that even for a day," said your man. "That is the least of my worries. I don't want anything but to get the hell out

of this cursed place. They will have no authority over me once I'm dropped over Ireland. I won't do a single thing for them over yonder—nothing whatsoever!"

Although I had made the suggestion myself, I was taken aback by the impudence of the statement and the mindset it revealed. Is it not a sad thing to deceive a person when he is in a bad way? This would ill become me, and I felt ashamed, but to tell the truth, there was nothing else I could do to leave the lonesome lad go free from the disaster that we saw coming, than to send him home across the sky on this expedition.[16]

There are several interesting points. First, it validates O'Reilly's statement about James being associated with various groups—in this instance, the SS intelligence service. Second, it is telling that at the time of this writing (1991), she still took offense at O'Reilly's ingratitude toward Nazi Germany. The names she mentions, Gerhard Pyper and Dr. Wilhelmi, are not otherwise listed in documents from the German radio service and might be pseudonyms.[17]

She then goes on to characterize O'Reilly as spoiled, saying that he was invited to every party thrown in Berlin, and—presumably in contrast to her own upper class self—that he was unpracticed in the ways of gallantry and high society. James recalled one incident where she was forced, she says, to defend the honor of Ireland when O'Reilly's bad behavior caused a woman to curse the entire nation owing to his conduct. She also regarded him as a traitor of sorts, because "once in Ireland, he did not wait a day before he had betrayed every single foreigner employed by the Rundfunkhaus, telling the British secret services stories both false and true." Later, when being questioned herself by MI5 officers, James assumed that some of the derogatory information in her file was courtesy of O'Reilly "who had turned traitor."[18]

In this, she was mistaken. Although interrogated at regular intervals by Irish Military Intelligence officers, O'Reilly revealed little of substance. The existence of an unofficial intelligence-sharing agreement between Irish Intelligence and MI5 permitted the British to forward pertinent questions to the Irish; both parties were understandably concerned to learn whether O'Reilly and John Kenny were the only two agents parachuted back to Ireland.[19] O'Reilly amused himself by playing with his captors and only admitted what he believed they already knew.

James's actual contribution to the Irland-Redaktion is difficult to assess. Her name does not appear in the surviving directory from October 1942, although considering the limited records available, that is not surprising.[20] Both the BBC and Irish Military Intelligence monitored German broadcasts directed toward Ireland from 1941 through 1943. In some instances the reception was poor, and only part of the program was heard. In very many others it was almost impossible to determine which speaker was at the microphone. Irish officials noted some thirty on-air names; some of them were pseudonyms but a surprising number were authentic. Monitors attempted to take verbatim notes on content but often could only note the date, speaker, and subject of the broadcast.[21] Taken as a whole, the preponderance of evidence suggests that James was an occasional contributor but not an integral part of what was, at best, a less-than-professional broadcasting troupe.

A *Fragebogen* (questionnaire) James completed during the war proves that was using the Nora O'Mara pseudonym by at least 1940, but the first on-air use of that name and surname initially appeared in a transmission from 14 March 1942. The name "Nora" appears in another broadcast intercepted on 1 August 1942, along with a male speaker self-identified as Sean O'Neill. By June 1943, James had evolved yet again, for the first time using the Róisín pseudonym that she would adopt in her postwar persona.[22] In one broadcast she gave a talk on the Treaty of Limerick.[23] Irish Intelligence likewise linked the announcer "Sylvia" with Róisín and Nora O'Mara. If that connection is accurate, Sylvia/Róisín/Nora/Rosaleen still had much to improve upon in her Irish identity quest; the stereotypical dialog and almost racist characterizations were counterproductive: "Well me mother was a banshee and me father was a spalpeen."[24]

Rosaleen James continued to work with Francis Stuart at the Irland-Redaktion, although by this time Stuart had taken up with Gertrud Meissner (who would eventually become his second wife, after Iseult Stuart's death). On 3 March 1943, for example, Redaktion chief Dr. Hartmann gave a talk in Irish, followed by an hour and a half play read by Stuart. The last item of the evening's broadcast included a recitation of "My Dark Rosaleen," some Irish dance music, and a woman who concludes the program with the words, "We who have spoken to you have had only just one wish, namely to participate in the festival in honor of Ireland's patron Saint. How much we would give in order to know if you've enjoyed it. Our thoughts will be with you through the rest of the evening. Good night, good night everybody. Good night Ireland." Irish Intelligence linked the unidentified female speaker to O'Mara.[25]

Perhaps owing to time pressure or editorial incompetence, many of the Irland-Redaktion programs were of very poor quality. On 5 August 1942, for example, "Nora" participated in a radio play that tried to explain the folly of stationing American troops in Northern Ireland. Convoluted dialog soon buries any point they were trying to make:

> NORA: But why doesn't the government do something about it?
> SEAN: Well, Nora, they did all they could do at present, they protested against the American invasion but as could be expected, without results. The Americans don't seem to love us any longer.
> NORA: Anyhow, what is the idea of getting the Americans on to this island? I don't see any results in the six counties, the North is still as undemocratic as before.
> SEAN: Perhaps you don't understand Nora, democracy is a secret recipe which is only shared by Britain, the U.S.A., and Soviet Russia. We'll be told about it only after the war but those American forces in the North have another mission besides. You see, Mr. Roosevelt is quite clever but he tried to beat the English at their own game. He requires a new base to cross the Atlantic and gives the British, for the first time, the opportunity of withdrawing their troops so that they can fight their own battles in the Near East or on the second front.
> NORA: Do you really think him so cute? Wouldn't the British see through that?
> SEAN: I suppose they would but what choice have they now, themselves beaten on all fronts and their promising ally Russia demanding quick relief by a second front?[26]

It is unlikely that any Irish listeners would be significantly enlightened by this exposé of evil Allied intentions.

There is a curious document in James's German file from this same period. On 12 March 1942, just two days before she appeared on the radio as "Nora O'Mara," the Propaganda Ministry dispatched a letter regarding "Actress N. O'Mara." Directed to a Herr Hilger, it reads as follows:

> As we have already discussed by phone, for reasons of particular merit from Herr Minister [Josef Goebbels], Frau O'Mara is being sent for 14 days of convalescence to Baden-Baden. Department T [Theater Department of the RMVP] would instruct you—if necessary under gentle coercion—to provide a decent theater engagement. Corresponding negotiations with theaters in the Reich are underway.
>
> Frau O'Mara is not at all at fault for her part in this dire situation. Department T, through the Ministry Office (Lt. Frowein) has been instructed to help Frau O'Mara in case of need; it is requested to appropriate 500 RM from the Goebbels Fund.[27]

This raises several questions. What was the nature of the "particular merit" that she performed for Josef Goebbels? How did she so suddenly come to be deserving of such attention? Whatever was at the heart of the matter, James was awarded a sum from what is properly called the *Spende Künstlerdank*, a one-time grant for deserving artists. The normal grant amount was between 100 and 300 Reichsmarks; James's grant was well above that.[28] It is especially curious since there is no record of her performing in any stage or theater productions during the war. In an attached memo, she was directed to report to the office of the director of the Berlin Theater, Eugen Klöpfer. There is no indication in the surviving documentation of any subsequent acting job.

In addition to being the Berlin Theater director, Klöpfer was a noted actor and simultaneously the overseer of the Dr. Goebbels Spende Künstlerdank. He was also a strident National Socialist, who was named in 1944 to the *Gottbegnadeten-Liste* (God-gifted list) of the most important artists in the Third Reich, all of whom were exempted from military service. Rosaleen James was not included. After the war, as part of the national denazification (*Entnazifizierung*) process, Klöpfer was questioned about his part in the death of renowned actor Joachim Gottschalk. Gottschalk, a beloved figure of the German stage, was married to a Jewish woman, and was subsequently sidelined when he refused orders from Goebbels (via Klöpfer) to divorce her. When his wife and son were ordered to the concentration camp at Theresienstadt, the Gottschalks committed suicide. Ironically, James claimed to have been a friend of Brigitte Horney, a famous German actress who risked her career to attend the Gottschalk funeral.

The Klöpfer connection was interesting in another way, too. In addition to his National Socialist administrative responsibilities, Klöpfer continued his acting career during the war. In 1941, he was a supporting actor in the role of "Duffy" in the film *Mein Leben für Irland* (My Life for Ireland), which was one of two Propaganda Ministry–controlled films about Ireland produced by Tobis (rival of the larger UFA studios, until it was absorbed). The plot opens in 1903 and was centered around two generations of Irish rebels. Michael, the father, was an active terrorist who was captured following an attack where he killed a British policeman. While waiting for his execution, he is secretly married to his pregnant fiancée, and gives her a silver cross inscribed with the words "My Life for Ireland," which is carried by only the truest Irish freedom fighters. Their son, also Michael, grows up in the atmosphere of British-controlled Ireland where, as the son of an executed rebel, he is unfairly subjected to abuse and humiliation at the hands of British teachers. He is seen as a re-education (*umerzogen*) project, an attempt to turn him from his Irish heritage and force him to follow the path of his colonial masters. There is a somewhat creepy romantic subplot involving Michael's mother and one of her son's classmates; a dedicated Irish freedom fighter is wrongly suspected of collaboration; and the school has an English informer in its midst. Finally, however, the long-awaited battle with the British occupiers begins; Michael learns the truth and rededicates himself to the Republican cause.

The film's message is clear: Germany and Ireland are both victims of British imperialism, and Germany's war is merely a continuation for the centuries-old Irish struggle for freedom. This dovetailed nicely with the guiding philosophy of the Irland-Redaktion radio propaganda message, the attempts to recruit Irish prisoners to fight against England, and the general tone of German intelligence and diplomatic operations concerning Ireland. Although the film had limited distribution because of the war, Klöpfer and the other members of the Reichstheaterkammer must have hoped it would serve as a public relations bridge between the two countries, and even to the Irish population in America that was, presumably, inclined to follow the idea that "England's difficulty is Ireland's opportunity."

The Nazi film review board (*Filmprüfstelle*), which was directly controlled by Goebbels' Propaganda Ministry after the Cinema Act of 1934, declared that *Mein Leben für Irland* was "artistically valuable" and "valuable for the youth." It is almost inconceivable that Rosaleen James did not see this movie—in part because film-going was the normal pastime for the overwhelming majority of wartime Germans, but also because it likely added to her gathering store of information about the Irish and what she must have presumed to be their social and political beliefs. By 1941, James was already passing herself off as Irish but without any genuine background or sufficient personal knowledge to complete the illusion. Piecing together that identikit meant using any sources available in Berlin: movies, books, and conversations with authentic Irish nationals. Indeed, the guiding pro-Irish, anti-British sentiment as expressed in her autobiography is uncomfortably close to the dialog and philosophy of this one movie alone.

There was, though, a second possible source of inspiration: the earlier film from 1940, *Der Fuchs von Glenarvon* (The Fox of Glenarvon). Set in a mythical seaside county, the story concerns a corrupt British landowner named Grandison who is assigned as justice of the peace in rural Ireland. His wife, however, is Irish and feels a natural sympathy to the plight and aspirations of her own people. Her husband is involved a diabolical insurance fraud scheme that results in the death of a local man. Meanwhile, Mrs. Grandison falls in love with a returned Irish patriot, and eventually leaves her mean-spirited British husband for the handsome son of Ireland. As with the later *Mein Leben für Irland,* the propaganda-driven political message overwhelms any entertainment value in the film. In both cases, Irish nationalists are seen as heroes, and the British are exclusively viewed in a negative light: abusive, corrupt, criminal, and immoral. The emphasis is again on the appeal to common cause between Germany and oppressed minority groups everywhere: that "we" are all brothers in arms against English tyranny and colonialism. The parallels between the Nazi film's narrative and political philosophy and that of Rosaleen James are obvious. Although the one likely did not cause the other, they are identical in kind and intent; life imitates art.

The last certain wartime mention of Rosaleen James comes from the response to a request from MI5. Irish Intelligence queried the Irish chargé d'affaires in Berlin, William Warnock. He responded:

> Regarding Nora O'Mara Mr. Warnock was unable to add anything to our information on the Sir Ian Hamilton story and could not

throw any additional light on the point as to whether she was an illegitimate daughter, or a ward, or adopted daughter of Sir Ian. Mr. W[arnock] met her only once, following an incident which occurred at an entertainment which was being given to soldiers who [were] going to the front. She apparently offered to provide an item in the show and was asked for her identity papers by the promoters; she could only produce a document such as is issued by the police to any "stateless" person and evidently was turned down. Apparently she made a claim that she was Irish and Mr. W was phoned next day and asked why he had not issued the necessary documents to her. He denied her claim and said he had no intention of issuing identity papers to her. Following this, he met her at a party when she upbraided him for what he had said concerning her claim. She did not appear to him as being quite sensible on the occasion. She was obviously pregnant although she was emphasizing that she was "Miss." He had no information on her "liaison" with a Russian count but believes that she lived with a Russian family for a time at least. He could not understand the part she was playing. She was an actress and he had met her on the occasion only. Mr. W. was of the opinion that she was responsible for a raid by the SS on [fellow broadcaster Liam] Mullally's flat, as the latter did not like her and was rather outspoken where she was concerned.[29]

From early 1944 through the end of the war, there is no further paper trail on Rosaleen James, and she omits this period in her autobiography. Absolute proof of where she lived and with whom, and what she did to earn a living are lacking, but there is an intriguing story from the final days in Berlin, involving a woman who claimed to be Irish.

10

Collapse

Possibly the final episode of Rosaleen James's wartime experiences comes not from her selected autobiographical tales, but from the survivors of Hitler's bunker. The war in Europe was in its final phase: Soviet troops had entered Berlin, and the Reich had only days to live. A handful of officers still served Hitler, among them SS-Obergruppenführer Hermann Fegelein, Heinrich Himmler's adjutant and the man married to Eva Braun's sister—and thus also Hitler's brother-in-law.[1] His meteoric career was built largely on connections, not military excellence. Had he lived, Fegelein would likely have faced prosecution for war crimes related to his activities on the Russian Front while commanding the 8th SS Cavalry Division "Florian Geyer." Good looks and excellent social skills propelled him to the pinnacle of power—but at this terminal stage of the war, any connection to Hitler was a liability, not an asset. While Berlin burned, Fegelein was planning his escape.

He had been missing from the underground *Führerbunker* since April 25, but the alarm did not sound until Hitler himself noticed his absence on the 27th and dispatched an SS colonel, Obersturmbannführer Högl, to an address in the Bleibtreustrasse where Fegelein was reported to keep an apartment with his mistress. Fegelein was there, hurriedly packing a valise. And there was also a young woman present. As Högl talked with the drunken Fegelein, the woman went into the kitchen and promptly escaped out a window. Högl secured his prisoner and the valise and returned to the Führerbunker. The bag contained jewellery, a significant amount of cash, and two passports—one of them British—made out to the now-absent female companion. Four survivors of the bunker recall

Collapse

having met the woman earlier, and their descriptions are interesting: they describe a person who more than casually resembled Rosaleen James. Hitler's SS adjutant, Otto Günsche, remembered her as a good-looking Irish woman who spoke German with an accent and at least two or three other languages.[2] She claimed to have a husband who was a foreign diplomat that none of the bunker personnel had ever met. They all agree about one thing: she worked in broadcasting but in a position that principally required translation work. They nicknamed her "Mata O'Hara." James's pseudonym was, of course, Nora O'Mara. Hitler's personal pilot Hans Baur, who remembered her as *claiming* to be Irish, first met her at a party held at Josef Goebbels's villa in Schwanenwerder, and the inference was that "O'Hara" had a more personal connection to the Minister for Propaganda.[3]

After her escape from the window, she was never seen again. Rosaleen James (Nora O'Mara) next appeared in Paris during the first week of May 1945.[4] What are the odds that they are the same person—Irish (or pretending to be), worked in broadcasting, language ability, and a connection to Goebbels?

Inside information about people and events in the German hierarchy had been leaked to the Allies for some time. The Bunker survivors believed that "O'Hara" was a British agent, and that some of the material she discovered was used on the Soldatensender Calais. The Soldatensender (Soldier's Radio) was not what it seemed—that is, a German radio station operated from inside occupied Europe by group of renegade SS. It was, in fact, a British "black" propaganda station operated in Sussex by the Political Warfare Executive from October 1943 until 30 April 1945. The idea was simple: broadcast contemporary music, sports, and news in a way that would be attractive to German servicemen, and use subtle techniques to mislead and affect morale, all while pretending to be an authentic German radio station. This clever distinction separates it from the "white" propaganda of the wartime BBC overseas service aimed at Germany, or even that used by James and Stuart at the Irland-Redaktion. At least until after the Normandy invasion, the Soldatensender never directly criticized Hitler—that would have been too obvious—but instead dropped occasional gossip about the circle around him, some of which hit uncomfortably close to home.[5] Could one of the sources have been Fegelein's "Irish" mistress?

Masquerade

That part of the story is unlikely. There were few bunker survivors, and none of them knew the truth: that Hitler's higher command Enigma messages were compromised, and consequently Allied intelligence had a wealth of data on the Third Reich, combined with thorough interrogations of senior German personnel who surrendered. Neither a British spy nor a German mole, Rosaleen James was needed to provide inside information; open-source German radio transmissions and reasonable guesses were more than sufficient. The listener's imagination, combined with a dash of paranoia, would do the rest.

11

Defense of the Realm

The exact nature of James's escape from wartime Berlin is a mystery. Other than writing of taking the next-to-last train out of the city with her small daughter, she is silent on all other details. She arrived in Heidelberg and—she says—was the impromptu guest of Ali Khan, who was at that time serving as a lieutenant colonel in the British Army. What she neglected to mention in her autobiography is that upon arrival in Paris she was pregnant for the second time; the father of this child—as was the case with her daughter born in 1940—is never identified in her autobiographies.

Her arrival did not go unnoticed by British intelligence. As of 12 February 1945, she had been on the list of renegade British subjects—those Britons who aided the Axis and who were subject to arrest and prosecution for treason. Well before the end of the war, British MI5 was hunting traitors in the Legion of St. George and the British Free Corps, as well as among the cluster of civilians who volunteered to work on Hitler's behalf. A special section within MI5, SLB3, was tasked with tracking the British and Irish renegades and bringing them to justice.[1] The head of this team was Lieutenant Colonel John (later Sir John) Stephenson; the team included such luminaries as Major R. W. Spooner and Captain W. J. Scarden. Stephenson was based in Paris following its liberation in August 1944.[2] Special Branch detectives detached to MI5 participated in assembling information and conducting interrogations.[3] Stephenson later wrote, "Our task was to find some 100 British collaborators and obtain evidence on which they could be prosecuted. . . . The few broadcasters, stool-pigeons, and those who were recruited into the pathetic little body which the Germans called first the Legion of Saint George and, later, the British Free Corps, fell far short of three figures."[4] Phyllis Ursula Rosaleen James, alias Nora O'Mara, occupied the 86th position on that list.[5]

In concert with the Renegades list and the other information gathered by the Allied War Crimes Commission, the western Allies published the CROWCASS (Central Registry of War Criminals and Security Suspects) Consolidated Wanted Lists in their effort to weed through the ruins of postwar Europe in search of war criminals.[6] This was likewise a cornerstone to the Allied policy of denazification. Despite this extensive listing of some 60,000 individuals (not all of them criminals; some were wanted as witnesses), there was some initial question as to whether sufficient evidence would be available. Military authorities and intelligence teams worked to gather probative evidence. Wanted individuals, witness statements, documents, and photographs were discovered as Allied forces tightened the noose around Germany.

James successfully appealed to U.S. Sixth Army Group commander General Jacob Devers, who was apparently impressed when James "claimed friendship with the Prime Minister and her connection with Sir Ian Hamilton." He sent her by car to the British embassy in Paris. According to the consulate report,

> When we heard of her pending arrival in Paris, we were asked by M.I.5 to keep them informed and not to give her any facilities to return to the United Kingdom until they had seen her. On arrival she was directed to the Elba Home but after taking a meal there, she disappeared and was not heard of again until I received a note a week later from the United States Army Medical authorities to the effect that she had been admitted to an American Army Hospital suffering from malnutrition and pregnancy. She had previously placed her daughter, aged four, by whom she was accompanied, with a friend living just outside Paris.[7]

James's postwar recollections of these events, unsurprisingly, testify to her outraged sense of Irish nationalism and identity: She later claimed that she told British agents that "this is not my war. . . . I am an artist, and moreover, I am Irish!"[8] She also admitted in her autobiography that she was less than forthcoming about her Berlin activities.[9] During the interrogation period, she was restricted to a refugee camp and placed under surveillance by a woman she names as "Madame Conscience." James opined that Madame Conscience would "probably not have to suffer the pains of hell" due to a couple instances of unexpected kindness to Rosaleen James and Francis Stuart, when the latter visited her at the camp.[10]

British consular officials were soon puzzled at MI5's sudden about-face. Intelligence officers had interviewed her, but a curious series of decisions in London soon placed Rosaleen James in a different category from the remaining renegades—a protected status. Within a two-week span, notations in the "renegades" file indicate that her condition went from "Detain and notify S.H.A.E.F. [Supreme Headquarters Allied Expeditionary Force]" to "Report to S.H.A.E.F. but do not detain unless special circumstances require it." In another notation, referring to a message from the consular section to "K Department" (MI5), it states, "Asks what her connections in England wish to be done in the matter." Her connections were indeed good. The final notation reports that "permission has been granted to her to return to this country." There was to be no further investigation, arrest, pending charges, or publicity. Outside of the secure internal communications traffic among the British consular section and the security services, no one ever reported a word about the link between the adopted daughter of a noble war hero and high treason. Even MI5's file on her was made to go away. "All serials marked destroyed on authority of G.E.W/R8," the handwritten notation on one of her statements reads. The only material that survived exists as scattered remnants in other files.[11]

Other volunteer Nazis were not so fortunate. Some found their way directly into British hands, others came via the U.S. Army, a small number were repatriated by the Russians, and one was reported killed while fighting in Berlin.[12] Italian partisans apprehended John Amery, the creator and ideological spark behind of the Legion of St. George, on 25 April 1945, as he and his companion Michele Thomas attempted to flee from Milan to Lake Como.[13] He was interned at Terni and briefly shared a cell with another renegade, former Irish Minister to Berlin Charles Bewley.[14] From his interrogation and the documentary evidence assembled after the German surrender in Europe, there was little doubt about Amery's guilt. He pleaded guilty to eight counts of treason and was hanged at Wandsworth Prison on 29 December 1945. Fellow collaborator William "Lord Haw-Haw" Joyce followed him to the gallows on 3 January 1946.[15]

A total of sixty-six files were sent to the Department of Public Prosecutions on various renegades, and many received prison time for their wartime roles.[16] Despite sufficient evidence to warrant prosecution for high treason, most were instead charged with violation of Sections 2A and 90 of the Emergency Powers (Defence) Regulations Act, 1939. The authorities seemingly took the view that the common motive was often more one of opportunism than treason, hence the reduced charge and seemingly disparate sentences. The Treason Act of 1351 was the governing legislation in effect. It specified, "If a Man do levy War against our Lord the King in his Realm, or be adherent to the King's Enemies in his Realm, giving to them Aid and comfort in the Realm, or elsewhere" then that person is guilty of treason.[17] But there were political, procedural, and security reasons why some cases would be better handled in more delicate ways.

The primary difficulty with the Treason Act is in the degree of proof necessary for conviction. It requires two witnesses to an overt act of treason, who may or may not be available to testify, depending on circumstances, and could well require the admission into evidence of privileged or secret information. This would have been a concern in Rosaleen James's case. The renegades file states that information on her came from two places: German official records and unspecified "secret sources." Sources and methods are highly sensitive, and in this instance the damage caused by airing them might be unacceptable. To circumvent just such an issue, and recognizing that wartime demands expediency, Parliament passed the Treachery Act of 1940, which covers similar ground as the Treason Act but has a lower threshold of proof, and without the necessity of two witnesses. The language of the Act is clear:

> If, with intent to help the enemy, any person does, or attempts or conspires with any other person to do any act which is designed or likely to give assistance to the naval, military or air operations of the enemy, to impede such operations of His Majesty's forces, or to endanger life, he shall be guilty of felony and shall on conviction suffer death.[18]

Defense of the Realm

The question then becomes this: Was Rosaleen James's conduct sufficient—under either the Treason Act or the Treachery Act—to warrant criminal prosecution? Based upon her selective admissions alone, as a British citizen, we know the following:

1. She knowingly and voluntarily broadcast propaganda for Germany, a belligerent with the United Kingdom after 3 September 1939, on multiple occasions from 1939–43.
2. At the Friesack Camp in 1941, she participated in an effort to recruit British prisoners of war for use as German agents.
3. She was a paid asset of German military intelligence.
4. She aided and abetted Hermann Görtz's covert intelligence mission to Ireland.

In most jurisdictions, intent can be inferred from conduct, which in turn means that by applying almost any standard but her own, she was guilty.

Others in similar circumstances to Rosaleen James were treated quite differently. The best example is Susan Hilton, one of James's colleagues at the Irish service of German radio. Born in 1915 to an Anglo-Irish family living in India, she briefly flirted with socialism before joining the British Union of Fascists (BUF) in 1936. She resigned in 1938 when she became uncomfortable with the BUF's increasing anti-Jewish tone. Hilton married a British mining engineer and was en route to join him in 1940; that plan changed when her ship, the *SS Kemendine*, was sunk by the German raider *Atlantis* in the Indian Ocean. The captured passengers and crew were then put aboard another captured vessel, the *Tirranna*, for transport back to German-occupied France. Her streak of bad luck continued: the *Tirranna* was itself torpedoed by a British submarine off the coast of France, and the survivors of this second sinking finally reached the shore. Freedom necessitated an identity shift, or at least an emphasis on a different nationality, and Hilton accordingly morphed into an Irishness of convenience. Accordingly, the Germans recruited Hilton to write a propaganda pamphlet entitled "An Irish woman's experience of England and the war at sea," published in 1942. Approached by German officials and asked whether she would be willing to undertake an intelligence mission to Ireland, the United States, or Mozambique, she refused. Instead, Hilton, by now a full-blown alcoholic, found work in a variety of

German radio propaganda ventures, finally being recruited by the Irland-Redaktion in early 1942.

Broadcasting under a number of different aliases (Susan Sweney, Ann Tower), Hilton worked for the Irish section for almost a year before her continuing alcohol problems began to affect her on-air performance and she was fired. While still there, she occasionally worked with Rosaleen James, saying that she and others had written some of James's scripts because they felt sorry for her. Hilton was never accepted by the Germans to the same extent as her pseudo-Irish co-worker, and the Gestapo put her under surveillance. In July 1944 she was arrested, and ended the war in the Liebenau internment camp. Although most other prisoners were released immediately, Hilton remained there another eight months under continuous MI5 interrogation, during which time she admitted broadcasting for the Germans. In December 1945, she was returned to England to stand trial for treason.

Unlike James, Hilton's nationality became an issue. In addition to her original British passport, she had obtained a temporary Irish passport from the Irish Legation in Paris—this was not difficult, apparently—as well as a Fremdenpass using her Ann Tower pseudonym. Since her original British citizenship was never in doubt, the trial went forward. Hilton ultimately decided to plead guilty on eight of ten counts in the indictment, all pertaining to her work on German radio, and the prosecution dropped the remaining two charges. She was sentenced to 18 months in prison.[19] Having neither James's pedigree nor her connections to mitigate her punishment, Hilton served her entire sentence. She died in 1983.

James's friend Mildred Gillars, "Axis Sally," was tried for treason in the United States in 1949. Although claiming a wide variety of defenses—including being under the Svengali-like control of her married German lover—she was convicted and sentenced to 10 to 30 years in prison. She was released in 1961 and died in 1988.

William "Lord Haw-Haw" Joyce was shot during his capture in 1945, recovered from his wounds, and was returned to England to stand trial in 1945; he was charged with three counts of treason. The wording of the charges against him could similarly be applied to Rosaleen James: "being a person owing allegiance to our Lord the King, and while a war was being carried on by the German Realm against our King, did traitorously adhere to the King's enemies in Germany, by broadcasting propaganda."

Joyce defended himself on jurisdictional grounds, claiming the he was properly an American citizen and thus beyond the reach of British justice. The trial court, Court of Appeal, and the House of Lords disagreed. Joyce was sentenced to death and hanged. He was reburied in Ireland in 1976. Although Margaret Joyce also made propaganda broadcasts, she was never tried.

While William Joyce was permanently out of the picture, Francis Stuart was not. Rosaleen James maintained her interest in him long after their relationship fizzled. In March 1946, she was staying in the Paris suburb of Rueil-Malmaison and wrote a peculiar letter to Iseult Stuart in Ireland, asking for information about him. Considering the fact that James and Stuart shared an intense physical affair in wartime Berlin, it is curious that she would write to Stuart's scorned wife for sympathy. Stuart was at this time a virtual refugee himself, wandering from place to place with his new girlfriend (and eventual wife), Madeleine Meissner.

The letter from James to Iseult begins as follows: "Excuse me for writing to you without knowing you but I feel so worried about your husband that I feel obliged to bother you with an enquiry whether you have had any news from him lately in Austria. I have heard so much about you and the two children that I almost feel as if I have had the pleasure of knowing you, knowing as I do your husband since his arrival on the continent in the early spring of 1940. . . . The Irish Legation told him, on his arrival, of my whereabouts, and he came to see me several times during his stay in Paris . . ." James's intent of using such language might be innocent enough, but the overall tone is one of intimate familiarity, with the intimacy in question inappropriately being between the letter's author and the recipient's husband.

Slightly later in the letter, she adds, "But I too feel, like dear Francis, that the misery and despair that one has absorbed during these fateful times bind one to those one has shared them with."[20] Still in transition from her wartime pseudonym to her postwar Irish persona, James signed the letter as Róisín O'Mara. There is no response from Iseult Stuart, who by this point had certainly come to accept that Francis had no intention of returning to his family or, seemingly, to Rosaleen James. Iseult Stuart died in 1954, never again seeing her husband.

12

1945 to 1977

The Theater, a Playschool, and a Museum in the West

After the war, James based herself briefly in France before she moved to Germany, first to Frankfurt, then to Lake Constance. Her two memoirs are the main sources for her whereabouts, but newspapers also provide sidelights on thirty years spent on a variety of personal projects. However, the only activities she wished to highlight herself in the memoirs were those undertaken to promote the Irish language. Only in 1977 did she decide to comment on Germany and World War II again.

But first, either in 1946 or 1947 and while still based in France, she undertook a risky trip to Berlin that lasted a few months, with the vague intention to see how her friends were doing. Characteristically, she does not let us know with whom she left her young children. Her commentary on postwar Berlin is striking. According to James, she witnessed GIs stationed in Berlin playing cruel games with children who wanted chewing gum or tobacco for the black market—and worse, discarding food while guarding the rubbish from needy Germans. Incredibly, she contrasts this with German soldiers who—so she believes steadfastly—had handed out food to the people of Warsaw when the war was over.[1] Her illusory views of Germany were only reinforced by her visit. She reconnected with Ruth Weiland—Francis Stuart's friend and publisher of *Irische Freiheitskämpfer*—for practical help, despite her obvious dislike for the woman, who was now turning to English publishers for a living. Through Weiland's help, she found work with a *Times* (London) journalist, John H. Freeman, as a chaperone for his young daughter.

James's dramatic rendition of this episode contains the curious claim, discussed in chapter 8, that sometime around 1943 she was commissioned by the German government to write an account of the English occupation of Ireland, which was supposedly intended to be used as a guide for what *not* to do in the occupation of Poland. In any case, the work never saw the bookshops: she claims that it was close to publishing but that the proofs were destroyed by an Allied bomb.[2] Now, in Berlin, jealousy between the two women came to a head, so James claimed, and Weiland—who was to marry Freeman in December 1947—tipped him off about James having been involved in publishing books (in the plural) for the Nazi regime. James describes her last outing to a PX Store with Freeman's daughter, her hasty departure, and the arrival of military police at her friend's house with dramatic force. She found out about Weiland's marriage to Freeman much later, and commented by paraphrasing an Irish proverb: "There is surely nothing more poisonous in the world than the jealousy of women."[3] She does not comment on whether or not her reconnoitering had been worth it; this interlude in the book appears as adventurous in character as it is preposterous in intention. If anything, it appears to have been written to settle old scores.

A reconstruction of James's whereabouts since 1947 and throughout the 1950s and 1960s relies to an uncomfortable degree on her second memoir, *I gCéin is i gCóngar* (At Home and Abroad), published in 2006.[4] As is the privilege of the memoirist, she selected what she wanted the readership to know very carefully, and as was the case with *Cé hÍ Seo Amuigh?* (Who Is She Outside; 1992), we wait in vain for any appearances of her two children (with one brief exception), let alone their fathers, and—more mysteriously by far—for an account of her marriage to the man "Vinard" whose name she carries in press publications of the 1970s and as author of her first memoir of 1992. When she surfaces in the Irish press because of her heritage projects in Connacht, she is called variously "Madame Róisín Uí Mheara-Vinard," "Mrs. Róisín Vinard," "a widow," "Swiss born [Miss] Róisín Vinard," "born in Switzerland," and "an enterprising Irish-speaking French woman, Madame Róisín Vinard."[5] All this seems to point to a (French-speaking) Swiss origin for the elusive Monsieur Vinard, and testify to the fact that James is comfortable telling many different stories about her nationality to many different audiences.[6]

James reconnected with her idealized Ireland at some time in the late 1940s, and again during the 1950s: having sworn never again to set foot in England, she travelled to Ireland via a steamer headed for the United States.[7] She describes Dublin of the late 1940s as a place abounding in melancholy and dilapidation, marked by the unemployed men roaming the streets—but with their Catholic faith seemingly intact. The country lay supine, under "the foreigners' yoke," and she comes to the conclusion that what was needed was a revival of its culture and of the Irish language in particular. While remembering her ideas, the older memoirist admits, "I was still very young." However, this idealism and drive were to sustain her over the next few decades of sporadic but energetic and direct involvement with the country. Some of her endeavors in Dublin were of a literary sort: she tells of many days spent in the National Library. Séamus O'Sullivan, editor of *Dublin Magazine*, published James's poem "Chú Chullain of Muirthemne" in 1955, of which it suffices to quote from the first verse: "Slain he lay. . . . The hills of Ulster shuddered in his blood."[8] After making the acquaintance of the productions director at Radió Éireann, she had two translations of French plays accepted for broadcast, as well as a piece of her own about James Clarence Mangan, which no longer survives.[9] Her return to radio did not involve speaking roles as it had in Berlin, however.

James chose to make much of these few months in Ireland, and does not mention that around the same time period, she lived in Frankfurt am Main and managed to reprise (or inaugurate) her theater career, while the children lived with her—Nadejda, now ten, and Roderich (Ruairí), around six years of age. In 1951, Nora O'Mara (her adopted name at the Irland-Redaktion) was listed among the cast of ladies at the Fritz Rémond Theater in Frankfurt.[10] Around 1945, she began receiving monthly payments from a fund Lady Hamilton had set up for her, and this may have continued for some time; otherwise it is hard to imagine how she made ends meet.[11]

At the theater, the only play in which she verifiably acted was John Galsworthy's *Windows* (*Fenster* in German), a social comedy from 1922. She was maybe a little old for the role of the daughter of the house, Mary March, a woman in her early twenties, but she brought an insider's knowledge of the British class system. She remained a member of the German Guild of Actors until 1955, sixteen years after joining them; but only one other involvement with German theater can be ascertained: her production of Samuel Beckett's *Fin de Partie* in the Intimes Theater, Munich, in 1958.[12]

It is apt, at this point, to compare her with another English actor and co-founder of the Gate Theatre, Dublin, who had likewise adopted an Irish persona for himself—namely, the London-born Micheál Mac Liammóir (né Alfred Willmore). He toured Germany in 1950 with a troupe that included Orson Welles, and Frankfurt was their first port of call in the very same year that James worked at the Kleines Theater am Zoo. Mac Liammóir later published a short piece about this trip ("Ó Chill Áirne go Berlin"). Not having lived in Germany, he expressed an ambivalent mixture of fascination and utter strangeness when it came to the country, and a clear distaste for its people. James, in one of her chapters on postwar Germany, dismissed the young people there as weak, without focus, if not shirking hard work.[13] Mac Liammóir, quite the opposite—though it might have heartened James to hear it—believed that racial superiority would come to the fore again: "That foolish regard for the superiority of this race or the inferiority of the other race was to blame for the rise of the Nazis, the movement that destroyed Germany. When the German race rises again from the ashes of crushing defeat, I have no doubt that they will begin again to apply the same sort of foolish regard to some other thing."[14] James's views on the postwar laxity among young Germans would be mirrored, twenty years later, by her disappointment with the young Irish generation that she witnessed during her long stay in the west.

Her visits to Ireland continued, and her circle of Irish-speaking acquaintances grew, a fact she celebrates in great detail in her second memoir. Fascinatingly, she sent her daughter, Nadejda Jakobi, to an Irish-speaking district in County Mayo when she was a teenager in order for her to learn Irish. One recent observer has found that it was no accident for James to seek out the west of Ireland, given her sympathy for the Germany of Hitler. German scholar Joachim Fischer comments, "The book [her first memoir] refers to intellectual and ideological relationships between aspects of the Irish cultural and religious discourse and fascism in the years 1933–1945, [and] also to the fascination with Hitler and the Nazis that played especially on the remote areas of the west, if often caused by mere ignorance."[15]

In *At Home and Abroad,* James never alludes to her life during the war, to her views of Germany then or now, and when this author spoke to persons who knew her on Inis Meáin, they expressed ignorance of her earlier life and of her views. It made sense for James to keep her counsel on these things in her second memoir, given how the first one was received in 1992–93. However, we will see how, in a regular European column for the Irish-language paper *Inniu* (1977–1982), she was later able to express her redoubtable views on the Germany-that-was and the Germany-that-is.

James's longest stay in Ireland began in 1969 and lasted nearly five years. She initiated two Irish-language projects in the west: one in the city of Galway, one on the middle of the three Aran Islands in Galway Bay. She withdrew from both of them short of funds and essentially disappointed with the lack of official support she encountered, though judging by the legacy they left, they were not failures.

The first venture in Galway city was a "cultural academy," that is, a school providing evening classes in languages, performance, arts and crafts, as well as readings and recitals, with an Irish language nursery school as mainstay. Galway was then approaching 30,000 inhabitants; it had hosted John F. Kennedy ten years previously, had opened a vast new cathedral in 1965, and was emerging from a long period of economic gloom.[16] This must have helped James initially. The academy was named An Durlas (The Fortress). The idea of immersing very young children in the language was not James's own; she credits precursors in the Irish language playschool movement.[17] In founding and running An Durlas she was greatly assisted and kept afloat by theater producer and actor Traolach Ó hAonghusa, and in early 1970 they even moved to larger premises on Mill Street.[18] The nursery school was a success: Mary Sheehan, who personally taught at the academy until 1983, was interviewed in 2004 about her work there and referred to James as "a prim and proper lady."[19] Within a year of opening, An Durlas also ran a theater company and had 150 students aged 2 to 80 on its rolls.

In her memoir, James claims that while her clientele at the academy derived from the middle classes, she could use her new connections and some of the money from theater productions for the people of the

Gaeltacht: her schemes included the teaching of Irish and German to factory workers in the Gaeltacht, and enabling people to make crafts.[20] Eventually, she was frustrated in her efforts to build a bridge between Galway and the Gaeltacht—owing to lack of government funding and other support, as she said.[21] Hampered by financial constraints, she finally sold An Durlas to the Gaelic League (an Irish non-governmental association for the Irish language) in 1973. Wrapping up her involvement in An Durlas, James managed to interest the *Irish Times* in her work: here, she is styled "Mrs. Roisin Vinard, a widow who was born in England but who has lived in a number of countries in the Continent and is of Irish descent," and holding a Swiss passport. "She is an idealist, in the truest sense, whose dream is to see Irish spoken throughout the country as a living language." The journalist concludes, "The goal of retrieving and breathing life into Ireland's heritage is a heartbreakingly difficult one. If one person could do it, that person would be Roisin Vinard."[22] It is clear that James's inventiveness came fifteen years too early: it was only in 1988 that an Irish-language association "presented compelling evidence . . . that promoting Irish led to significant socio-economic benefits," and a new umbrella body began promoting the use of Irish among Galway businesses.[23]

James then relocated farther west, on the middle of the three Aran Islands in Galway Bay which had been long recognized as a Gaelic cultural stronghold. In the same newspaper article she displayed a well-meaning but ultimately patronizing attitude that can only have been a hindrance for her next project: "The people of the islands are better; their backs have not been broken. There is not so much defeatism on the islands. I am trying to teach the people on Inishmaan how to make these plaques for instance. . . . The people on the islands spend all winter long doing nothing. If you give them something to do, it will encourage them."[24]

As with many visiting antiquarians and linguists before her, James made a home in an Irish-speaking house. For James, this represented the perfect "Ur-Irish" experience, where she could become immersed in an Ireland unspoiled by the modern world, and where it was possible to tap into her imagined well of the "real" Ireland.

Within three months, James collected artifacts, found a suitable building, and gathered support, and her new Museum of the Islands was opened on Inishmaan in August 1973 by the government minister responsible for Irish-speaking districts. This was a good news story and was covered by local and national papers, which refer to James as a Swiss woman with fluent Irish, although her own diffidence about her linguistic abilities strongly contrasts with this depiction. The minister Thomas O'Donnell is the only person excepted from her generally condemnatory comments on the Irish government and its low level of support.[25] Her memoir lists the acquaintances and friendships she forged with people during her months on the island. However, based on comments from her former landlady, Máire Phaidín Uí Mhaol Chiaráin (Maura Paudeen Mulkerrin), from a woman who worked with her at the museum as a young girl, and from James's memoirs, we get the impression instead of a well-meaning outsider, a "prim and proper" lady, and a dramatist, who admires the peasants but wishes they weren't so stubborn in their ways.[26] "Happy people of Inishmaan! Rich and of a humble heart, they were still in good spiritual health! I had a glimpse of the Garden of Paradise that God created according to his own wish."[27]

It will remain a matter of speculation how James chose to speak of her war years, and the kudos she may even have received for her continued pro-Nazi stance. Her landlady does not remember her talking about her past. When controversy flared up about her book in 1992–93, she called on the people of the west, whom she used to "discuss things with," to be her character referees.[28] The fact that many Irish people, especially in the remote west of Ireland, were sympathetic to Hitler and his Reich has been the subject of a few academic studies.[29] In Germany, this Irish admiration for Hitler was revealed by novelist Heinrich Böll's *Irisches Tagebuch* (1957).[30] In Ireland, Hugo Hamilton's *Speckled People* made it known to readers of a new generation.[31] A recent television documentary, *Glaoch ón Tríú Reich* (2013), showed how German radio broadcasts found interested listeners in Connemara and included a statement from retired philologist Gearóid Mac Eoin, whose parents' pro-German stance during the war went back to German support for the Easter Rising.[32]

However, in the absence of indications that James spoke with people about her past or her views, it is unfair to presume she would have been met with sympathetic ears.

It is important to investigate James's idea of race, to see whether what she learned early in life carried over into her experience in the west of Ireland, whose people she portrayed so admiringly. Her view of the islanders is of a romantic cast, and while the subjects differ, they are of the same cast as the generalized laudatory and defensive racial remarks about the Germans in *Cé hÍ Seo Amuigh?* (Who Is She Outside). According to James, Germany took over from Ireland the role of Teacher of Europe: the Germans worked diligently among the barbarians, followed calls for help from far-away countries "in the name of Christ" (presumably referring to the Crusades), and spread "culture" (their own?) between St. Petersburg (the Teutonic Knights), Strasbourg, and Prague.[33] When she talks of out-and-out Germans—for example, the spy Hermann Görtz and the Abwehr officer Kurt Haller—she calls them honest people, "*gan cham gan chlaon*" (undeceiving and unbiassed).[34] There had been leaders before Hitler, she believed, who were moralists above all else, dreamy visionaries who did not have their feet on the ground, but whose people were their blind disciples.[35] Hitler would have been very pleased with this, having made great efforts to cast himself as a philosopher-Führer: according to Hitler, Germans were "a metaphysical people who violently opposed the superficiality of western democracy."[36] James herself goes so far to say they were the "bright race" (*an cine geal*) that was the only one that would "defend civilization from the tyranny and the barbarity that was threatening to take over the world and smash Christianity itself at the time."[37]

All this smacks of a mix of propaganda, taken on board wholesale and regurgitated even fifty years after absorbing it. While it is one thing, for example, to express praise for the Germans having become colonialists in Africa without using force back in the 1940s—a prevalent but grossly inaccurate view even then—it is quite another thing to do so in 1992.[38] If she criticized Germans at all, it was for their credulity, for their self-sacrificing willingness to help (and reform) others, and for not being able to distinguish between friends and foes.[39] And in all this, she sails close to the winds of the racial laws she witnessed being institutionalized in Germany. Also, in *Cé hÍ Seo Amuigh?*, James gives us a glimpse into her personal racial ideology when she comments that in lowland Scots, there was "a good drop of Teutonic blood mixed with the pure native blood of the Gael."[40] The poor Germans, in her view, were in fact filled with respectful suspense for the "sophisticated Gauls" over in France (i.e., the Celts whom Julius Caesar and Tacitus reported about), only to be rebuffed because the French feared their pan-Germanic ambitions. The

Gauls were a race easily offended and honor-bound—traits shared by the Irish, according to James.[41]

How, then, does James speak about the "pure Gaels" in the west of Ireland? In asking this it has to be borne in mind that her second memoir was tame in comparison to her first, which had caused an uproar, and did not speak in racial terms; her publishers would have made sure of that. Here is what James found to be true of the people of Inishmaan:

> The people of Inishmaan are a brave lot, unafraid of danger, smart as well as energetic by nature. They are a philosophical people in their outlook, pious and patient above all else. Also, they are well-mannered and talkative, their conversation is full of imagination when they are night-visiting, as it used to be once in the deep winter by the fire, or outside by the garden fence during the short summer nights.... And the children with their well-articulated speech! Anywhere in Ireland you would not hear the likes of their dignified talk and the unceasing sweetness of their sound.[42]

She finds no fault with the islanders except for their giving in to modern lifestyles, blue jeans, and electricity. There is an elderly woman, "Mamó" (grandmother), whom she befriends and pities for the stain attached to her family (an illicit marriage had taken place, maybe between first cousins). The fact that islanders were restricted within their tight circle for mates made James think her museum might work as a meeting point for young people of the area, the islands and mainland Connemara. It was not to come off as she envisioned.[43]

In James's sweepingly positive judgments of the Germans as well as the "Gaelic" peoples, even though she never comments on physical attributes, it is obvious she was inspired by theories of racial purity coursing through Europe since the eighteenth century,[44] and likely by the idea of a *Germanentum*, which the National Socialists derived from the *völkische Bewegung* (ethno-nationalistic movement). Her anti-Semitism, as expressed in *Cé hÍ Seo Amuigh?* and her European newspaper column, is unmistakable, even if she wraps it round with concern "for these scattered people" who needed to be contained in ghettos during the war, in order to safeguard the German offensive in the East."[45] Certain influences from the *Blut und Boden* (blood and soil) ideology, a mythical and mystical connection with the land and a promotion of folklore, which encouraged Germans to hearken back to their true ethnic identity, are a little less ostensible. The precise roots of these ideologies in James's upbringing and formative years abroad, although now untraceable, are obvious.

If racially motivated, James is not consistent, of course. Her unconcealed disgust for "Aryan, but not Celtic!" Britain after the war came from a mixture of her disdain toward her adopted family, a hatred of Churchill and his politics, and an obvious identification with the Irish attitude toward "perfidious Albion." There, she is caught in a bind between the two "races," and could not argue her way out of the fact that Anglo-Saxons and Germans were of the same "race." While the Germans were outdone by the jealousy of their neighbors (not by their own hubris), the people of Inishmaan were to be outdone by alien modern lifestyles.

James lived on the island for the better part of a year. As she had planned at the outset, she left the museum to local people to run when—just as in Galway—her resources began to run out. Her achievement is undebatable, and was lasting. Nonetheless she expressed that she was frustrated in her grand ambitions for the islanders, blaming her dissatisfaction characteristically on the State, including the social welfare payments that discouraged people from engaging in knitting and other old crafts, and on the arrival of "the modern times":[46]

> Thanks be to God, I came there just in time, and while I knew the place, the local peoples' lives were not yet being disturbed, and there was nothing to pollute their imagination. . . . I left them and it was then that modern ways of life invaded them, coming over the communal threshold of this secretive Celtic place, trampling on the Gaelic gladness, and extinguishing the fire on the hearthstone itself with its various gadgets, but especially the television."[47]

This cultural pessimism is mirrored by statements she made another time about the Germans of the postwar period. James stayed tenuously connected with the museum, even until the early 1980s. There is no question but that she left an impression on the islanders.

Again, she was not short of an idea as to what she could do next *ar son na cúise* (for the good of the [Gaelic] cause). Her plan was to translate the Irish epic *Mad Sweeney* into German. She returned to Germany, living in the countryside of Übersee in Upper Bavaria (near Chiemsee), where the translating venture developed into more scholarship, bolstered by a new friendship: that with the historian and churchman—and later Cardinal—Tomás Ó Fiaich, of whom more later.

While this is the next step described in her memoir, she only just barely mentions her journalistic writing of the column, "Letter from Europe," for an Irish-language publication, a venture that lasted for three years.[48] It was in *Inniu*, a small weekly, that she first gave voice to her opinions about the German people, the unfairness with which they were treated after World War II, the false claims made by the Allies (from her point of view) about the deaths of Jews in German camps, and the relations between Ireland and Germany during that period.

13

Letters from Europe, 1977–1982, and *In Search of Irish Saints*

From November 1977 to the end of 1980, James contributed a regular column, "Letter from Europe," to the Irish weekly newspaper *Inniu* (Today). The paper provided no forum for discussion, and her views seem to have gone largely uncommented upon by those who read them. As discussed previously (chapters 2 and 7), James had adopted the Irish last name O'Mara as early as 1940, when she published an essay in an edited volume. And when she became a member of the association of stage practitioners, she did so under the name Nora O'Mara. She forgot this when she said in *Cé hí Seo Amuigh?* that it was only in 1969 that she decided to call herself after her foster mother's family—the Scottish Muirs—and mistakenly decided on the Irish surname O'Mara as an equivalent.[1] As indicated in chapter 2, "Muir" is of a Germanic, not a Gaelic, derivation. By the time the weekly column "Letter from Europe" appeared, she had gone for the Gaelic rather than the Anglicized form of that name: "Ní Mheara."

It is important to look closely at the paper *Inniu*, which hosted James's "Letters," and the organization that founded it. It is unlikely that James knew of the paper in its heyday during the 1940s, but it sheds a sidelight on Ireland during the "Emergency," as World War II was called (and perceived) there. *Inniu*'s mother organization was the Irish-language movement Glúin na Bua, roughly translated as "Hosts of Victory." The movement was founded in 1942 with the main aim of offering a service to Ireland by strengthening the native language; but a monoglot Ireland was their ultimate dream. In this they were in no way isolated:

they followed like others in the wake of the 1937 Constitution of Ireland, which endorsed the Irish language as the first official language. However, they were frustrated with the lukewarm efforts made by the mainstream Gaelic League and had split away from it. Their own approach to the problem of an Anglicized Ireland was to hold marches, print pamphlets, stage dances and plays, and screen films, all with an emphasis on activating young people: nationalism, Catholicism, republicanism, and socialism were aspects of varying importance to the movement's raison d'être.[2]

In founding Glúin na Bua, its first members distanced themselves from a previous affiliate of theirs, Gearóid Ó Cuinneagáin. His own 1942 right-wing organization, Ailtirí na hAiséirghe (Architects of the Rebirth), was a political party that reached its apex in 1945, ironically "at the precise moment when newsreel footage of the Nazi concentration camps were being displayed on cinema screens across Ireland."[3] Ó Cuinneagáin's organization did not imitate the Nazis, aiming instead for a missionary totalitarian state where a Catholic ideology would reign; where, within five years of governing, Irish would completely replace English; discrimination against Jews and Freemasons would be enshrined in the constitution; and a remade Ireland would reconquer Northern Ireland by means of a blitzkrieg carried out by a new conscript army. Despite their early success and support from mainstream politicians like Ernest Blythe, Oliver J. Flanagan, and Dan Breen, the party soon suffered from splits and from Ó Cuinneagáin's unyielding *Führerprinzip* (leadership principle), about which only few members agreed. Ailtirí na hAiséirghe played only marginal roles from the late 1940s onward.[4]

The Glúin had parted ways with Ó Cuinneagáin precisely because of his politics, and while Irish military Intelligence, G2, had an eye on the Glúin, they were early persuaded that it was a cultural organization and kept their eye on Ó Cuinneagáin and the Ailtirí instead.[5] It has to remain specualtion whether James had much of an inkling of this during her time in Berlin. It is possible that Francis Stuart used one of his talks on the German airwaves to persuade Irish voters to support the Ailtirí and the republican party, Córas na Poblachta, in the elections of Spring 1943.[6] And certainly James, then living with Stuart and in a whirligig of Irish and IRA connections, was aware of the Ailtirí, if not the Glúin. Upon becoming firm friends with one of the Glúin's (and *Inniu's*) founders, Proinsias Mac an Bheatha (Francis McVeigh), there is no doubt that many interesting conversations were had between them about the (from an Irish-language perspective) very active and hopeful 1940s. It would be very interesting to know whether James ever met Ó Cuinneagáin, who continued to live in Dublin until his death in 1990.

Intended as a mouthpiece for the movment, the paper *Inniu* was founded in 1943 by two of Glúin na Bua's members: Ciarán Ó Nualláin, the brother of well-known satirical writer Brian O'Nolan (also known as Myles na gCopaleen),[7] and Proinsias Mac an Bheatha, a civil servant working for Customs and Mail. Mac an Bheatha was a late learner of Irish. Born in Belfast in 1910, his family left the north after an outbreak of sectarian violence, and he was brought up in Dublin. He developed a deep interest in the Irish language, even publishing a primer in 1946. Although working in the civil service throughout his working life, he was involved with Irish language organizations such as the Glúin, wrote regularly for the national press, and published 13 books in Irish (essays, historical studies, novels, and poetry).[8] *Inniu* was published from March 1943 onward (weekly from 1945) and survived, thanks to government funding, until August 1984, when funding was withdrawn. Ciarán Ó Nualláin stayed *Inniu*'s general editor until his retirement in May 1972, and then went on to become its literary editor.[9]

While it is nowhere said, it is reasonable to assume that it was the friendship with Proinsias Mac an Bheatha that gave James scope to write for *Inniu*.[10] They first met in 1971, and her friendship with the family continued on until Proinsias's death in 1991. He also proofread her first memoir for her, though he did not see it published. As an aside, it is also interesting to speculate whether Mac an Bheatha had heard James's voice long before he met her: in his memoir, he recounts listening to the German radio very frequently in and around 1941. His reference is to the sentimental song "Erika," which the German radio was "forever playing" at the time, and for which he had written an Irish version.[11] If Mac an Bheatha was, in fact, such a keen listener, he more than likely heard the programs produced by the Irische Redaktion, though he was not so keen to talk about that twenty-five years later.[12] In any case, as one of the co-founders of Glúin na Bua and *Inniu*, he remained intimately involved with the paper as one of its board members and by writing regular columns for it. It may well have been he who suggested that James contribute her column, "Letter from Europe," to the Irish language cause, informing the Irish readership of anything she found striking that went on in "Europe."

As the importance of the Glúin waned in the early 1950s, *Inniu* became a decidedly nationalist and predominantly conservative paper, read widely, if not so much by native Irish-speakers then by enthusiasts outside the Gaeltacht.[13] Its standard of Irish was very high, and it did much to add to a modern Irish vocabulary and standardize the spelling. However, regarding its standard of journalism, as an expert in the matter put it, "you would find more opinions than reportage, and although the opinion pieces were of merit, a proper distinction was not always made between the two."[14]

In the period of nearly three years during which James contributed a regular column, "Letter from Europe," the editor was Tarlach Ó hUid (1917–90). His life is a fascinating parallel to James's own, from their shared passion for Ireland and its language, to the point of denying their origins and upbringing. Born Augustus Walter Hood in London just 17 months before Ursula James, Ó hUid was of Irish extraction with an Ulster Unionist and Methodist background. As a young man he converted to Catholicism, and while still in London he had a connection with the London branch of the Gaelic League. He denied his upbringing and adopted as his own the culture, language, and heritage of Ireland. In 1936, he joined the Irish Volunteers, self-admittedly for "a love of Ireland, a desire for heroic deeds and Romanticism, as well as for a lack of understanding of Irish history,"[15] and in 1940 spent time in prison in Belfast for his membership in the IRA. His memoir, *Ar Thóir Mo Shealbha* (Seeking My Estate), describes this process, and severely criticizes the IRA, something that drew fierce attacks upon him from Irish writer Máirtín Ó Cadhain.[16] While in Crumlin Road Prison, Ó hUid edited the paper *Faoi Ghlas* (Locked Up) under the name Tarlach Bhillí, and he began contributing to *Inniu* also. On his release, he joined the above-mentioned Architects of the Resurrection, as did other republicans who became leading figures in the organization.[17] He told an interviewer that his publishing policy was "to praise anything that was for the good of the nation and to condemn anything that would do harm to it."[18] He remained editor until the end of the paper in 1984.

We know little to nothing of Ó hUid's attitude toward James, whose column, "Letter from Europe," began in November 1977, became a weekly column by 1978, and terminated as such at the end of 1980. She contributed another article on 12 March 1982, and (likely) an unsigned one in October 1983. It is maybe notable that in November 1983 she wrote to Mac an Bheatha, wondering whether Tarlach Ó hUid had something against *Róisín i gCéin* (Róisín Abroad).[19] But since this likely relates to three unsigned feature articles about the upcoming anniversary of St. Virgil in Salzburg, in which she played an administrative role, it is hard to make a connection with her previous, more controversial, articles in the paper.[20] There is no further sign that Ó hUid was seriously set against her or that she had upset anyone among the readership in the previous years to explain her column's demise.

What does she write about? As is typical for the journalistic letter genre, James is given free rein to report on whichever European matters seem of import to her, matters that can be presumed to be met with interest by its readership, and to offer her own opinion on them.[21] Since she was based in Germany, it is understandable that most of her news was from that country. In choice of subject matter and in delivery, the "Letters" have an Irish nationalistic and a conservative tone, often praising old regimes and their "heroes" and criticizing contemporaries for either a lack of moral fortitude or failure to learn from heroic predecessors. Her very first sentence for the column in 1977 sets the moral tone: "*Ní minic, faoraoir* [sic], *a fheictear an gníomh gaiscíochta sa lá inniu*" (Alas, it is very rare that one sees a heroic deed these days).[22]

She emerges as a cultural pessimist for whom coming generations are not strident enough, not following ideals of a certain cast, not cherishing their roots sufficiently: this all finds parallels in parts of her memoirs. While autobiography does not come into this directly, James, of course, chooses her material by whether her own past experience helped her form an opinion about it. Her style in her "Letters" is identical to that of her memoirs—often declamatory and sometimes cast in dramatic dialogue. There is some humor also, but more often of the ironic rather than the light sort. She rarely lists her sources, presumably many of them items in the European press.

Irish language matters, an issue she was concerned with all through her postwar life, do not recur frequently in her "Letters," given that she was writing from the continent, but when they do, she either criticizes the Irish government for not doing enough or praises foreigners for taking up the language.²³ England is still acting perfidiously by spreading news designed to ruin the Irish economy and saddling Ireland with an ugly image in the eyes of the world, with "step-mother" Thatcher ruling Ulster like the French run Corsica.²⁴ All things "Celtic" are tellingly of a noble or valiant hue; nations are usually compared with the "ancient" Celts and either fall short of the mark (Poland) or are sweepingly (and partly unhistorically) declared Celtic (France).²⁵ The case of Poland is interesting, however: after John Paul II's accession to the Papacy, James portrays the country as a long-suffering nation much in need of liberation from the Soviet yoke.²⁶ The Communist regime is just like the English rule during penal times in seventeenth and eighteenth century Ireland. Communists and those not standing up to them (the German government) are very frequently targets of her scorn; Socialist democracies, so she maintains, cause tax-havens to flourish.²⁷

Unsurprisingly, overtly modern art, like an unworthy underground theater from Munich that was going to bring its play to Dublin, brings only a "pollution of standards."²⁸ In many ways—and this is perhaps intended—this brings to mind the National Socialist term *Entartete Kunst* (degenerate art), with all the social and racial overtones that implies.

Germany and its people are blameworthy only for not standing up for themselves; otherwise there is praise for their philanthropy, diligence, talent, and learning.²⁹ In terms of politicians, German strongman politician and leader of the Christian Socialist Party (CSU) Franz-Joseph Strauss is a praiseworthy figure, while Chancellor Helmut Schmidt of the Social Democratic Party (SPD) is uselessly in thrall to the East and to the American West and cannot write policy that might keep the number of immigrants down.³⁰ She shines her approving limelight on Berliner Philharmonic director Herbert von Karajan; test pilot, lifelong Nazi, and teacher Hanna Reitsch, whom James says failed to save Hitler but who educated U.S. pilots after the war; Winifred Wagner, unfairly a victim of denazification measures, according to James; Rudolf Hess, who was treated inhumanely as a prisoner in West Berlin, so James believed; and UN secretary general Kurt Waldheim, the peace-worker, as she would have it. To these is added—shockingly—Herbert Kappler, former head of the police and Sicherheitsdienst (SS intelligence service) in Rome and, according to James, ultimately a victim of the Allies and Italian Communists.³¹

Letters from Europe, 1977–1982, and Irish Saints

The list is meaningful. Von Karajan was acknowledged worldwide as one of the greatest conductors of all time, and his Deutsche Grammophon recordings with the Berlin Philharmonic are still considered the gold standard for symphonic music. His motivation and record during the Nazi period are a matter of debate, although he joined the Austrian Nazi Party in 1933 and enjoyed the patronage of both Hitler and Goebbels until well into World War II.[32] His contribution as Germany's postwar cultural ambassador of classical music is likely what resonated with James, with the added benefit that he had significance in the Third Reich.

Hannah Reitsch has no such ambiguity. She was a gifted pilot who broke many records in the 1930s and 1940s—a particularly difficult feat considering that women were largely excluded from aviation.[33] She earned and kept Hitler's favor, even flying a light Fieseler Storch aircraft into Soviet artillery fire during the final days of the Reich, so that she and Generaloberst Ritter von Greim could meet with Hitler one last time. After the war she continued to fly, continued to set records, and continued as an unreconstructed National Socialist. In one of her final interviews, Reitsch said—much in parallel to James's pessimism:

> And what have we now in Germany? A land of bankers and carmakers. Even our great army has gone soft. Soldiers wear beards and question orders. I am not ashamed to say I believed in National Socialism. I still wear the Iron Cross with diamonds Hitler gave me. But today in all Germany you can't find a single person who voted Adolf Hitler into power. . . . Many Germans feel guilty about the war. But they don't explain the real guilt we share—that we lost.[34]

Winifred Wagner is similar in some ways, although without the heroics of flight. She was the wife of composer Richard Wagner's son and the living apostle of Wagner at the annual Bayreuth festival that Hitler attended until 1939. Winifred and James shared things: both were British, both were adopted, and both championed extreme views in place of the values of their childhoods. Wagner had a problematic marriage, and her introduction to Hitler in 1923 freed her in some ways. There were rumors that Wagner had a deeper relationship with Hitler, but that was apparently not the case. Nevertheless, Hitler was always a welcome guest at Haus Wahnfried, Richard Wagner's villa in Bayreuth. Even in the decades after World War II (Wagner died in 1980), she maintained contact with extreme political elements (Oswald Mosley and others) and never backed away from her affection for Hitler.

Rudolf Hess is well known and was the last of the Spandau Prison inmates sentenced at the International Military Tribunal at Nuremberg. An early member of the National Socialist party, Hess participated in the Munich putsch in 1923 and acted as Hitler's aide during a brief imprisonment in Landsberg Prison. Rewarded for his loyalty, Hess rose in party ranks but became less influential after the Nazi party assumed control of Germany in 1933. By the time of his bizarre flight to England in 1941, he was showing early signs of the mental health issues that only increased in severity as the years passed. During his forty-year incarceration, the plight of the former Deputy Führer became a rallying cry for right-wing elements inside and outside Germany. He committed suicide in 1987.

Herbert Kappler is in a class by himself: he was a murderer. As SS-Obersturmbannführer (lieutenant colonel) and Chief of Police in Rome in 1943–44, he was responsible for the arrest and deportation of Roman Jews to extermination camps. In 1944, Kappler organized and carried out the Ardeatine Cave massacre, in which 335 Italian hostages were murdered in retaliation for resistance attacks on SS personnel. He was brought to trial in 1947 and sentenced to life imprisonment. Due in part to the intervention of Irish Monsignor Hugh O'Flaherty, he was baptized a Catholic and eventually moved to a military hospital on grounds of ill health. He escaped in 1977 and fled to West Germany; the German government refused Italian requests for his extradition. Kappler died in 1978. James maintained that the Italian hostages were put to death according to the rules of war and that Herbert Kappler was ultimately a victim of the Allies and Italian Communists.

About ten of James's just over one hundred "Letters" carry a section dealing with the Second World War and with its aftermath. In essence, her idea of Germany's tragedy can be summed up by these points: the Hohenzollern family had been good rulers and ought never to have been dethroned in 1918; Churchill's deaf ear to German peace overtures and his merciless military decisions caused the conflict to become a war of attrition; and the partitioning of Berlin was a "devilish act" by the Allies, matched by the fact that 32 years after the war there was still no peace treaty.[35]

Letters from Europe, 1977–1982, and Irish Saints

The most controversial of the "Letters" is from 13 January 1978 entitled "The Prisoners Who Died in the Camps of Bergen-Belsen."[36] It is in close parallel to statements she made later in her autobiography, *Cé hí Seo Amuigh?* She begins the article by criticizing the Federal Republic of Germany's abject and unchanging remorse about its war crimes, as manifested by Israel's Foreign Minister Moshe Dayan's visit to Germany and his success in raising international loans for Israel—after a commemorative visit to Bergen-Belsen. James states, "I'd say that the German government will never have the courage or the boldness to throw off this yoke, this tie that they have been carrying for the last 30 years."[37]

The inscription upon the plaque Dayan unveiled at the camp was, according to James, belied by statistics and by other facts. It was not, she claimed, that 30,000 Jews were exterminated here, as the plaque said. Her take on it was that 7,000 people died there of typhoid fever, many of them criminals, and only a few of them Jews. James claimed that the primary cause of death struck the camp in 1945: the Allies (Churchill is singled out) were bombing Germany's railways day and night to cut off supplies and to break the civilian population's spirit; famine was widespread; and the camp commander Joseph Kramer made the brave and sensible decision to keep the camp gates closed to avoid the potentially looting, perishing masses from going out into the surrounding countryside: "For himself, it would have been easier to get out of the affair like that."[38] According to James, it was after the Allies took over the camp that the majority of the 7,000 died, and the Allies took the opportunity to take "awful pictures" and send them all over the world. The only source she chooses to quote is a document on "Missing People" allegedly published in Arolsen.[39] She also, unbelievably, decides to quote an unnamed text by Hannah Arendt, who had studied the events of the war closely, according to James, and who stated that the pictures were in fact misleading in that they only showed the state of affairs at the very end of the war. The Arendt citation is nonsense and fictitious.

Bergen-Belsen was originally established as Stalag XI C but became a SS concentration camp for Jews starting in 1943, with the aim of exchanging them for Germans held prisoner overseas. The facility soon became desperately overcrowded, and Russian prisoners were housed at a neighboring camp. Of both groups, tens of thousands died—as many as 35,000 from untreated typhus in the first few months of 1945—despite the fact that Bergen-Belsen was never designated a *Vernichtungslager* (extermination camp). SS-Hauptsturmführer Josef Kramer and forty-three of his male and female SS staff were put on trial in September 1945 and charged with war crimes in the mass murder and torture of Allied prisoners.[40] Eleven of the defendants, including three women, were sentenced to death by hanging. The testimony established a pattern at Belsen where random murder, physical torture, and deliberate starvation were the norm.[41] Ironically, although James refers to the International Tracing Service (ITS) archive at Arolsen proving that "only 7,000" died at Belsen, the archive actually cites a death figure of fifty thousand concentration inmates and at least twenty thousand Soviet prisoners of war.[42] Seven thousand dead from typhus fits with her Holocaust-denial mindset; seventy thousand dead from murder, starvation, and disease does not.

James would take this up again in *Cé hÍ Seo Amuigh?* The theory (conspiracy theory?) used in postwar newsreels to explain away corpses by means of typhus had been widely sown, even at the time the news was still fresh. The above-mentioned Irish fascist organization Architects of the Rebirth carried an article by Deasún Breathnach in July 1945, in which he reviewed a newsreel:

> We're able to see through the lie: the corpses had been exhumed from the ground. Furthermore, I myself observed (from the Press Association!) that 4,700 people have died in Germany of typhus, and that of this number 1,500 were in Buchenwald. A couple of days afterward I was speaking with a German who said that the Germans place those suffering from typhus in typhus camps. Can it thus be seen that Belsen and Buchenwald were typhus camps? When people contract typhus they quickly become emaciated....[43]

It must also be said that, any anti-Semitic intentions completely aside, according to historian Clair Wills, Irish commentators on the first reports from death camps had been generally skeptical, partly owing to the old enmity towards Britain, and took the horrific coverage for exaggerations of British propaganda.[44] However, James's statements in the 1978 article and her memoirs date thirty and forty years later and do not fall within the context of widespread denials that occurred just after Belsen was discovered. At all times, her own anti-Semitic intentions—which cannot be of any doubt, given other statements made in her 1992 memoir—are well disguised; her own express desire is to clear Germany of guilt. Tellingly, the other piece of news she chose to impart to her Irish readers that week dealt with the Irish greyhound, the *cú Gaelach*. With a note of irony, she tells the story of famous German actor Hans Clarin using such an animal to keep his fans at bay: the ideal twinning of Irish and German, body and spirit, was much to James's liking.

The article about Bergen-Belsen in particular gives rise to the question as to whether any readers reacted to her views. Unfortunately, until about 1982 there was no regular "Letter to the Editor" page in *Inniu* that would have given a forum to readers. Rarely, letters appeared near the editorial, and only one of them referred directly to James, although it did not comment on the Bergen-Belsen article.[45] Dr. Dorothy Ní hUigin, an expert on *Inniu*, confirms the lack of responses from members of the public reacting to James's articles.[46]

Beginning in the 1970s and continuing for the next decade, James carved out a scholastic niche by translating Irish works for a German audience. Her first effort, *Der König der Bäume*, is a wonderful achievement, a new translation from the Middle Irish texts (as stated in the book's blurb and the introduction). The book would not have made a "big splash" academically speaking, but it reached the shelves of the Bonn University Institute, for instance—currently the only remaining university in Germany teaching Celtic languages.[47] James—now styled O'Mara—had no formal academic training for this undertaking, which makes the achievement the more remarkable. This is the case even if the work lacks a full academic apparatus: neither the introduction nor the text carry appropriate references or textual notes about the two recensions that formed the basis of the new translation.[48] The project took her a decade—between first noting it to Cardinal Tomás Ó Fiaich in 1975 and delivering the book to him in Armagh. Judging by her acknowledgments, she not only managed to gain permission to see medieval manuscripts in a large number of prestigious institutions and repositories, but even received special treatment from the director of the National Museum of Ireland and from the National Monuments Service (or the Office of Public Works [OPW]), who invited her to join a scholarly expedition to the ruins of Abbey of St. Moling.[49] Characteristically, James denies the Royal Irish Academy, one of the repositories of the original texts, its "Royal" origins whenever she gets the chance.⁵⁰ To the extent that any of these institutions knew of her past, no one seems to have held it against her.

James thereby boldly reinvented herself yet again, this time as a scholar. The introduction to *Buile Shuibhne* (Mad Sweeney) catches the reader's imagination and shows why James chose to translate this piece over others:

> The reader is presented with a wide range of viewpoints. Vivid depictions breathe life into the 11th/12th-century courtly milieu with its etiquette and customs, lore of healing, and superstitions. We see a theatrical backdrop of the 7th century with a number of historically valid and believable topographical and hagiographical details. Often, a rougher wind from earlier times blows across the open scene; at times we are touched by a whiff of the La Tène which the monastic scribe cumbersomely attempted to erase. It is a joy for the reader that he did not manage to completely overlay the phantoms behind Suibhne's form. . . . The mantle of Christian edification lies on [Sweeney's] shoulders only loosely. The dress underneath turns out to be a patchwork of pagan saga embroidered with pearls of nature poetry. . . .⁵¹

The book's factually incorrect author description is interesting in terms of James's self-refashioning: she is introduced as "the author of many works regarding Ireland. She is a resident of Bavaria, on the Chiemsee, and a resident of the west of Ireland, where she founded a cultural institute and a museum, both serving the Irish language. A strong advocate of unadulterated translations directly from the original language, she works on the transmission in German of classical texts in her Gaelic mother tongue."

Only an extended trawl through south German and Austrian newspapers will show whether the first claim is realistic. The Gaelic mother tongue is an invention, if a logical consequence of the long journey taken by Phyllis Ursula "Rosaleen" James to cast off her hated British name and origins and to fabricate a Gaelic identity now capped off by that elusive thing, her Ur-language.

Staying in contact with Ó Fiaich, James became one of a number of collaborators who assisted him with his *Gaelscrínte san Eoraip* (Irish Shrines in Europe), an acclaimed monograph, not yet superseded, about the medieval Irish saints and scholars who worked on the continent.[52] Ó Fiaich, in James's telling, had intended to take this work further in a "more extensive study of those regions potentially converted to the Christian Faith by Irish evangelists," and asked for James's assistance. Because of his untimely death, she herself went on to do this, so she explains in her foreword to her follow-up, *In Search of Irish Saints*,[53] by adding many places not covered in Ó Fiaich's *Gaelscrínte san Eoraip*. An extended edition of James's work appeared as *Early Irish Saints in Europe: Their Sites and Their Stories*.

Through the 1980s James was involved with Irish events and seminars on the Continent. The years 1984 and 1989 brought the anniversary celebrations of Saints Virgil (Salzburg) and Kilian (Würzburg), for both of which she was working in a liaison capacity. She also assisted pilgrimages to the Continent by the Armagh Historical Society; the Cardinal, she felt, was relieved to take opportunities such as this to leave Northern Ireland and its troubles.[54] She talks with relish about the wrangling that accompanied organizing an event in Vienna involving both Church and state. Filmmaker and journalist Bob Quinn described the excitement arising from hearing the Ó Riada[55] mass in Vienna, but committed a journalistic blunder in James's favor: "To hear Irish sung for the first time in a thousand years in this cathedral was enough to make every atavistic fibre quiver. The person responsible for this event was Róisín Ní Mheara-Vinard, late of Galway, now living in Bavaria. That evening the city presented her with a specially struck medal."[56] It was in fact Ó Fiaich who was honored with the "*Großes Ehrenzeichen*" by the Province of Salzburg's president (Landhauptmann).[57]

In the autumn of 1987, James organized a Celtic seminar in Vienna, and toward its organization was awarded £1,200 from lottery funds by the Department of Foreign Affairs.[58] In August 1988, James was mentioned in a social column of the *Irish Times*, in a report about that year's Merriman summer school in Lahinch, County Clare: "Róisín Ní Mheara-Vinard lives in Austria and organizes Celtic seminars and other events in Salzburg, Vienna and Munich. 'I had the Chieftains over a fortnight ago,' she said."[59]

The celebrations of St. Kilian's 1,300-anniversary in Würzburg in 1989 also took more than a year's preparation, beginning with a pilgrimage from Armagh in 1988, and James was involved in helping with both. For instance, she compiled a list of churches dedicated to St. Kilian for the priests leading the pilgrimage.[60] A year's program of church celebrations, exhibitions, and popular festivals was planned.[61] Ó Fiaich was the principal celebrant at the mass on 2 July 1989, which was celebrated in German and in Irish, and which opened Würzburg's folk and beer fest in honour of the saint.[62] James describes seeing the cardinal in the cathedral, flanked by two Irish priests and resembling the saint and his co-martyrs Totnan and Kolonan: "A notice of warning to me regarding a self-sacrifice in the name of God."[63] She refers to Ó Fiaich's death the year after.

Besides having a hand in organizing these and other scholarly cultural events,[64] James seems to have been writing pieces about Ireland and organizing radio programs, talks, concerts, and screenings of films related to Ireland. For instance, in 1985 she met the famous singer Seán Ó Sé in Cork in preparation of a concert that year; she met Bob Quinn in Carraroe to prepare a film screening in München; and she was doing research at University College Dublin's folklore archives in preparation of a lecture on the Irish Halloween.[65] During the late 1980s she also went to Newry intending to teach children Irish through puppetry (without recompense). Her friend Mac an Bheatha drafted a press article on this plan of hers and went as far as to call it a "movement."[66]

Whether all these ventures amounted to full-time employment is guesswork, but it is hard to believe it could have paid enough to make a living. While experiencing shortages of funds every now and then, the impression one gets is that James had some independent means, and by this stage was also supported both by social pension arrangements in Germany and maybe by her children.

In September 1988, and while still planning for the celebrations of St. Kilian, she tells Mac an Bheatha that she would from now on stay out of "international Celtic events," excepting maybe those that were of more significant and with a real benefit to Ireland. Quite naturally for her age (she was by now 70), she was getting tired more often.[67]

Cardinal Ó Fiaich's death occurred in 1990 when James was working on the last drafts of her memoir. There is no proof she ever discussed the writing with him. Even if their friendship was built on sporadic correspondence and work-related meetings in Armagh and in Irish pilgrimage sites on the continent, one speculates that Ó Fiaich must have become aware of James's views on World War II, if only from her writings in

Letters from Europe, 1977–1982, and Irish Saints

Inniu. He was an early subscriber to *Inniu*, was outspoken in its support when government funding was eventually capped,[68] and despite his increasing cares during that period—having been appointed Archbishop of Armagh and Primate in 1977 and made cardinal in 1979—it seems unlikely that her views escaped him. His private thoughts on this will remain unplumbable—maybe until James's own papers come to light, containing his letters to her. It is just possible that, in a pastoral way, he helped divert her focus to an area in which she had a natural interest and that she was well placed to explore—the lives of the medieval Irish missionaries and churchmen on the continent—and away from her self-serving recollections that touch on other, more controversial subjects.

James's legacy in Armagh is considerable: besides publishing the book *Irish Saints in Europe* and a number of papers with Seanchas Ard Mhacha, they accepted her offer to arrange and list the cardinal's own papers for use in the commemorative library and archives that were opened there in his name in 1999. It is her arrangement and list that are still key to the collection now.[69] In a fundraising volume highlighting some of the holdings of the Cardinal Tomás Ó Fiaich Memorial Library and Archives, the introductory chapter makes reference to James's presence at the opening of that institution: "Author and friend of Cumann Seanchais Ard Mhacha, Róisín Ní Mheara-Vinard travelled from Austria for the occasion and, again emphasizing Cardinal Ó Fiaich's interest in early Irish links with Europe, Dr Peter Ochsenbein, librarian of the Stiftsbibliothek, St Gallen, Switzerland, crowned the day with an illustrated talk on the Irish treasures in the famous St Gallen Library."[70]

James had indeed come a long way.

14

Accessory after the Fact

Holocaust denial is not a new phenomenon. It has gained momentum since the 1960s, and perhaps reached its apogee in 1998 with the action brought by David Irving against Deborah Lipstadt, an American historian who had labelled Irving as a Holocaust denier.[1] Through his many historical works, Irving gained a reputation as a highly competent military historian, but with each succeeding work he manifested an increasing bias in favor of Hitler and Nazi Germany. This came to the forefront in 1977 when he published *Hitler's War* and made the case that Hitler was ignorant of the Holocaust until it was too late to stop it; Irving further offered a bounty for anyone who could produce a signed Hitler document that showed otherwise. Irving's work, speeches, and appearances thereafter made it abundantly clear that he was, for reasons of his own, entirely sympathetic to Hitler and Nazism. The Lipstadt trial was the first to tackle the issues of evidence and historical truth as they relate to Holocaust denial. This issue is relevant when considering the degree to which Rosaleen James was a Nazi sympathizer and whether she subscribed to a belief that denies or minimizes the organized murder of millions of human beings.

Holocaust denial (or "revisionism," to use the deniers' preferred label) can generally be understood to contain three main elements: (1) that while there was unfortunately some killing, there was no systematized, official German policy to do so, certainly not one directed by Adolf Hitler; (2) that the gas chambers at Auschwitz-Birkenau were a myth; and (3) that the total number of those killed was in the thousands, perhaps hundreds of thousands, even slightly over a million, but not approaching

Accessory after the Fact

the traditional figure of 6 million usually cited. There are, of course radical elements even inside the radical school of Holocaust denial, who maintain that no Jews were killed at all. In most instances, the pillars of denial are linked to an imagined universal Jewish conspiracy to distort and manipulate the truth.

As seen in the previous chapter, Rosaleen James's overt anti-Semitism first surfaced in January 1978 in her column for *Inniu*, "Letter from Europe." In this letter she put the subject of Jews and the Holocaust at center stage, and presents views she will more fully develop more fourteen years later:

> No doubt, a political visitor has no more effective way of exerting pressure on Germany than by mentioning the war crimes. . . . I'd say that the German government will never have the courage or the boldness to throw off this yoke, this tie that they have been carrying for the last 30 years. Even though it is clear (despite the inscription [in Bergen Belsen]) that 7,000 died there, according to the registry of Missing People in Arolsen. In addition, a lot of the prisoners were criminals and only a few were Jews. The main cause of death in the camp was typhus, a disease that hit it in 1945. At the time, the air raids occurred day and night, of course.
>
> Germany was under attack on both fronts, the railways were being targeted and goods trains were stopped when their drivers were killed by machine guns from warplanes. The carriage of goods stopped in all regions, and this had been decided by Churchill in order to break the spirit of the civilian population. Famine followed this everywhere, not only in the camps. Two paths were left to Joseph Kramer, manager of the Bergen-Belsen camp: he could open the gates and expel the looting, perishing masses into the surrounding country (for himself, it would have been easier to get out of the affair like that)—or wait until the war was ended and the enemy arrived.
>
> He made a decision, . . . but in the meantime the number of people dying in the barracks increased every day. For that reason, when the English arrived on 15 April 1945 they were met with a very sorry sight. Many of the 7,000 there that died, however, died after that date. The enemy seized the opportunity to take ugly

pictures and spread them all over the world: ". . . the world shall remember. . . ."

Along those lines, Professor Hanna[h] Arendt—an American Jew herself—, wrote after having studied WWII: "It is right to say that these pictures deluded people in that they display the situation in the camps at the end of the war when the awful events of the world war had taken place everywhere in the last months, and it [is] hard to get a proper account of them still."[2]

James follows this with a "Letter," published on 28 April 1978,[3] concerning a "recent threat from the U.S." when a delegate from the American Jewish Committee approached the organizers about changing the text of the drama for the Oberammergau Passion Play in 1980, because of parts that gave offense to Jews. Despite a polite and reasoned request from the German government, the local production officials refused, and preparations for the next play "are underway with Judas Iscariot [i.e., the Jew] as ugly as he was first conceived for this play in 1534." She hoped that many Irish would visit in 1980 and give their support to the "honest, pious, and loyal people there. They will not be disappointed." Given this predicate attitude, her comments in her 1992 memoir *Cé hÍ Seo Amuigh?* (Who Is She Outside?) are unsurprising. The tone of those comments, though, grew more entrenched and specific in the fourteen years between her articles and the publication of her memoir.

We can date the genesis of the memoir to the mid-1980s. In a letter to Mac an Bheatha dated 3 June 1985, James wrote: "As regards the 'memoirs,' I have more than 150 pages done, and Máirín Ní Dhomhnalláin continues happily to help me! She says that the contents 'run along smoothly in Irish!' I will be working away in Dublin whatever the story, and I hope that FNT will be satisfied!"[4] As soon as it was published by Coiscéim,[5] it raised a sharp but short-lived outcry from critics and journalists, a politician, and a handful of citizens, and has since been nearly forgotten. Rather than an autobiography proper it is better styled a memoir, because although James proceeds chronologically, she is selective and leaves out important information. For example, both her children are presented as four-year-old and two-year-old faits accomplis without fathers. She elaborates on certain aspects of the Nazi regime by quoting selective works underpinning her views.

The publishing house Foilseachán Náisiúnta Teoranta (FNT; connected with *Inniu*) was James's first choice, but after FNT's liquidation in 1988 she wrote to her friend Proinsias Mac an Bheatha about finding another one, preferably one that could pay an advance.[6] Characteristically, she states that this publisher would thereby do a good deed "*ar son na teangan in Éirinn*" (for the cause of the Irish language in Ireland). Furthermore, she says, "It will be a lavish book in two parts and with illustrations. The only hindrance for publishing it is long-lived F.S. [Francis Stuart]!! (He's written to me since.)"[7]

It seems extraordinary that she wanted to wait for Stuart's death to publish the book, cosidering that she only gave him the role of a friend and cohabitant in it, and that she omitted the difficult relationship described in Stuart's *Black List, Section H* (1971), which talks in great recognizable detail about "Susan," alias Ursula "Rosaleen" James. She allowed Mac an Bheatha at this stage to mention the book to a friend (the writer Proinsias Mac Aonghusa) but professed herself still unhappy with it. Whether or not the draft was shown to Mac Aonghusa, he proved to be one of her most scathing reviewers when it was published, illustrating his review with an image of Hitler and another of "the horrors of Buchenwald."[8]

A few friends helped James with her book: Máirín Ní Dhomhnalláin was mentioned again in a letter, with James recognizing she was *traochta* (worn out) by the work, which by then ran to 250 pages.[9] Ní Dhomhnalláin was a published poet and a librarian who worked for forty-two years for the Royal Irish Academy. Her father, the widely known and esteemed writer and *Gaeilgeoir* Pádraig Ó Domhnalláin (formerly Donlon),[10] was one of the foremost pioneers of the Irish language and of the Gaelic League. While it would appear that Ní Dhomhnalláin did the most needful early work, it is surprising that she is not mentioned in the book's foreword; she died only in 2006. Mac an Bheatha died in 1990, two years before the book's publication, but James had shared drafts with him, and he is given prominence in her acknowledgments for having urged the task of publication on her: "He was saying it was my duty to write this account."[11]

Ignoring Ní Dhomhnalláin's input, James gives Mac an Bheatha credit for early help with "the language of our forefathers which I did not have the luck to learn in my youth."[12] She also gives brief nods to Micheál Ó Cuig, long associated with the Taibhdhearc Theatre in Galway; to lecturer and poet Ciarán Ó Coigligh, who edited the text; and to writer Aogán Ó Muircheartaigh who worked on the photographs.[13] It seems that only one of the people who saw the drafts warned her about its contents: according to Ó Coigligh, Mac an Bheatha advised James against publication because it would bring trouble, and "he was right in the end."[14] Ó Coigligh himself, by contributing a glowing introduction to the author and the book, drew some trouble upon himself.[15] So did the publisher, Pádraig Ó Snodaigh. James was sure of herself and her contribution to the Irish language—so sure that she dedicated *Cé hÍ Seo Amuigh?* to "the people of Ireland."

The title, *Cé hÍ Seo Amuigh?* (Who Is She Outside?), is immediately recognizable to Irish-language enthusiasts as the slightly adapted beginning of the Munster ballad "Éamonn an Chnoic," or "Ned of the Hill."[16] With that, James makes an obvious statement connecting her outsider status with her Gaelic credentials. One of the reviewers, Bríona Nic Dhiarmada, summed up the expectations that this outsider's book raised: she had looked forward to reading something so unusual from a woman author who discussed international politics and whom she did not know—a rarity in Irish-language circles. It was for the politics, but also for James's style, that she ultimately condemned the book, a view echoed by most reviewers.[17]

The single most troublesome point of the book for Nic Dhiarmada and the others is James's insistence on her view that the Holocaust did not happen as has been widely proven. Fourteen years after first airing her views in her 1978 "Letter" in *Inniu*, she reiterates what she said—except that now she names the one and only source for her beliefs: a French cook who worked in one of the camps (Buchenwald or Bergen-Belsen, she was not sure) whom she met in Paris soon after the war.[18] The woman also told her that the "foreign" internees had in fact been fed very well until the Allies' infamous bombing of supply trains, since they were carrying out hard work, so much so that the German internees began to complain about it. She also said that meantime, in camps in the east, internees were given the choice of either staying until the Soviets arrived, or being brought west: "Alas, they chose the second option!"[19] According to the cook, when the trains arrived in her own camp (Buchenwald or Bergen-Belsen), many people who had died during the journey fell out: they only died because a journey that had previously taken three days now took three weeks, thanks to the Allies. The heaps of corpses from the trains, left there until the U.S. Army liberated the camps, were welcome fodder for the "Yankees." James attributes a breathless quote to the unnamed woman: "That is how it was! They were documentary pictures of the ignominious treatment they gave us and that they [the Yankees] themselves with their bomber planes were the cause of! They killed the head of camp, the doctors and the wardens without leave for anybody to defend themselves, and without hearing them out!"[20] According to James this woman was trustworthy, so the question for James was, why were such lies told about the camps? In her memoir she also goes further, retelling another Allied hoax with the same intent of blackening Germany's name: a young American GI whom she met in Paris soon after the war told her of having taken photographs—by order of his superiors—of German civilians who had died during the Dresden bombings and who were disinterred for the purpose of taking photographs. He was one of a small band of disturbed young men who needed to tell their tales. Her story is contradictory as well as deeply untrustworthy: the GI told her another story illustrating German high-mindedness and American baseness, although he was still stationed in a border town in East Germany.[21]

Compared to *Inniu*, James's readership was now slightly wider. In her shrill effort to counter the overwhelming body of historical evidence to the contrary, she comes across as a conspiracy minded crank with a reactionary political agenda. The majority of commentators—there are ten reviews, four reports, and an interview following the publication of *Cé hí Seo Amuigh?*—condemn the book. One of the earliest commentators, and the first reviewer who wrote in English for an Irish newspaper—that is, one of a few reviews guaranteed to reach many readers—was Cathal Mac Coille, at the time a staff writer for the broadsheet *Sunday Tribune*. His review of 24 January 1993 called James's memoir "by far the nastiest book I have read in the Irish language" for "its ill-founded challenge to the facts of mass-murder."[22] . . . Suffice it to say that this unpleasant addition to the David Irving school of denying facts that are too horrible to contemplate contains not a shred of credible evidence to make anyone doubt what has been chronicle [*sic*] of Jewish suffering. What it does contain is a series of impressions, opinions and hear-say of the vaguest kind."[23]

Mac Coille also pleaded that Bord na Leabhar Gaeilge, a body within the Department for the Gaeltacht[24] that at the time allotted funding to Irish-language publications, "not shame us by grant-aiding its publication."[25] The following week, Minister of Equality and Law Reform Mervyn Taylor, a member of the Jewish community, was quoted in the same paper as saying, "It would be scandalous if this book were to receive any help from a government-funded agency."[26] Two weeks later, an Irish journalist working in London took this point further and gave the book its most international airing. *The Independent*'s Leonard Doyle reported on 8 February 1993 that "the authorities in Ireland have subsidized an anti-Semitic memoir in the Irish language, which may be in violation of international laws forbidding the incitement of racial hatred. The book states that there was 'no proof that the Germans intended to exterminate' the Jews and that pictures of Nazi concentration camp victims were corpses exhumed after the 1945 Dresden bombing."

Doyle claimed that the grant of £1,095 had been paid, and that Seán de Fréine, secretary of Bord na Leabhar Gaeilge ("a quango"), denied the book was anti-Semitic. De Fréine had earlier defended himself to Mac Coille by pointing out that his organization was not a censorship board, but he obviously found it necessary to defend himself to Doyle more strongly. Where was the publisher in all this? Coiscéim's Pádraig Ó Snodaigh is quoted by the London *Independent* as offering whatever grant money he may receive to any Jewish charity. Regarding his decision in favor of publishing the book, he was given a voice by the *Sunday Tribune*, calling *Cé hÍ Seo Amuigh?* "a marvelous historical document," and saying, "It gives an excellent insight into the English ruling classes during the second world war and indicates how many of them accepted what was going on in Germany before the war. I don't like the lady who wrote the book and I dislike some of the things that she says but I am not going to get involved in the censorship of a book. The first thing that Hitler did when he came to power was to burn the books that he didn't like."[27]

The debate about grant-aiding reached its greatest notoriety when Irish independent and socialist county councilor Joe Higgins took part in a protest against the grant-aiding held by the Irish branch of "Youth Against Racism," quixotically staged outside the wrong offices.[28] The question of whether the book was grant-aided or not was never taken up again. James's second memoir, published by the Armagh Historical Society (Seanchas Ard Mhacha), was grant-aided by the same agency. But unsurprisingly it mentions neither the first book nor the *Inniu* column

"Letter from Europe," and the only time it mentions Germany in conjunction with the war is at the beginning, when James repeats Irish people's expression of sympathy for the poor war-riven Germans.[29]

However, the "paper debate" is as fascinating as the semipolitical debate was not. The arguments to and fro between freedom of the press and censorship were taken up by reviewers again and again. Of fourteen discussions of the book in the press, three reviewers tended toward censorship (if only by not giving government funding to support the book), while three were outspoken for the freedom of the press. Proinsias Mac Aonghusa, then President of the Gaelic League, called the book "likely a dangerous book," warning that young people may read it who have no knowledge of the facts and will take the "squeaky clean look" that fascism gets in the book at face value.[30] Although not against its publication, he had misgivings about its grant-aiding, and pointed realistically to the fact most baffling to any non-Irish person: that there would have been "never-ending trouble" had the book been published in English or German.[31] Published in Irish only, it merely raised a storm in a teacup: proof of the irrelevance of the Irish language to the "real world?" More forceful in advocating censorship through the denial of grant-aid is Cathal Mac Coille's plea to the Bord na Leabhar Gaeilge (mentioned above). The most prominent advocates of censoring the book for grant-aid, in accord with London *Independent*'s Leonard Doyle, were Minister Taylor and President Mary Robinson: "Ireland's President, Mary Robinson, a constitutional and civil rights lawyer, was said to be 'distressed and embarrassed' over the government grant, according to Dublin sources."

On the other hand, there were advocates for freedom of the press, among them Alan Titley (*Books Ireland*), editor of the monthly magazine *Comhar*, Tomás Mac Síomóin, and columnist Marie Ní Chonchubhair (also of *Comhar*). Titley's article begins by stating, "This is a good book. Before I am misquoted and garotted I should explain. It is a good book because (a) it tells a story which is not often told, (b) it is generally well-written with a regard for style and pungency, and (c) it raises emotions in us which are well worth arousing."[32] Titley also points to the fascinating glimpses of the English upper classes and of Francis Stuart ("no mean collaborator himself") that James's writing provides. Although Titley believed the author held "weird opinions," and told "nauseating lies," it did not make him think "that this book should be banned or not supported in the normal fashion. . . . [It] should be widely read because it is a ringing refutation of itself."

Mac Síomóin went a step further to praise the publisher for his work in general and for his personal sacrifices. As regards censorship, he agreed with other reviewers about the appalling nature of the author's message, but again referred to de Fréine of the Bord na Leabhar Gaeilge who "will understand also that it is difficult to rein in the censorship horse once it has bolted—[it will go for] the Right today, the Left tomorrow, particular dialects the day after, and further on the work of Máirtín Ó Muilleoir, Proinsias Mac Aonghusa, *Comhar*, extreme republicanism, extreme obscenity etc. etc.?"[33]

Along similar lines, Ní Chonchubhair (like Mac Síomóin) chose to use the book to argue that the Irish laws of defamation ought to be reviewed.[34] She quotes Ó Snodaigh extensively, and he is reported to have said that there is no paragraph in the book that refers directly to Nazism—if he did, he could be easily and multiply refuted—as well as that there were received views as to what the Irish language can be used for: "We are always hoping that Irish is squeaky-clean. . . . It is applied censorship to say that it is not in order that money be spent on a book of this sort."[35] However, Ní Chonchubhair does not depart from her main theme, and although she lambasts Leonard Doyle for talking of a book he could not read, her own knowledge of the book was very limited.

Entirely different in tone, a satirical piece also in *Comhar* poked fun at the whole matter, by referring to "Salman Mac Coille['s]" article in the *Sunday Tribune* and a protest by the Gaelic League against James's book. The protest, according to the satirist, happened because "it was a scandal that an Irish book was published which anybody was interested in."[36]

Unsurprisingly, every one of the reviews dismissed the book's claim to historical veracity where German Nazism and the Holocaust are concerned, and most condemn the racism they found inherent in it. The book was "a vindication of Hitler's Germany," wrote Proinsias Ó Drisceoil, that coincided with "the revival of neo-Nazism in Europe."[37] "I do not remember having read any book that is so openly anti-Jewish as this piece of work," offered Mac Aonghusa in *Anois*; while Nic Dhiarmada judged the book to be "propaganda for the worst and most ugly philosophy that took root in the Europe of the 20th century, i.e., Nazism."[38] She refers to James's description of the Scottish lowlands where a "good portion of

Teutonic blood [was] mixed with the true native blood of the Gael," to illustrate this statement.

Alan Titley satirized James's pro-Hitler attitude and notes that "her story is a catalogue of weird opinions and very particular special pleadings. . . . Everybody was out of step except our Gerry. That nice homely guy, A.H. was forced to attack Russia. . . ." Yet Titley did not find the book particularly anti-Semitic; "insofar as she doesn't appear to particularly like the Jews she has far greater disdain for most other nations, classes, and groups, particularly if they are not German."

Both Mac Coille and Nic Dhiarmada point to victims of the Holocaust whose testimony refutes James's opinion about the extermination camps: Mac Coille cites a friend and Irish resident whose father was put to death, and Nic Dhiarmada refers to a recently published book by Helen Lewis, *A Time to Speak*.

The only reviewer taking James's side, Eoghan Ó Súilleabháin, attacks the other writers' "sharp tongues" while agreeing to many of their verdicts on James and her book.[39] The article is long and carefully interspersed with quotations from the book. Ó Súilleabháin's principal message is that hypocrisy reigns where Germany's Nazi period is concerned, that there were many sympathizers in Ireland, and that the left-leaning Proinsias Mac Aonghusa and another colleague writing for *Comhar*, T. Ó Raghailligh, issued apologetics for Stalin that did not meet with a similar outcry.[40] Their criticism of James where she opines that "the pitter-patter of parliamentary democracy . . . was forced on us"[41] rings false, according to Ó Súilleabháin, since their own democratic credentials were lacking. "If we would like to defend democracy, we had better understand causes and dynamics of the movements opposing democracy, and this woman's book is a great help towards that."[42] Ó Súilleabháin insists also that there is no propaganda or deception in James's book, but rather the complex thoughts of a person molded by difficult conditions. This aside, he admits that her grasp of historical fact is slender, and that she uses statistics only to bolster her argument, to the point of calling her account evasive and glib in places.[43] He names her long conditioning in England, where her social class, in particular, was in sympathy with Hitler, as well as her years in Germany,[44] as reasons for her pro-Hitler stance: "Hitler was a very clever politician who was able to hide his evils very well."[45] Ó Súilleabháin's apologia for James on the grounds of her conditioning hardly accounts for her unbending stance, which goes so far to deny the Holocaust based on the unsupported testimony of a French woman she claims to have met only once, immediately after the war.

One argument by Ó Súilleabháin in defense of the book was echoed by Titley, Nic Dhiarmada, and Ó Drisceoil—namely, that James provides rare and at times critical insights into the English upper classes and personages such as Axel Munthe, William Joyce, "Axis Sally," Seán Russell, and Frank Ryan.

How did readers see the person behind the book? Ó Drisceoil judged her to have assumed "what she considered to be the full Gaelic identikit," meaning her (assumed) conversion to Catholicism, Gaelicization of her adoptive mother's maiden name, and assuming the language as her own ancestral one. He did not question where her need for an "identikit" came from, but examines her ideology: she managed to "retain her reverence for aristocracy which she combined with extreme nationalism, leading to a form of monarchial republicanism in the case of Ireland and Nazism in the case of Germany."[46] Titley concurred: her "snobby upbringing" may have instilled in her a "hatred of the British ruling class, but it left her indelibly marked with a disdain for all ordinary people."[47]

When interviewer Desmond Fennell asked James later whether she was a snob, she told him to ask the people in the west of Ireland, deliberately misunderstanding a question that might have aimed at her upper class upbringing or her racial favoritism (Gaelic, German). In judging the person behind the book, Nic Dhiarmada is the most outspoken about James's racism, saying she found it hard finishing "this ugly book," and she points to the large amount of make-believe that had a claim of "true Irishness" running through it. Ó Súilleabháin complained later that nobody could see the sense of humor betrayed in the book, such as her mocking her own inability to cook.

It is interesting that Eoghan Ó Súilleabháin, otherwise positively inclined to James, claimed she showed an inclination to like German men, but not the women. When asked by Fennell about this later on, James dismissed the question as "silly."[48] There is no doubt that James's descriptions of Ruth Weiland and Lale Anderson are less than sympathetic, but in her pieces in *Inniu* and her second memoir there are a number of likeable and admirable women such as Rudolf Hess's wife Ilse, pilot Hanna Reitsch, and Bayreuth administrator Winifred Wagner

(*Inniu*), as well as women she knew personally, Máire Phaidí and Mamó on Inis Meáin.[49]

Few reviewers discussed James's style. The most outspoken was Nic Dhiarmada, who called it false, old-fashioned, and affected, making the book hard to read. She regrets that the book is put before the readers as "another deed for the revival of the language."[50] Eoghan Ó Súilleabháin pointed out that because of the book's themes, quite different from the old traditional topics of rural life, it "shows where the language can go." Ó Súilleabháin points rightly to James's great linguistic ability in this, her fourth language, and gives examples of turns of phrase, highlighting her "joyful descriptions of a world of affluence," and her bringing to life the atmosphere in Berlin during the war years.[51]

James was given a chance to reply to her critics when Desmond Fennell interviewed her in November 1993. Here she argued that she was an eyewitness but she was lambasted for opinions derived from what she had seen and heard. As for "liberals" warning against her book, she said that "truth begets something bad—bitter or tough, one has to swallow it sometimes."[52] Asked outright whether it was a lie that the Nazis killed millions of Jews on purpose in camps like Bergen-Belsen and Buchenwald, she is evasive and returns to an oft-repeated point about the bad treatment of Germany after World War I:

> There was no talk of that then. I have mentioned the first account one had of it. I got it by chance, in Paris. Scares came along of every sort, in every place, and from every side—*á la guerre comme á la guerre* as was said in France before. Of course, there was no need for the enemy to be pushed to the last, as was done with Germany, while the country was trying to come to a solution. Millions of people would be saved from death if only an honorable peace were made in time. And whatever happens, it is not right to hit somebody who is lying on the ground. And another thing, it is not right to judge the person that didn't have a chance to defend his case. There are always two sides to a story.[53]

James and the Irish people were too innocent and needed to wake up to certain realities, she further implies. Asked about her love for Germany, James expounds a belief—echoing the book itself—that if there had not been Hitler, somebody else would have tried to remove the weight that 1918 placed on Germany. Since 1945, Germany has been "schizophrenic." She seems to mean that it was drained of its lifeblood, because Europe, according to James, is the poorer without its "buttress of support": "Philosophical and spiritual works and discoveries are lacking."[54] She also repeats her belief that the French Revolution was a step in the wrong direction, because "Europe went astray" with it and "has been wandering ever since." Her cultural pessimism, as expressed in her columns in *Inniu*, comes to the fore again—"There is only the irrational path of materialism and of nihilism before us. . . ."—though she derives hope from faith: "God is there and He is strong."[55]

As for James's aloofness about her private life, Fennell tackled this by asking about her love life, but got nowhere with it. "Síle Ní Ghadhra is my love!" [56] James maintained, rebuffing Fennell's and the readers' curiosity about the real woman behind the politics, the cultural chauvinism, and the gaps in her telling, and pointing to another make-believe woman. As an eye-witness, her testimony is untouchable. As a private person making her choices of what to tell us and what to leave out, she did herself no favors with this interview.

After Fennell's interview, no further comment was made on James's outlook. As Joachim Fischer in a study of Irish-speaking literature regarding Germany said, the opportunity that her book and the controversy seemed to offer for discussing Irish ideological positions during the war was lost.[57]

James's affection for the Irish language and its people is beyond doubt, and it seems unlikely that she chose to air her opinions in Irish in order to escape censure. Censure there was: many of the "people of Ireland," to whom she arrogantly dedicated the book, rightly protested against it in disgust and subjected it to a certain amount of critical analysis. It is doubtful that many people in the west of Ireland read it: Nóirín Uí Ghoill, who used to work for James at the Inis Meáin museum, found her second memoir hard to read. Sometimes, when a person writes in a second or third language, the style will be convoluted. However, it is obvious that James would have been put before a much larger and even more critical jury had she written *Cé hÍ Seo Amuigh?* in her mother tongue, English. Irish, as writer Gabriel Rosenstock once pointed out in an entirely different context, gives freedom:

Newspapers don't bother to review us. TG4[58] refuses to air a book programme. We can say what we like. Nobody's interested. Who will rein us in and say we are too far to the right, too far to the left, too folkloric, too experimental, too spiritual, and too materialistic? Nobody. Being invisible, we can come and go like the gentry (by which I mean the fairy folk)![59]

In 2006, James (as Róisín Ní Mheara) published *I gCéin is i gCóngar: Cuimhní Cinn a Dó* (At Home and Abroad: Memoirs 2). With a nod to the nickname she gave herself in correspondence with friends, Róisín i gCéin ("Róisín Abroad"), this was the second instalment of her memoirs, published by the Historical Society of Armagh, which was favorably inclined to her for her friendship with Cardinal Ó Fiaich.[60] It is here that she talks of her postwar life. In four chapters, she describes early visits to Ireland, the Durlas, and Inis Meáin projects.

Apart from expressing disappointment with the Irish government's handling of the language question, she avoids politics. But she does not avoid racial stereotyping: the true Gael of the islands is held up as an ideal, and the pollution of the ideal by way of modern dress and electric appliances finds loud condemnation. There seems to have been no review of the book.

Reviews of her two works on the Irish saints did not make reference to her journalism or controversial autobiography; she is simply a "disciple" of Cardinal Ó Fiaich, and one whose work provides "a graceful broad sweep with an evangelistic message to engage spiritually in pilgrimage with those stalwart and compassionate saints."[61] Eight years later, the same reviewer, regarded the expanded new edition of that work (*Early Irish Saints in Europe: Their Sites and Their Stories*) in even more friendly terms: "Róisín Ní Mheara does not need my praise: a friend of the Armagh Diocesan Historical Society, a friend of the late Cardinal Ó Fiaich and the generous donor to the library founded in his memory."[62] Ó Muirí might have found it inappropriate to comment on the author's life, but the juxtaposition of the Irish saints and Róisín's hard and cold eye on what went on around her in Berlin makes for bitter reflection. Aside from the warm and glowing reviews by an editor at her publishing house, it may speak for itself that there appear to be none from the academics and colleagues of Ó Fiaich.

James's version of European history in the 1930s and 1940s stands in stark contrast to the historical record, and she cannot let go of the notion that the Jews were the agitators, the corruptors, and the malicious hand behind what happened to the Germany that lived in her imagination. The second chapter of her memoir *Cé hÍ Seo Amuigh?* tells the story of her first sojourns as a young student in Berlin, sojourns that were interspersed with prewar holidays in Monte Carlo with the Hamiltons. This is interwoven with commentary on European politics, Hitler, and the Jews, helped by the fact that the Hamilton's set overlapped in Monte Carlo with the Churchills', and the Vansittards'—Sir Robert Vansittard having been made Whitehall's Minister of Foreign Affairs. Once back in Berlin, bureaucracy forced her to find documents to prove she was not of Jewish descent, and this sets her off on a long passage plainly supporting the National Socialists' anti-Semitic policies:

> These rules were put in effect in Germany in order to keep the inordinately tight influence that the Jews had on the country in the post-war years in check. Especially in cultural things it was judged that this was harmful and that this infiltration was the cause for the dangerous decrease in the moral standards of the cities. Maybe that was true, it is not for us to judge that.[63]

However, judge it she did, with full approbation:

> After those Jews who were long settled in the country had obtained power over finance and business, the others came to direct the arts, literature, the media and education. It could not but begin to go against them, and the day came that the populace was moving towards the right, and the small number that had been lucky had to give up their domineering ways and leave their powerful positions. ... The majority preferred to leave the country, given they had family connections abroad. They were encouraged to do so when they were permitted to take a great part of their belongings with them.[64]

James's rhetoric echoes that frequently found in *Der Stürmer*, perhaps the most degrading of all Nazi publications and one that characterized Jews as a subhuman virus attacking the healthy body of Aryan Germany.

Accessory after the Fact

The forty-five years since the end of World War II had not changed James's beliefs. Writing about the Nürnberg Laws of 1935, which effectively deprived German (and later, Austrian) Jews of their most basic civil rights, James agreed with the Nazis and further commented on what she thought to have been Nazi Germany's humanitarian concern for the Jews:

> But all through the '30s Germany had to deal with the large number of Jewish refugees from the East, and Germany developed schemes for resettling them in a Zionist state outside Europe. The "Madagascar Project" was the most ambitious of them all, and Germany only gave this plan up in 1942 when the war kept going on, and when it was impossible going ahead with it. . . . But England seized Madagascar in 1942 with a heavy hand and that was the end of those recommendations.[65]

Whatever the fierce loyalty to Germany James had early on identified with—as the maligned underdog of her early childhood—she goes several steps too far in attributing good impulses to a ruling elite that was planning for genocide:

> Whatever happened after that, it is impossible to deny that Germany was seriously looking for a permanent sanctuary for the Jews. . . .
>
> It always fell on them to find a practicable way for a re-settlement program of the same type when the large number of other Jews were taken by the German army at the mobilisation of the ample regions of the East. That army could do nothing but to gather the Jews, by their own admission their fierce enemies, into ghettoes, postponing a solution for the problem of that class until after the war. And there are plenty of documents in evidence of this good plan.[66]

The following passage leaves the reader in no doubt about her alarming beliefs and her membership to that amorphous but dangerous community of anti-Semites and holocaust deniers able to couch their views in solicitous language:

It is clear to anybody reading the newspapers of that era that the specifications of the restraining laws which Germany implemented against the Jews in 1935 were made under duress. . . . Beyond that, it is certain that it was the Europe-wide show of indifference to the policy that caused Hitler to underestimate the danger to his own nation inherent in the Jewish question, alas! Similarly he underestimated the declaration of war that the World Organization of Jews made against Germany after he came to power in 1933.[67]

Thus far, the teichoscopy James presents has been just her own. But at the end of her observations, she boldly and offensively claims them for the entire Irish nation:

At the end of the day, it is right for us Irish to observe from the sidelines . . . there is plenty of evidence that the Germans did their serious best to solve the "Jewish problem" humanely. It cannot be denied either that the other nations put obstacles in the way of that sort of thing. Since secret documents of great import are still under lock and key by the authorities ruling now, we cannot pass judgement, or fault people. There are two sides to a leaf—or to a boat, as said in Connemara![68]

Throughout her writing, James's use of "us Irish" serves to remind the reader that James is one of them, a true Irishwoman, and one unafraid to tell the truth about what happened even if the non–Irish-speaking world refuses to accept it. Such fantasies aside, she seems unable or unwilling to distinguish between virulent anti-Semitic propaganda and fact.

James's general attitude seems to be one of confirmation bias: sifting information until she can isolate one piece for the "Aha!" moment that proves what she already believed, and rejecting the weight of evidence or scholarship that shows otherwise. In the case of the Holocaust, her position became somewhat more refined over the years. From that earliest public mention of it in 1979 she gravitates to the deaths at Bergen-Belsen, and seemingly argues that if 30,000 people were not killed there, then the entire structure of the Holocaust is a fiction. There is no mention of Auschwitz-Birkenau, Treblinka, Sobibór, the million murdered by the SS-Einsatzgruppen, or any of the other facets of National Socialist

Germany's elaborate mechanism for the biological extermination of the Jews and others.

This version of Holocaust denial is not new.[69] In many aspects, James's stripe of anti-Semitism and Holocaust denial is similar to British historian David Irving's: the deaths in camps were due to disease, not intentional biological extermination; the Jews deserved what happened; Churchill was a greater war criminal than Hitler.[70] Irving's libel suit in 1996 against historian Deborah Lipstadt and Penguin Books brought the specifics of Holocaust denial to a judicial forum. As part of the defendant's case, a noted historian of modern Germany, Richard Evans, studied and evaluated Irving's works and ascertained the degree to which he had manipulated or fabricated evidence as part of a plan of Holocaust denial.

Considering the number of times that the Jews surface in James's narrative and the way in which they are depicted, it might be fair to apply Richard Evans's evaluation of David Irving's aim to her: "suppression and manipulation of the historical record in the service of the principles of Holocaust denial."[71] Commenting on the deniers' central themes, Gill Seidel observed, "They all purport to show that Jews are liars and tricksters holding the world to ransom and continuing to extract war reparations. This is a continuation and an extension of the anti-Jewish prejudices and practices. The implication is that after all this time Jews are still liars, parasites, extraordinarily powerful, and fundamentally dishonest—and that maybe Hitler was right."[72]

In the aftermath of his own losing effort to promote Holocaust denial as truth, Irving was convicted in 2006 of violating Austrian law against Holocaust denial; he served seven months for statements he made in 1989 that there were no gas chambers at Auschwitz.[73] Although initially contrite and penitent, he reaffirmed his previous views immediately upon release from custody. But although she was also a resident of Austria at the time of Irving's conviction, Rosaleen James did not attract the same kind of attention.

Conclusion

Even among the cast of characters who betrayed their countries and willingly pledged allegiance to Hitler's cause, Rosaleen James was, on the surface, only a bit player in a more significant production. She was not a person of influence, made no crucial decisions, did not possess important military or political information (with possibly the Fegelein incident excepted), took no part in actual fighting, and even her contribution to Nazi propaganda work never rose above the mediocre. By all rights, she should have remained in her well-earned place as a minor footnote to the larger story of the Second World War. But perhaps the lure of stardom was too tempting, and her craving for attention—whether positive or negative—was too strong for her to simply to slip into her manufactured, Irish-themed obscurity.

Starting in 1945, amid the confusion of a destroyed Europe and safely away from the people who had known her earlier and who therefore knew the truth, she was reborn. Phyllis Ursula James would never reappear. She instead dug into her wartime past and emerged with suitably Irish names that would serve: she had used Nora O'Mara since 1940—Nora was her birth mother's name, and O'Mara was what she (wrongly) believed was the Irish equivalent of Lady Hamilton's family name, Muir; she had used the Irish version of her pet name Rosaleen—Róisín—since a propaganda radio broadcast in 1942. This wasn't a seamless or immediate process. Until the middle 1950s, she went by the hybrid of Róisín O'Mara before going the whole way, in the linguistic sense, and evolving into Róisín Ní Mheara.

Conclusion

This mantle of Irishness became the hub around which James's next decades revolved. The transformation was striking: from having no knowledge of the language, she learned it to an exceptional degree and threw herself into a variety of activities to broaden her base. The process of linguistic and cultural assimilation was necessary to provide context for the next step: holding herself out to the world *as* Irish. The less nuanced attempts at this during the war were only partially successful and collapsed when confronted by genuine Irish acquaintances (Stuart, Ryan, Irish chargé d'affaires William Warnock, and others). However, when surrounded by Germans who had little if any knowledge of Ireland, her performance was sufficient. She refined this role over time, retaining the parts that bolstered the desired image and discarding those that did not.

Having little in the way of advanced education—that process seems to have ceased by the time she was seventeen—Rosaleen James is very much an autodidact, entirely self-taught with no chance to learn the formal intellectual tools that provide a framework and filter. Instead, her writings as a much older adult indicate that she practiced confirmation bias to an extraordinary degree. She eagerly accepts any shred of information, regardless of source, that reinforces the ideas she holds most dear. If, as apparently she believes, Churchill forced World War Two on a blameless Germany, then any affirming statement from any source, no matter how ludicrous or patently false, must be true. In many instances where she does this, the historical or literary damage is negligible. Crank opinions or conspiracy theories are usually harmless. If people choose to believe that Elvis is alive, that the Apollo moon landings were faked, or that space aliens manipulate street signs, then they are deluded, perhaps comical or annoying, but not dangerous.

Holocaust denial, however, is something far more sinister. In denying that event, in disregarding tens of thousands of eyewitnesses, in rejecting the authenticity of tons of German documents that testify to every aspect of the evolving genocidal plan, deniers seek to erase the murder and untold suffering of millions. There are two possible forms of denial: negative and affirmative. Rosaleen James employs both. On the one hand, she rejects the central fact of the Holocaust: that millions of Jews (and others) were systematically murdered in an effort to eradicate them from the planet. At the same time she advances the case for affirmative denial:

if Hitler and the Nazis acted, they were compelled to do so by outside forces, and anyway, the Jews were a parasitic influence on society. Thinking back on what she regarded as the glory days of the German occupation of Austria, James commented, "As regards the city of Vienna, this powerful minority [Jews] now had to pay for the dissatisfaction of the people."[1] This statement wasn't written in at the time of the Anschluss in 1938 but rather in 1992—after Auschwitz, after Buchenwald, after the Nuremberg Trials, after Anne Frank's diary, after the Eichmann trial in Jerusalem, after the thousands of original photographs and documents detailing the killing machinery, and after the newsreel footage of piles of murdered, tortured, and mutilated men, women, and children. This is not the case of someone who was merely caught up in the passion of the moment; it is a sober reflection—a deliberate, considered decision more than fifty years after the fact—that Hitler was right, the Jews were a pestilence, and that if something bad happened to them it was hardly Germany's fault.

James first aired these views in print in 1978, although they became more strident and specific over the next decade. Her vehicle for this initial airing was the Irish language publication *Inniu*, and while the rest of the English-speaking world would have had no way of knowing the growing anti-Semitic content of her writing, anyone reading *Inniu* would have. These musings were also an important means of establishing legitimacy within the Irish community. Despite this, she connected with several important linguistic and religious figures, the most significant of whom was certainly Cardinal Tomás Ó Fiaich, Archbishop of Armagh, and Primate of All Ireland. In addition to being a historian and Irish language scholar, Ó Fiaich was generally considered to be at least sympathetic to the Irish republican position and the idea of a unified Ireland. From her perspective, Rosaleen James could not hope for a better sponsor in her quest for Irishness. There is no evidence whatsoever that Cardinal Ó Fiaich supported or shared James's anti-Semitism, but as an Irish language enthusiast, he could not help but to have known her views; they were readily apparent to anyone reading her *Litir ón Eoraip*. Yet she continued to interact with the Cardinal, and later worked for a considerable time at the Cardinal Tomás Ó Fiaich Memorial Library and Archive in Armagh.

The Cardinal was not James's only sponsor. The Irish state did its part, too, in the allocation of lottery money in 1988.[2] Most of the people, but

Conclusion

not all, could be forgiven for thinking that she had moved on from her earlier position and was following a new path. However, when her book *Cé hÍ Seo Amuigh?* came out in 1992, everyone who could have plausibly claimed ignorance no longer had an excuse; her views were discussed both in the Irish-speaking community and, at least in Ireland, in the mainstream press. Yet, she was not ostracized. The momentary furor over the book's anti-Semitic content passed, and after 1993, there is no further mention of it in any publication, in any language, anywhere.

James published *In Search of Irish Saints* in 1994—a good, if unscholarly, look at the travels of Irish missionaries in central Europe—and enlarged on this in 2001 with *Early Irish Saints in Europe: Their Sites and Their Stories*. James must have learned something from the negative reaction to *Cé hÍ Seo Amuigh?*, though, and in the second volume of her memoirs (*I gCéin is i gCóngar*) there is not a single word about Jews. She focuses instead on her postwar activities and returns to the earlier theme of all the good work she has done on Ireland's behalf. She could not entirely let go, however. Early on, she states that Irish people in the immediate postwar period were insatiably curious about news from the continent, particularly about "those from whom victory had been wrenched away [i.e., Germans]." This immediately goes into a short segment of stilted, invented dialog in an effort to show the Irish people's concern for Nazi Germany: "From Germany is it that you're coming, you don't say? And how are they doing, those poor people? Is it possible that they can come around again, after that great mangling they got? With God's will, and isn't it disastrous the way they fared?"[3]

Much like her first effort, this second book was printed in exceptionally small numbers, caused no stir, and reached no one outside a severely restricted Irish-speaking audience. It is apparently difficult, for some in that community, to strike a proper balance between contributions furthering the Irish language and the simultaneous use of that same language to express views that are reprehensible to the civilized world. The idea that Irish—a language with meaningful connections to a rich culture—should be twisted to justify and deny the worst of human horrors is not an easy concept to accept. Yet justify and deny she did. And so did some others when discussing James's work.

Psychologists use the word "schema" to mean the framework a person uses to view the world, the hardwiring that allows us to acquire and evaluate new information and the filter through which we view the many relationships around us. Rosaleen James's schema was formed by an unfortunate confluence of events: uncertain parentage, distant and elderly caregivers, an atmosphere of pro-German sentiment at home, the lack of an advanced education, and formative years spent in a culture where moral and political values were perverted from what they once were. Her formative world—one that coincided with the triumph of fascism in Germany—was truly a vision through the looking glass. And James accepted that down was up, fiction was truth, evil was good. Writing of another pro-Nazi expatriate Englishwoman, David Pryce-Jones observes, this woman was "impelled to seek abroad the adventure, the identification, she had not found at home. The more dramatically colored and outlandish the new values, the more thoroughgoing their adoption."[4] Rosaleen James's "new values" were those of National Socialist Germany and were, in so many ways, a rejection of truth, morality, and human kindness.

The most disturbing part is not that James shaped her postwar life on these skewed values, but rather that so many people who knew of her extreme beliefs preferred to look the other way. In most Western countries the law provides that if a person abets, encourages, or facilitates another in committing a crime, then they are guilty along with the person who commits it. What about a person who justifies murder after the fact? How guilty, then, is Rosaleen James—and, in turn, how culpable are those who read her words and yet praised her accomplishments or provided money so that she could continue to meander along the path of Holocaust denial in her quest for Irishness?

James's linguistic prowess has never been doubted, despite her own ongoing misgivings in *I gCéin is i gCóngar* (At Home and Abroad). Coiscéim's manager Pádraig Ó Snodaigh remembers that she communicated with him only in Irish, and that her Irish was impeccable.[5] In her continuous attempts to "belong" and build an Irish identity for herself, James applied her purist views on who constitutes a real Gael/Irish person to herself and everybody around her, conveniently forgetting her birth mother's surname and misappropriating one of her adopted parents' names. She took this as far as dismissing Irish people born and bred in the country as "foreigners": describing her choice of speakers for the 1,200th anniversary celebrations in Salzburg, she wrote to Mac an Bheatha that she was seeking good speakers and trying to avoid the usual

Conclusion

people, such as (Peter) Harbison and (Etienne) Rynne (both academic archaeologists) because of their being *gallda*, that is, of Anglo-Irish stock and maybe not Irish speakers.[6] In an illogical turn typical for her, she contrasted the harpist Gráinne Yeats (whose surname is Anglo-Saxon) with Harbison and Rynne.

Recently, I read with fascination a memoir by another English woman who spent the war years in Berlin: Christabel Bielenberg née Burton. Her background provides a few additional parallels to Phyllis Ursula James's, with Bielenberg's maternal connections to the peerage and her liberal upbringing. Like James, Bielenberg humorously refers to her lack of cookery and housekeeping skills. Bielenberg is genuinely Anglo-Irish on her father's side, but although she and her husband chose to make their home in Ireland after the war, she did not make a cultural issue of it. Where their later lives differ is in their types of homes. James took her urge to "belong elsewhere" from her past as an orphan with a question mark over her father's identity and being sheltered by adoptive parents who were less than committed (not giving her their name), less than affectionate, and also rather old. Although James was provided with a good education at a series of finishing schools, like Bielenberg, James's and Bielenberg's respective families differed in their outlook: James's family was pro-German and militaristic, Bielenberg's was neither. Both women had happy early experiences in Germany, but while Bielenberg married a lawyer who was to be involved in the unsuccessful coup against Hitler, James decided to burn her bridges to England and associate herself with Ireland (her imagined homeland) and Germany (whose ideology she embraced completely). Her association with Francis Stuart sealed this by introducing her to members of the Abwehr and of the IRA. Ironically, Bielenberg and her one-time daughter-in-law Charlotte O'Connell sided with Máire Mac an tSaoi in 1997, who called on Stuart to resign his Aosdána membership:

> The question still remains: should Francis Stuart have been honoured by Aosdána, considering that he worked as a broadcaster/propagandist during the Nazi regime? For anyone who lived in Germany at that time, as we did, any person working for the Ministry of Propaganda had to be an active Nazi sympathiser. . . . No-one wants to persecute an elderly man, whose years in Germany

represent only a very short time in his life. It is his lack of regret, or expression of regret, that is incomprehensible in the light of what happened during the Holocaust. . . .[7]

In short: there could not be two English women further opposed than James and Bielenberg. There is no public record of Bielenberg reacting to James's book; even if she could not read it in Irish herself, she may have read the various reviews in English.

With that parallel life in mind, how does one sum up James's life and message? It is very tempting to explain her complete immersion in German and Irish affairs by her unhappy-if-privileged upbringing and her feelings of being an outsider wherever she went. However, for an intelligent woman who could acquire the Irish language, make sense of medieval texts and mindsets, and make friends with the academic and larger-than-life prelate that was Cardinal Ó Fiaich, her continuing embrace of a pro-Nazi stance does not leave much space for sympathy.

Almost seventy years ago, Robert Jackson, the American prosecutor at the International Military Tribunal at Nuremberg, gave a masterful closing statement where he discussed the relationship between guilt and denial. Referencing Shakespeare's play *Richard III*, he recalled Gloucester standing by the body of the king he has just killed.

> He begged of the widow, as they beg of you: "Say I slew them not." And the Queen replied, "Then say they are not slain. But dead they are. . . ." If you were to say of these men that they are not guilty, it would be as true to say that there has been no war, there are no slain, there has been no crime.[8]

Despite what Phyllis Ursula "Rosaleen" James would have us believe, there was a war, there were slain, and there was a monstrous crime.

Postscript

Phyllis James died in 2013. Somehow, despite this, her self-published book *Recollections* appeared in December 2015. It is an edited, English-language version of *Cé hÍ Seo Amuigh?* with some (mostly inconsequential) matter

Conclusion

omitted and some (mostly inconsequential) matter added—although in the book James makes no mention whatsoever of the 1992 work and, more predictably, its small but loud group of critics. The selective candor, curious omissions, and peculiar asides of the original are all present and accounted for.[9] While it is impossible to determine when it was composed, internal evidence and correspondence with Mac an Bheatha suggests that it was after the initial Irish language publication, although conceivably it could have been used as a basis for the Irish publication (i.e., a working draft in English, the language with which she was most familiar).

Tellingly, *Recollections*, unlike *Cé hÍ Seo Amuigh?*, is not dedicated "to the people of Ireland," but the Irish veneer remains in full flower, and the work is now more widely accessible in a way that was impossible with the Irish-only text. Likewise, the pro-Nazi and anti-Semitic material is mostly unchanged, but there is one striking instance where a reference to "the Jews" in her earlier work has been removed. The following passage appears in the 1992 edition:

> Nobody makes a fuss of the blood spill and the persecution which [the Germans] suffered, although the main media churn out unceasing propaganda about the horrific results of Germany's dilemma where the Jews were concerned. There was no longer any permission to talk about this. We have no evidence at all that Germany meant to annihilate its worst enemy. They had had a policy before to keep them under control until an international decision could be made for that place in the world where a state could be founded for them. The ghettos had a long tradition in Europe for this race of people that had been for ages without a country, without soil. During the Second World War, the ghettos were the only solution for safeguarding the German offensive in the East.[10]

The passage, however, is missing from *Recollections*. This does not mean James softened her beliefs in the intervening years. For example, she retains the scene where the French cook allegedly informs her about the "truth" of the Holocaust, as well as the discussions on the relative merits of the Nazi Madagascar plan, and the many dismissive instances where she holds Jews (and others) in contempt, particularly vis-à-vis the Germans.

The adage about leopards and spots seems quite apt.[11]

Notes

Abbreviations

AJHL — Archives of the James Hardiman Library
ChÍSA — James, Ursula Phyllis (as Róisín Ní Mheara-Vinard), *Cé hÍ Seo Amuigh?*
CÓFLA — Cardinal Ó Fiaich Memorial Library and Archive, Armagh
I gCéin — James, Ursula Phyllis (as Róisín Ní Mheara Vinard), *I gCéin is i gCóngar* Armagh: Seanchas Ard Mhacha, 2006
IMA — Irish Military Archives
KCL — King's College London
LH — Lady Hamilton
NA-Ireland — National Archives of Ireland
NA-Kew — National Archives, Kew
PAAA — Politisches Archiv des Auswärtigenen Amts
UCDA — University College Dublin, Archives

Introduction

1. James, *Cé hÍ Seo Amuigh?*, vii—hereafter abbreviated to *ChÍSA*.
2. Mac Eoin, *The IRA: 1923–1948*, 925.
3. Fennell, *Cutting to the Point*, 88.
4. James, *ChÍSA*, v, where she wrote, "I would find it hard to refuse any work for Ireland's good!" (Is deacair dom saothar i leith na hÉireann a shéanadh!)
5. In fairness, the publisher, Pádraig Ó Snodaigh, made it quite clear that he repudiated James's extreme views (Letter from Ó Snodaigh to author, 9 October 2009; and Ó Snodaigh, "Dublin Gave Subsidy"). Her anti-Semitism was evident much earlier, as will be shown.
6. Evans, *Lying about Hitler*. The David Irving libel trial will be discussed further.

7. She simultaneously lived with, and had an affair with, noted Irish writer and expatriate Francis Stuart, who broadcast German propaganda back to Ireland under the aegis of the Foreign Ministry.

8. When James felt the heat from British intelligence interrogators, though, she admitted the truth, or at least a version of it: "She claims that her parents were English and that she is the adopted daughter of Sir Ian Hamilton, but has no papers to establish her claim. She is supposed to be married to a Russian nobleman, present whereabouts unknown." NA-Kew, KV 2/119, summary of O'Reilly contacts, 3.

9. The title originates from the traditional Irish song, "Éamonn an Chnoic." One version has the line "Cé hé sin amuigh" (Who is he outside, over there?). The feminine version, with a more immediate demonstrative pronoun, is "Cé hí seo amuigh?" See more below, in chapter 13.

10. The usefulness of Irish other than as a statement of ethnicity and culture remains an issue. For national, ethnic, and cultural reasons, the Irish state insists on official bilingualism. For example, all proceedings in the Irish parliament, the Dáil Éireann, are recorded in English and then translated into Irish—in a country where 100 percent of the people speak fluent English and only a minority speak fluent Irish.

11. The trend is not unique to Ireland, of course. Even inside the British Isles, one may find a similar practice in Scotland, Wales, Cornwall, and the Isle of Man. It is likewise a global practice whenever the issue of ethnicity and national identity is in the foreground.

12. This is not a contradiction; Ireland had become thoroughly English-speaking after the Great Famine (1845–49), and, especially when dealing with agencies abroad, it was (still is) simply easier using an Anglicized form.

Chapter 1

1. Celia Lee, *A Soldier's Wife*, 11.
2. Winston Churchill's book, *Ian Hamilton's March* (London, 1900), helped make Hamilton into a national figure and cemented a friendship between them that survived until the late 1930s.
3. He wouldn't have had long to wait. Lord Roberts died in 1914, and Lord Kitchener perished when the *HMS Hampshire* struck a mine in June 1916.

Chapter 2

1. James affirms this version in her autobiography (*ChISA*, 117). She describes herself as a World War I "orphan" owing to her Irish father dying in the war, having "been enticed to fight for England on the understanding that by way of compensation, there would be independence for Ireland." Not so much.

2. *ChISA*, 2. James adds that "because that girl (Holman) was a friend of my poor mother in London, and because she was also Irish, I think that this account is the most believable one of the versions available."

3. General Register Office, Application 1979251-1, registered 30 July 1918. On wartime documents, James would later list her birthplace as both Philadelphia and London.

4. Phyllis Holman—later Phyllis Holman-Richards—was subsequently the founder of the Phyllis Holman-Richards Adoption Society, which later merged into Family Ties, part of the Adolescent and Children's Trust.

5. KCL, LH Diary, 14 July 1918.

6. "Our History," *Royal British Legion*, accessed 24 June 2016, http://www.britishlegion.org.uk/about-us/our-history/.

7. KCL, LH Diary, 8 July 1918.

8. NA-Kew, KV 2/423.

9. The electoral rolls for 1919 of 131 Gloucester Terrace list a Sir William Jamieson as resident; electoral registers were not prepared during the war. Michelle Goodman to author, 4 September 2010, City of Westminster Archives Centre.

10. Hill, *English Domestics*, 51. See also Marks, *Metropolitan Maternity*, 105. Nora James married a Mr. Thorn in 1920 and died in Wandsworth in 1974, age 81 (Michelle Goodman, City of Westminster Archives Centre). To judge only from James's published work and private documents, she never made an effort to find or see her biological mother.

11. KCL, LH Diary, 8 June 1904. Lady Hamilton expressed many sentiments in the same vein. "It is no use telling me sexual passion is a beautiful thing, even if I had not been carefully trained from childhood to feel as I do . . . The most beautiful and refined face is disfigured by that look of wild beast desire—it terrifies me when I see the glimmer of it."

12. Ibid., 2 October 1906.

13. Ibid., 26 March 1904.

14. In her ad nauseam connections to all things Irish, James notes in her 1992 book that "Sir Ian was not overjoyed about my arrival, despite my Irish background." *ChISA*, 6. John Lee (*A Soldier's Life*, 266) notes, "Ian referred to them as 'her' children and seems to have had little to do with their upbringing."

15. KCL, LH Diary, 7 January 1919. She also stated that a pregnant Clementine Churchill advised against adoption, instead offering to give the Hamiltons one of her own children, should she have twins. The child in question, Marigold—born in November 1918—died of septicemia in 1921. Lady Hamilton settled on the surname "Knight" for Harry, as Sir Ian would not allow her to name him Hamilton (Celia Lee, *A Soldier's Wife*, 207).

16. "Sir Ian took no interest in this venture. The children had their own attendant and at Lullenden occupied the Barn." Hamilton, *The Happy Warrior*, 438.

17. Lullenden was located at Dormansland, East Grinstead, Sussex. The Hamiltons originally rented it and later purchased the property from the owner, Winston Churchill.

18. KCL, LH Diary, 1 August 1920, 30 September 1920, and 4 October 1920. Lady Hamilton was never at a loss for pithy comments concerning two-year-old Rosaleen: "She looks sweet . . . but speaks with the most boring drawl at present and with a vile accent." Ibid., 5 October 1920.

19. Ibid., 1 July 1922.

20. Ibid., 27 July 1922.

21. Ibid., 3 June 1923.

22. Ibid., 31 January 1922. Adoption records from the General Registry Office are unavailable for years before 1927, so the results of the adoption process for Phyllis "Rosaleen" James and Harry Knight are impossible to confirm.

23. KCL, Hamilton Papers, Hamilton to Wingham, 24 September 1941.

24. Ibid., 10 September 1928.

25. *ChÍSA*, 8. As discussed earlier, the preponderance of evidence demonstrates that James has no Irish ancestry, other than the wishful thinking kind.

26. Ibid., 15. This is a good example of the Irish fantasies which appear again and again in James's book, *ChÍSA*. However, the name Comiskey is not mentioned by Lady Hamilton as being one of the household servants. James goes on to give the noble etymology of the name, citing it as Cumascach.

27. *ChÍSA*, 15, 44–46.

28. Pryce-Jones, *Unity Mitford*, 31.

29. *ChÍSA*, 23–24. The derivation of Ó Meara (female Ní Mheara) from Muir is mistaken, as James points out herself. Ó Dochartaigh identified "Muir" with "Ó Meara" (Anglicized O'Mara), while in fact it appears to have a Germanic (Norse) origin, for somebody dwelling on or near a moor. See Black, *Surnames of Scotland*, 617. James herself complicates this by claiming the "Ó Mórdha" tribe (Anglicized Moore) for herself, as an Irish population group that settled in Scotland later. See de Bhulbh, *Sloinnte uile Éireann*.

30. PAAA, I 28044 (Nora O'Mara), Fragebogen "Spende Künstlerdank," 13 March 1942. She signed this document as "Nora James O'Mara."

31. *ChÍSA*, 31.

32. As an example, a search of the Times Digital Archive from 1933–45 reveals no matching entries under any of the names she was known to have used, a peculiar result for someone coming from such a prominent family.

33. KCL, LH Diary, 22 September 1935.

34. KCL, LH Diary, 23 September 1935: "She has not heard from her friend in Berlin yet. . . . She might be more loving while she is still with me."

Chapter 3

1. Thompson, "Who Goes Nazi?," *Harper's Magazine*, August 1941.

2. KCL, Hamilton Papers, Hamilton to James, 23 October 1935.

3. KCL, LH Diary, December 1935. This might well have been the home of Helene von Nostitz, niece of Field Marshall Paul v. Hindenburg, a socialite

and author who ran a famous salon in Berlin. Frau v. Nostitz was among the 88 German authors and poets who in 1933 signed the infamous *Gelöbnis treuester Gefolgschaft* (Vow of Faithful Obedience) to Adolf Hitler.

4. KCL, LH Papers, Moyra to LH, 1 January 1936.

5. KCL, LH Diary, October 1935.

6. KCL, Hamilton Papers, E. C. Warner to Sir Ian Hamilton, 16 November 1933. Italics added for emphasis.

7. Ibid., LH to Warner, 16 December 1933.

8. Ibid., Hamilton to James 3 February 1936.

9. Ibid., James to Hamilton, February 1936.

10. Probably Friedrich Schiller's "Die Jungfrau von Orleans," which was staged many times in the 1930s and 1940s. National Socialist commentators frequently turned Schiller's Romantic period message into an affirmation of Nazi values, the *Sieg des Glaubens* (Victory of Faith). Eicher, Rischbieter, and Panse, *Theater im "Dritten Reich,"* 31.

11. *ChÍSA*, 60–61. KdF sponsored a number of free public activities to include concerts, theater performances, and holiday vacations aboard specially chartered ships. The Volkswagen Beetle, originally called the "KdF-Wagen," was designed along the same philosophical lines: to provide low-cost transport to ordinary Germans.

12. *ChÍSA*, 69.

13. *ChÍSA*, 69.

14. There is almost no end to pro-Nazi comments in James's autobiography. For example: "Hitler was on his guard. Although popular at home and abroad while the movement was growing in strength, I don't think that he sensed the real power of the invisible players behind his back, well-schooled players who held the puppet strings in their hands" (*ChÍSA*, 69). "Hitler knew that the programme of reform he was planning was bold, but with a loyal people behind him he trusted his luck. It was a mistake of judgement to hope that somebody would understand his good intentions, and the appeals to good sense that Hitler often came out with. The Germans had been treated unfairly according to themselves, and a new, rightful solution was needed" (*ChÍSA*, 70).

15. The Redesdales (after 1933) were at 2 Grosvenor Crescent; Unity briefly attended the Art School of the London Country Council.

16. To the end of her life, Diana Mitford remained unrepentant of the pro-Nazi stance she adopted in the 1930s and 1940s, not unlike Rosaleen James. Concerning Hitler, as late as 1989, Mitford said that he was "extraordinarily fascinating and clever. Naturally. You don't get to be where he was just by being the kind of person people like to think he was." Lovell, *The Sisters*, 516.

17. Pryce-Jones, *Unity Mitford*, 65. The accuracy of the grass-eating episode was reinforced by Harold Nicholson's diary entry made two years later in 1938: "Dined with Rob Bernays and Miss Mitford, Unity's cousin. She says that Unity does not hope to marry Hitler. It is mere adoration. Hitler likes her because of her fanaticism. She wants the Jews to eat grass." Ibid., 66.

18. *ChISA*, 40. In fact, Unity was staying at an informal but well-regarded finishing school run by Freifrau Laroche. Lovell, *The Sisters*, 167.

19. *ChISA*, 41–42.

20. Lovell, *The Sisters*, 182.

21. KCL, LH Diary, 2 January 1937. There is no trace of Karl Eidlitz the sculptor. There was, however, a Karl Eidlitz the actor (1894–1981). Weirdly, he was in the cast of a 1965 television movie, *Leinen aus Irland* (Irish Linen).

22. KCL, LH Diary, 1 August 1937.

23. *ChISA*, 50. By what means she could have possibly gone to Holyhead, and further to Dublin as a passenger on a private channel-crossing boat in a fit of fancy, is unclear.

24. *ChISA*, 51.

25. *ChISA*, 51.

26. *ChISA*, 52–55.

27. UFA (Universum Film AG) was then—and is now—located at Babelsberg, a Berlin suburb. As with all film production during the Third Reich, it fell under the control of Josef Goebbels and the Ministry for Propaganda. UFA produced most of the German films during World War II.

28. MacDonogh, *1938: Hitler's Gamble*, 107–9.

29. *ChISA*, 108.

30. *ChISA*, 105.

31. *ChISA*, 106.

32. Lovell, *The Sisters*, 242.

33. Sereny, *The Healing Wound*, 7–8.

34. United States Holocaust Memorial Museum, *Holocaust Encyclopedia*, s.v. "Vienna" and "Sicherheitsdienst" (Security Service).

35. *ChISA*, 107.

36. *ChISA*, 86.

37. United States Holocaust Memorial Museum, *Holocaust Encyclopedia*, s.v. "Vienna." To this total one should include the more than 18,000 Jews who had fled to Austria from neighboring states before the Anschluss with Germany. Deportations to the East started in 1939 and continued until 1944, as more space became available in the East and the killing plan crystallized after the 1942 Wannsee Conference and subsequent Aktion Reinhard.

38. "1933 Reichgesetzblatt," pt. 1, 661, 22 September 1933.

39. "Verordnung über die Aufgaben des Reichsministeriums für Volksaufklärung und Propaganda vom 30. Juni 1933."

40. "Reichgesetzblatt," pt. 1, 247, 15 March 1938. The same decree also prohibited Jews from displaying the German national flag.

41. Ehrenreich, *The Nazi Ancestral Proof*.

42. KCL, Hamilton Papers, James to LH, undated letter.

43. PAAA, I 28044 (Nora O'Mara), Reichstheaterkammer Personalfragebogen, 9 August 1944. The annual listing of member actors (*Deutsches Bühnen-Jahrbuch*) does not feature her until 1940, however.

44. KCL, Hamilton Papers, 14/2/1, "Report of the Dinner given by the Committee of the Anglo-German Association to Herr von Lineiner-Wildau [sic], M.d.R." *Major der Reserve* Friedrich von Lindeiner-Wildau (d. 1963), winner of the *Pour le Mérite* in the Maji-Maji Rebellion, later gained attention as commandant of Stalag Luft III, the historical setting for "The Great Escape." Considering his humane conduct at Stalag Luft III and acrimonious relationship with the Nazi hierarchy, v. Lindeiner would likely have been less than receptive to much of the A-G Association's later aims.

45. KCL, Hamilton Papers, 14/2/3, Hamilton to Frau v. Flesch-Brunningen, 30 November 1933. Luma v. Flesch-Brunningen (d. 1934) was a well-known artist.

46. Ian Kershaw, *Making Friends with Hitler*, 56.

47. Ibid. See Also Garfield, *The Meinertzhagen Mystery*.

48. Hamilton, *The Happy Warrior*, 448. The ceremony was also attended by *Generaloberst* Werner von Blomberg, defense minister, and the man considered most responsible for making the German Army compliant with Hitler's wishes.

49. NA-Kew, KV 5/6, Dienstelle Ribbentrop.

50. "Hitler Lent Me a Tooth-Brush," *Sunday Referee*, 7 August 1938.

51. 8 August 1938, *Daily Mail*. A few historians have since speculated that Deputy Führer Rudolf Hess's bizarre 1941 flight to Scotland was made for the purpose of contacting Sir Ian Hamilton, rather than Douglas, 14th Duke of Hamilton. This was apparently the story that Rosaleen James told Francis Stuart (Geoffrey Elborn, *Francis Stuart: A Life*, 133), and she repeated it again in her autobiography (*ChISA*, 179–81).

52. Kershaw, *Making Friends with Hitler*, 57.

53. Kershaw, *Making Friends with Hitler*, 23.

54. *ChISA*, 91.

55. In law, hearsay is a statement (or quote) made in court of something said outside of court, used to prove the truth of the matter. "Totem pole hearsay" refers to a string of such unauthenticated statements, with reliability decreasing with each addition.

56. *ChISA*, 95.

57. Ibid., 96.

58. KCL, Hamilton Papers, Hamilton to J. Goebbels, 29 September 1938.

59. KCL, Hamilton Papers, 14/2/12, Hamilton to C. E. Carroll, 25 March 1939.

Chapter 4

1. *ChISA*, 116.
2. Ibid., 115–16.
3. Ibid., 121–22.
4. Ibid., 71.

5. Lovell, *The Sisters*, 299.
6. *ChISA*, 126.
7. Browning, *The Origins*, 32–33. See also Blanke, "Modern Europe," 580–82. Review of Włodzimierz Jastrzębski, *Der Bromberger Blutsonntag: Legende und Wirklichkeit*, and Andrzej Brożek, *Niemcy zagraniczni w polityce kolonizacji pruskich prowincji wschodnich (1886–1918)*.
8. *ChISA*, 125. Contrast with Operation Tannenburg, a German SS/SD operation in 1939 using Selbstschutz (ethnic German militia) in an extermination action against Polish elites. Tens of thousands were murdered.
9. Former Polish transmitters at Katowice and Razyn were also used by the Propaganda Ministry for this purpose.
10. There is no evidence, in any case, under the names and pseudonyms James is known to have used. As with so many of the events of World War II, absence of evidence does not necessarily mean evidence of absence. Much official German documentation was destroyed during the course of the war.
11. *ChISA*, 135.

Chapter 5

1. NA-Kew, KV 2/769, summary, section "Abw. Activities of Rosaleen James @ O'Mara"; and Elborn, *Francis Stuart*, 133.
2. Elborn, *Francis Stuart*, 133.
3. NA-Kew, KV 2/769, Kurt Haller statement, 23. This document also lists James's MI5 file number, PF92, 437. Haller stated that her cover name, given at the time of her hire by Abwehr II, was "Dornröschen" (meaning "little rose of thorns"; it is the German name for "Sleeping Beauty").
4. Ibid., 24.
5. NA-Kew, KV 2/769, "Extract from statement of Phyllis Ursula Rosaleen James," 29 April 1945. In his own statement to MI5, Haller dismissed this version of events.
6. Ibid. In contrast, she paints a suspiciously positive picture of Haller in her memoirs, likening him to Hermann Görtz as "honest, undeceiving, and unbiased." To this she added that St. Brigid's cloak must have saved him from harm beyond 1945, because of his kindness to the Irish in his care. *ChISA*, 158.
7. Although referring to himself as both "Dr." and "Professor," Fromme was neither. Stephan, "Die Vergessene Episode," 5. Due to his travels and writings, Fromme was involved in Foreign Office and Abwehr affairs concerning Ireland, Iceland, Sweden, and Flemish nationalists. In 1934 he contributed an essay, "Zwei verwandte Freiheitsbewegungen," to a collection entitled *Deutscher Aufstand: Die Revolution des Nachkrieges*, drawing a link between the Irish and Flemish separatist movements. He died in 1960.
8. *ChISA*, 138–39.

9. Ibid., 140.

10. This is a matter of some confusion. Görtz flew to Ireland as a Leutnant der Reserve (reserve lieutenant), and was eventually promoted (while in captivity) to Hauptmann (captain). As part of their larger plan to fool Görtz into thinking he was secretly in touch with his Abwehr headquarters, his Irish Intelligence captors "promoted" him to major. In life, Görtz never rose above the rank of captain, but by the time of his funeral in 1947, his Irish friends responsible for carving the headstone plaque had done one better: the inscription gave his rank as lieutenant-colonel. Hull, *Irish Secrets*, 244, 258.

11. Ibid., 81.

12. Ibid., 84–87.

13. In her responses to a questionnaire in 1942 (which she signs as "Nora James O'Mara"), she cites her membership in the Reichstheaterkammer as dating from 1938. The annual listing of the German Stage Yearbook (*Deutsches Bühnen-Jahrbuch*) for the 1940–41 season lists her as "Nora O'Mara."

14. ChÍSA, 144.

15. Ibid., 141.

16. ChÍSA, 154.

17. James relished in the Nazi's April 1945 execution of Admiral Canaris, an opponent of Hitler and the Nazi regime: "He was to die for high treason early in 1945, but as the proverb says, 'a traitor is never caught in time.'" ChÍSA, 152.

18. Stuart, *Black List, Section H*, 304.

19. This part of the operation did not go well. Görtz landed in the wrong place, hiked overland to Laragh after first stopping at the local police station to ask directions—in partial German uniform—before surprising Iseult Stuart. She sheltered Görtz for a few days before passing him along to James O'Donovan of the IRA. Information about her involvement later surfaced, and she was tried for aiding a belligerent. Despite a confession and overwhelming evidence of her guilt, she was acquitted.

20. Stuart, *Black List*, 300.

21. Ibid., 303–4.

22. Kiely, *Francis Stuart*, 131.

23. One of many poetic names for Ireland; see W. B. Yeats's eponymous 1902 play where an old woman—Ní hUalacháin—comes to a house where a wedding is being prepared and calls the groom away to join the French who are just landing. As if in a trance, he leaves his bride and her dowry and goes with the old woman to fight for Ireland.

24. ChÍSA, 144.

25. In Kiely's discussions, Stuart's complex attitudes toward the relationship emerge. Part was purely physical (Stuart describes James as "the most beautiful woman he had ever known and, by implication, that he had ever slept with"), and, in another aspect, James "was willing to partner him since she, too, had a

taste for bohemian living which was somewhat curbed by wartime restrictions on food and alcohol." Kiely, *Francis Stuart*, 136.

26. *ChÍSA*, 162.

Chapter 6

1. As to the result of the campaign, James observes in her autobiography: "The people of Paris witnessed Germany triumphantly marching through its streets, but giving the *Arc de Triomphe* a wide berth, so as not to hurt the public morale. For sure, the Germans did not take possession of the whole country but in the part they occupied, the authorities put in place there were under order to deal with the people respectfully. A spirit of renewed kinship blossomed again, and the emphasis was on the affinity of the arts of both peoples. . . . It was the policy of rekindled friendship that was behind Germany not taking any stand against its [the Vichy government's?] reign in France between 1940 and 1944, except under duress, and apart from the terrorist acts by the communist Maquis." *ChÍSA*, 175–76.

2. Ironically, the bombing campaign, or S-Plan, was the singular event that convinced German intelligence that the IRA was a viable partner in the war against England. That was a serious error in assessment.

3. America was critical to IRA fund-raising, and that is still the case today. Members of the American-based ultra-nationalist *Clann na Gael* organization had been rerouting money from the Irish Hospital Sweepstakes, which was illegal in the United States, although enormously profitable. After the outbreak of war in September 1939, direct transatlantic service between the United States and Ireland was suspended, effectively cutting off the quick delivery of funds to the IRA.

4. *ChÍSA*, 167. This is one of the instances where James's speculation borders on delusional. There is no evidence for this theory. She simultaneously applauds Dr. Edmund Veesenmayer for his work in Russell's case. *ChÍSA*, 168. Veesenmayer was sentenced to 20 years imprisonment in one of the successor Nuremburg Trials for his part in organizing the 1944 collection and deportation of approximately 450,000 Hungarian Jews to the Auschwitz-Birkenau death camp.

5. PAAA, I 28044 (Nora O'Mara), Reichstheaterkammer/Fachschaft Bühne, Fragebogen—August 1944.

6. Kiely, *Francis Stuart*, 131.

7. *ChÍSA*, 164.

8. O'Donoghue, *Hitler's Irish Voices*, 51, from a 1989 interview with Stuart. As O'Donoghue notes, Stuart radically changed his version of the relationship between 1950 and 1989. In a 1950 article for *The Bell*, Stuart wrote, "It was then that I got to know him well and we became close friends.

9. Kiely, *Francis Stuart*, 136.

10. Fisk, *In Time of War*, 16. See Doerries, *Prelude to Easter Rising*, for the complete documentary examination of Casement's activities in Germany.

11. Fisk, *In Time of War*, 129.

12. Carter, *Shamrock and Swastika*, 124. The recruitment goal of this hypothetical unit was 2000 volunteers, at least according to Carter; this fact is unverifiable by other sources.

13. Stephan, "Die Vergessene Episode," 378, interview with Sonderführer Kurt Haller. The Germans, with their limited prewar interactions with Ireland and her politics, never developed a reliable understanding of what "Irish" meant. In some cases, a person having a name they wrongly believed was of Irish provenance was sufficient to classify that person as Irish and thereby anti-British.

14. The restriction on foreign nationals in the German Army was relative. French volunteers were grouped into Infantry Regiment No. 638 (7th Infantry Division), though later transferred to the 33rd SS Panzergrenadier-Division 'Charlemagne.' Spanish soldiers comprised the Wehrmacht's 250th Infanterie Division, called the 'Blue Division,' as part of the 16th Army.

15. Elborn, *Francis Stuart*, 135. The camp was Stalag XX A, near Frankfurt.

16. NA-Kew, PRO KV 4/9, Liddell Report, 94. Irish volunteers to Nazi Germany presented a particular legal problem. Irish premier Eamon de Valera had declared his country neutral on 3 September 1939, but legally Ireland was still a member of the British Commonwealth. Commonwealth countries had the right, under the 1931 Statute of Westminster, to remain neutral, but "as British subjects, those who give aid and assistance to the King's enemies rendered themselves liable to be charged with treason." In addition, Britain was still technically responsible for Ireland's foreign diplomacy, and no foreign ambassador could be appointed to Dublin without the consent of the British monarch. Despite this, all the Axis nations maintained an official wartime diplomatic presence in Ireland.

17. *ChISA*, 190.

18. IMA, G2/4949, John Codd statement. The authenticity of this quote is open to question. The affiant, Sergeant John Codd, was prone to exaggeration, although at the time of the statement he seemed unaware that the "Mr. Richards" he described was actually Frank Ryan.

19. Carter, *Shamrock and the Swastika*, 124. The actor Denholm Elliot was among those interned at Stalag III B, Lannesdorf, though he was not snared by the German recruitment effort.

20. IMA, G2/4953, Appendix III, statement of Father O'Shaughnessy. Private Patrick O'Brien was the soldier jailed by the Germans for rape in May 1942. He was later sent to Stalag III D and probably joined the British Free Corps. Private Frank Stringer (Royal Irish Fusiliers) previously served in the Royal Navy but was discharged for unspecified reasons and joined the Army. Both he and Private James Brady were captured on Jersey in July 1940, where they had been under penal confinement after a conviction for attempted murder.

21. Kriegstagebuch der Abwehr II, entry of 6 October 1941, Bundesarchiv-Militärarchiv (MA), RW5/v. 497. Two separate operations, *Möwe* (Seagull) I and II, were also planned with others from this group of traitors, but were aborted in June 1942.

22. IMA, G2/4949, Codd statement of July 1945, Appendix II.

23. Ibid. Two of them, Privates Frank Stringer and James Brady, seem to have likewise joined the SD and were last seen on the Eberswalde sector near Berlin on 16 April 1945, three weeks before the German surrender.

24. Elborn, *Francis Stuart*, 166.

Chapter 7

1. In a letter to a Mr. Wingham dated 26 February 1942, Sir Ian's solicitor states, "Lady Hamilton meant to cut her (Rosaleen) clean out of the Will because, as she said to me more than once, 'I can't treat Fodie the same as Harry and she has her Trust so will never want.'"

2. KCL, Hamilton Papers, W. Stephens to Mrs. Shield, 30 June 1941.

3. Ibid., Nadejda Muir to Annie, 26 June 1941. James's main source for family news was Nadejda's sister Feo, in Sofia, Bulgaria. Although Bulgaria was an Axis partner with Germany, letters could still get through using the United States as a conduit. *ChISA*, 213.

4. KCL, Hamilton Papers, Muir to Chou Guepin, 11 November 1941. In an earlier letter, Sir Ian reports, "I do not know Miss James' address. Letters come from her, and answers go back, via Lady Muir's sister, Madame Guepin." KCL, Hamilton Papers, Ian Hamilton to Messrs. McGrigor, Donald & Co, 6 November 1941.

5. KCL, Hamilton Papers, Hamilton to Wingham, 24 September 1941.

6. Kiely, *Francis Stuart*, 143–44. Stuart would later marry Gertrud (Madeleine) after the death of Iseult Stuart in 1948.

7. Ibid. Ironically, Horney appeared in the 1937 British film *Secret Lives* (U.K. title)/*I Married a Spy* (U.S. title).

8. Rote Kapelle was the RSHA (Reichssicherheitshauptamt—Reich Security Main Office) for the group.

9. Kiely, *Francis Stuart*, 143. Schulze-Boysen's position was further complicated by the fact that he was a serving officer in the Luftwaffe; Libertas worked in the as a film critic and sometime press officer for MGM. Die Rote Kapelle (The Red Orchestra) was the name given to their group by the Gestapo; it was one of several independent espionage networks operated by the GRU (Soviet military intelligence) but the only one with the primary objective to provide political resistance and compile information about atrocities.

10. *ChISA*, 114–15.

11. *ChISA*, 159.

Chapter 8

1. Kiely, *Francis Stuart*, 126. Kiely draws on conversations with Stuart.
2. *ChISA*, 146–47. Stuart's novel *The Great Squire* had been published in 1939 and was now being translated as *Der Herr von Baravore* (1940), but it does not seem that he was working on a novel at the time.
3. *ChISA*, 147. By contrast, in Stuart's telling, "Susan" was his typist only in connection with his translation work for the Drahtloser Dienst AG (Wireless Service AG), a journalistic service for the radio, and he does not mention the 1940 publication under discussion here. Stuart, *Black List Section H*, 340.
4. Francis Stuart, "Einleitung," 7–16. Stuart openly criticizes Parnell, who although (according to Stuart) he "achieved as much through the art of statesmanship as any of the soldiers," was essentially weak like all who adhere to constitutional means, by underestimating the adversaries' ability for *Hinterhältigkeit* (perfidy). Stuart blames Parnell for denouncing the militarists ("The Invincibles"), and for not seeing that force can sometimes be the only way to make an impression. Ibid., 9.
5. Weiland, *Irische Freiheitskämpfer*, "Lernen wir führende Köpfe Irlands kennen, die sich hundertfältig für die Freiheit der sagenumwobenen Bardeninsel Eire eingesetzt haben."
6. Ibid., 7.
7. *ChISA*, 140. See Hull, *Irish Secrets*, 53.
8. McBride, *Im Dienste einer Königin*, 68–79. Weiland quotes from a letter she received from Maud Gonne in August 1939. Weiland, *Irische Freiheitskämpfer*, 78.
9. For commentary on Francis Stuart's contribution, see Kiely, *Francis Stuart*, 137; and Roth, "Francis Stuart's Broadcasts," 408–22, 411.
10. For basic biographical information and Mühlhausen's membership of the National Socialist Party (and SS), see Broderick, "Under the 'Three-Legged Swastika'," 195–209. Mühlhausen knew Séamus Ó Duilearga, head of the Irish folklore Commission, and it would be surprising if he had not introduced him to Hyde; see Mühlhausen, *Die kornische Geschichte*, 3. Mühlhausen's photographs of Donegal were included in a military operational booklet; see Hull, *Irish Secrets*, 106.
11. Born in Clontarf in 1900, Coyle graduated from University College Dublin and became managing director of the United Potash Syndicate, which he had joined in 1923; he died in Berlin in 1943. See the BBC *WW2 People's War* archive (http://www.bbc.co.uk/history/ww2peopleswar/), for which this information was gathered from the Coyle family. James does not mention him in her memoir.
12. *ChISA*, 287.
13. Weiland, *Irische Freiheitskämpfer*, 95.
14. *ChISA*, 148.
15. *ChISA*, 172.

16. James [as O'Mara], "Pádraig Pearse," 80. "Das irische Blut siegte wieder über das englische. Pádraig Henry Pearse, Sohn eines englischen Vaters und einer irischen Mutter, in Dublin geboren, fühlte sich irischer als Ossian selbst."
17. Ibid., 95.
18. See "Geschichte der Universitätsbibliothek," *Humboldt-Universität zu Berlin*, accessed 13 February 2011, http://www.ub.hu-berlin.de/ueber-uns/geschichte.
19. James [as O'Mara], "Pádraig Pearse," 95. See Aldous, *Great Irish Speeches*, 67.
20. Ibid. 145.
21. *ChÍSA*, 188.
22. James claims that this work—not giving a title—was published in German during the war, and is probably still unknown to the Irish. Instead, it seems that the novel was never published. On 20 August 1942 Stuart received a refusal from the Ministry of Propaganda over his application for publication of his new novel *Winter Song*. He stopped writing the novel, whose manuscript was never found. See Elborn, *Francis Stuart*, 153; Kiely, *Francis Stuart*, 156.
23. *ChÍSA*, 189.
24. *ChÍSA*, 189.

Chapter 9

1. *ChÍSA*, 193.
2. Ibid., 194.
3. O'Donoghue, *Hitler's Irish Voices*, 46.
4. Ibid., 97.
5. Ibid., 197–98.
6. The sheer number of collaborators who worked for the Berlitz School in Berlin is staggering, although there were limited alternatives for unemployed non-German-speaking foreigners in the capital.
7. Just as with "Lord Haw-Haw," there were at least two contenders for the title "Axis Sally." Gillars's rival was Rita Zucca, who broadcast from the German propaganda station in Italy. Zucca, also an American citizen, but one who had surrendered her nationality, was ineligible for prosecution by U.S. authorities. She was later convicted in an Italian court and served nine months.
8. While she deliberately cultivated a sexy image on the radio, Gillars was more accurately described as "theatrical" and "horse-faced" at her 1949 trial. "Treason: True to the Red, White and Blue," *Time*, 7 March 1949.
9. Lucas, *Axis Sally*, 97.
10. Ibid., 131.
11. *ChÍSA*, 200.
12. NA-Kew, KV 2/119, Ahlrichs to Menzel, 21 November 1942.
13. O'Reilly, "I Was a Spy in Ireland," *Sunday Dispatch*, 17 August 1952, 9.

14. NA-Kew, KV 2/119, Appendix III, O'Reilly's Broadcasting Contacts. The precise meaning of "intimate" in this situation cannot now be established, but depending on how the relationship ended, might help explain James's later antagonism toward O'Reilly.

15. This should properly be the Reichs-Rundfunk-Gesellschaft, which in 1939 became known as the *Großdeutscher Rundfunk*.

16. *ChÍSA*, 210–11.

17. She gives a brief synopsis of Dr. Wilhelmi: "[He was] head of the Department for Radio Plays. He had held a permanent position as a director of the German Theatre of New York, but he left when the war began. He called on me to join his crew of radio translators, and I stayed there until that international service was terminated when the war drew to a close" (*ChÍSA*, 193). Her confirmation of the radio translator job is important when evaluating the testimony of the survivors of Hitler's bunker.

The Deutsches Rundfunkarchiv has no listing of a "Dr. Wilhelmi" but does for an "Ernst Wilhelmy": "Wilhelmy worked as an administrator with the German shortwave transmitter, in other words, the German European Station, specifically for the English language programs." Deutsches Rundfunkarchiv, correspondence from Andreas Dan, Archivist, 17 March 2010.

18. *ChÍSA*, 252.

19. Hull, *Irish Secrets*, 206.

20. Deutsches Rundfunkarchiv, correspondence from Andreas Dan, Archivist, 17 March 2010.

21. In one example, the monitor notes, "'Sylvia' spoke on 24.3.1942 and told some funny stories and a pointless anecdote about two sparrows named Mr. and Mrs. Lops."

22. A January 1943 note from Irish representative in Berlin, William Warnock, to the Department for External Affairs confirms this. He lists some of the personnel in the Irish section, adding, "A Miss Nora O'Mara, born in England of Irish parents, but not an Irish citizen, speaks occasionally, I believe. She has been in Germany for some years." James herself would be the likely source of this information.

23. The 1691 Treaty of Limerick ended the war between Jacobite and Williamite forces in Ireland. Irish nationalists historically referred to the "broken promises" of the Treaty, which was likely the anti-British message of this radio segment. The "Wild Geese"—Irish expatriates who served in foreign armies after the Treaty—date from this event. James mentions this several times in her autobiography.

24. IMA, transcript of 24 March 1943 broadcast. *Spalpeen* (Irish Gaelic): a rascal.

25. IMA, transcript of 18 March 1943 broadcast. On 14 March, under the name Nora O'Mara, she read poems by Michael Robert and David Mortier. The announcer noted that in the following week Francis Stuart would read a letter to Ireland in the name of the Irish colony in Germany.

26. IMA, G2/2014, Francis Stuart file, radio intercept transcription, 5 August 1942.
27. Bundesarchiv, I 28044, Frowein to Hilger, 12 March 1942.
28. Alan Steinweis, *Art, Ideology, and Economics*, 99.
29. IMA, G2/0214, Nora O'Mara, 15 July 1944.

Chapter 10

1. Hermann Fegelein would have been Hitler's brother-in-law for a very brief time. Hitler married Eva Braun early on 29 April 1945. Survivors' accounts differ as to whether Fegelein was executed on the 28th or 29th of April.
2. There were no authentic Irish nationals in Berlin at this time, and the Irish Legation had since moved after a 1943 bombing raid which destroyed the Drakenstrasse premises.
3. O'Donnell, *The Bunker*, 198–212. This is confirmed by Rochus Misch, the SS soldier who worked as Hitler's radio operator and was among the last to leave the Führerbunker. Misch, *Hitler's Last Witness*, 2640 (Kindle edition).
4. In her autobiography, James states that she and her four-year-old daughter left Berlin in March 1945 by squeezing through the window of a train about to depart. She does not elaborate on the circumstances. *ChÍSA*, 219.
5. Its powerful signal also operated in proximity to the genuine German national broadcast channel, the Deutschlandsender, often overriding it. When Calais fell in 1944, the name of the station changed to Soldatensender West, and began to be more sharply critical of Hitler, including very accurate details about his declining health and appearance.

Chapter 11

1. NA-Kew, PRO KV 4/9, Liddell Report, 73.
2. O'Donoghue, *Hitler's Irish Voices*, 209.
3. West, *Guy Liddell Diaries*, 198.
4. *London Times*, 23 March 1987, quoted in O'Donoghue, *Hitler's Irish Voices*, 205. John Stephenson was knighted in 1962, and served as a Lord Justice of the Appeal Court from 1971 to 1985. He died in 1998. Ironically, Sir John's father, Sir Guy Stephenson, Assistant Director of Public Prosecutions from 1908 to 1930, was involved in prosecuting Sir Roger Casement for treason. Author interview with Professor Eunan O'Halpin, Trinity College Dublin, 2 June 2000.
5. The Paris Consulate to MI5 letter also mentions her using another alias, Wehrli. There is no file associated with that name in the MI5 information released to the National Archives.

6. This was a necessary foundation for the later war crimes trials held by the International Military Tribunal, the Nuremberg Military Tribunal, and the great many trials conducted by the individual nations under Control Council Order No. 10. CC10 also allowed for German authorities to assume responsibility for denazification proceedings.

7. National Archives UK, FO 369/3547-52, letter of 7 May 1945, Consular Section Paris to MI5.

8. *ChISA*, 231

9. *ChISA*, 249.

10. *ChISA*, 247.

11. National Archives UK, KV 2/431, Renegades and Suspected Renegades, Case number 86 (Phyllis Ursula Rosaleen James, alias Nora O'Mara), file notation.

12. As a measure of reciprocity, the British were obliged to return captured members of Andrei Vlassov's Army of National Liberation, a unit of former Red Army soldiers who fought with the Germans.

13. *Daily Herald*, 2 July 1945, 1. There was some initial confusion with the story of Amery's arrest. His companion was described as "Amery's wife," prompting the real Mrs. Una Amery, herself a former prostitute, to come forward and rebut the misidentification. For good measure, she also described her errant husband as a "sexual pervert." "Archives Reveal Truth about Fascist Traitors," *The Independent*, 8 February 1995, 8.

14. "Minister Charles Bewley—activities during the war," NA-Ireland, DFA SOF P.14, 1 Oct. 1947. Bewley, a Quaker who converted to Catholicism, was sacked from his Berlin post in 1939 for being avidly pro Nazi. Bewley's own selective version of his activities is contained in his posthumous autobiography, *Memoirs of a Wild Goose*.

15. O'Donoghue, *Hitler's Irish Voices*, 167. Under the existing law, the only possible sentence was death. As of 1998, with the passage of the Crime and Disorder Act, this changed to life imprisonment.

16. Thurlow, *Fascism in Modern Britain*, 168.

17. *UK Statute Law Database (legislation.gov.uk)*, Treason Act 1351 (c. 2), accessed 21 July 2016, http://www.legislation.gov.uk/aep/Edw3Stat5/25/2/contents.

18. Treachery Act 1940 (United Kingdom), 3 & 4 Geo. VI c. 40, paragraph 1, "Death penalty for treachery," accessed 1 August 2016, https://en.wikisource.org/wiki/Treachery_Act_1940_(United_Kingdom).

19. O'Donoghue, *Hitler's Irish Voices*, 205.

20. NA-Ireland, DFA A72, O'Mara to Iseult Stuart. Stuart did in fact see James in Paris. Based on conversations with Stuart, his biographer Geoffrey Elborn states, "It was awkward for Stuart, who was worried about Madeleine, but he felt he should visit Nora for the sake of their past relationship. When they met, Nora was desperately unhappy. When she heard that Stuart wanted to be with Madeleine, she was tearful and emotional. Elborn, *Francis Stuart*, 182.

Chapter 12

1. *ChÍSA*, 281–82.
2. *ChÍSA*, 188.
3. *ChÍSA*, 189.
4. Also published in Irish as *I gCéin is i gCóngar* (hereafter *I gCéin*).
5. *Inniu* (6 July 1973, 1); *Irish Times* (13 March 1973, 6); *Connacht Tribune* (3 August 1973, 29); *Connacht Tribune* (10 August 1973, 46); *Irish Times* (29 July 1975, 9). The Swiss nationality is repeated in pieces in *Inniu* (10 August 1973, 1) and in the *Irish Independent* (3 August 1973, 1).
6. The pattern of this is interesting. With the sensibility of a stage performer knowing the audience, she is careful never to make the mistake of telling a German listener that she is German or an Irish listener that she is native to Ireland. Instead, the narratives only work when the Germans think she is Irish, the Irish that she is Swiss and/or French, etc.
7. *ChÍSA*, 253, and again in *I gCéin*, 2. From her narrative, it is unclear where the children were during this period, but they were almost certainly not with her.
8. James [as Ó Mara], "Chú Chullain of Muirthemne," 7.
9. The plays are by Maurice Maeterlinck, *The Miracle of St. Anthony*, and Armand Salacrou, *Marguerite*. UCDA, P261/ 2252 and P261/ 3734 (RTÉ Radio Dramas). They are undated.
10. *Deutsches Bühnenjahrbuch*, 179. The theater is now named Kleines Theater im Zoo.
11. *ChÍSA*, 253f. She says this was independent of the inheritance she was entitled to.
12. "Anhang: Liste der deutschsprachigen Aufführungen," in *Materialien zu Becketts Endspiel*, 132. In her memoir, James praises Beckett for his powers of tragicomedy. *I gCéin*, 10.
13. "The young postwar generation in Germany was losing all cultivation ('going savage') at the time, thanks to being given some sort of muddied education that forced liberalism upon them. . . . " *I gCéin*, 11.
14. Mac Liammóir, *Ceo Meala Lá Seaca*, 172; see also 180–81, more specifically about the younger generation of Germans.
15. Fischer, ". . . 'thar lear' chomh hiomlán . . . ," 128–54, 136.
16. See especially Cawley, "Trends in Population," 681–702, 685–87.
17. *I gCéin*, 26.
18. James's memoir (*I gCéin*, 37), which gives Ó hAonghusa a smaller role, disagrees with testimony from Ó hAonghusa's son, who remembers his father's long working hours and physical work on the buildings during those years.
19. Hayes, "Ahead of Her Time." The playschool was run by the Gaelic League from 1973 to 1983, and was revived a few times after that. Ppersonal comment from Peadar Mac Fhlannchadha, Gaelic League branch manager Galway, 20 March 2013.
20. *I gCéin*, 33. See also Finlan, "Durlas an Dochais."

21. *I gCéin*, 35; and Finlan, "Durlas an Dochais": "The Department of Education, beribboned with red tape, will not recognise the school nor contribute a shilling to its support."
22. Finlan, "Durlas an Dochais."
23. Walsh, *Contests and Contexts*, 391. See also 378–79.
24. Finlan, "Durlas an Dochais."
25. *I gCéin*, 71.
26. Author interviews with Máire Phaidín Uí Mhaol Chiaráin, 4 June 2011; with Nóirín Uí Ghoill, 14 July 2012.
27. *I gCéin*, 79.
28. "Snob mise, an ea? Chuirfeadh sin iontas gan amhras ar mhuintir an Iarthair a mbíodh plé acu liom." Fennell, "Agallamh le Róisín Ní Mheara."
29. Fischer, *Das Deutschlandbild der Iren*, 362–460.
30. During Böll's holidays on Achill Island during the 1950s, he had an encounter with a local he calls "Padraic" who expressed admiration for Germany and Hitler. In a comical scene, Böll tells a few truths about Hitler over pints, acting as a "political dentist" who needs to pull bad teeth. Böll, *Irisches Tagebuch*, 42–46.
31. Hugo Hamilton, *The Speckled People*, 21–22. The book contains an account of his mother's bicycle trip through Ireland and her encounter with people unwilling to hear the same truths Böll peddles so successfully.
32. "Glaoch ón Tríú Reich" (Mind the Gap Films, 2013). Fischer judged in 2000 that Tim Pat Coogan's dictum of 1966, "Ireland's attitude to Hitler has never been objectively assessed," was still valid. Fischer, *Das Deutschlandbild der Iren*, 402.
33. *ChÍSA*, 36–37.
34. Ibid., 158.
35. Ibid., 175.
36. Quoted in Sherratt, *Hitler's Philosophers*, 81.
37. *ChÍSA*, 173.
38. German colonial history was not extensively studied until the 1960s, and it is maybe no surprise that James did not delve into the subject before repeating, in 1991, what she had been taught early in her life. For a very recent study of the Namibian (German South-West African) genocide of the 1880s. See Olusoga and Erichsen, *The Kaiser's Holocaust*.
39. See especially *ChÍSA*, 175, 198.
40. *ChÍSA*, 22.
41. Ibid., 114.
42. *I gCéin*, 49. This and other passages in the book would have benefited from editing.
43. *I gCéin*, 93–94.
44. See Burleigh and Wipperman, *The Racial State*, 36, and their summary of Social Darwinism with its proponent, the elective German Englishman Houston Stewart Chamberlain.
45. *ChÍSA*, 79–80, and 298 (ghettos). This is discussed again in chapter 13.

46. *I gCéin*, 100.

47. Ibid., 49.

48. Ibid., 105. She only mentions it as her occupation at the time of her pen-friend Ó Fiaich returning from Rome with the cardinalship, 1979. She surprisingly avoids any other mention of this work *ar son na cúise* (for the cause).

Chapter 13

1. *ChÍSA*, 23.

2. See the memoirs of one of the founders, Proinsias Mac an Bheatha, *Téid Focal le Gaoith*, and a collection of essays by Mac an Bheatha, *Téann Buille le Cnámh*. Much of the above is described in *Téid Focal le Gaoith*. For a critical study of *Glúin na Bua* and *Inniu*, see Ní hUigín, "Craobh na hAiséirí," 74–110.

3. The quotation is from Douglas, "Ailtirí na hAiséirghe" in the magazine *History Ireland*; for a detailed discussion, see Douglas, *Architects of the Resurrection*, 220–21.

4. Maume, "Ó Cuinneagáin."

5. IMA, G2/X/1320, memoranda of March and April 1943, May 1944 (all unsigned).

6. If so, the talk is phrased very obliquely. See R. M. Douglas, *Architects of the Resurrection*, 188–89; and Barrington, *Wartime Broadcasts*, 123–25.

7. O'Nolan, in his guise as Myles na gCopaleen and his column "Cruiskeen Lawn," summed up *Glúin na Bua*'s plan for "youth marches" in characteristic satirical fashion. *Irish Times*, 13 December 1943.

8. See Mac an Bheatha's autobiographical works, *Téid Focal le Gaoth*, *Téann Buille le Cnámh*, and *I dTreo na Gréine*.

9. The paper and its history were discussed by founder member Mac an Bheatha in his essay in *I dTreo na gréine* (see Ó Nualláin, "Eagarthóir"). For the most extensive study of the paper, its editors, contributors, and content, see Ní hUigín, "Craobh na hAiséirí."

10. Their surviving correspondence postdates her last contributions to the paper but makes reference to it.

11. Mac an Bheatha, *Téid Focal le Gaoith*, 91.

12. In a very insightful television documentary, "Glaoch ón Tríú Reich" (A Call from the Third Reich), Professor Emeritus and native Irish speaker Gearóid Mac Eoin, University of Ireland, Galway, speaks of his memories of listening to Hans Hartmann on the radio during the war.

13. Ní hUigín, "Craobh na hAiséirí," 101–2.

14. Ibid., 110.

15. Quoted by Ní hUigín, "Craobh na hAiséirí," 82.

16. Writing in the monthly Irish-language magazine *Feasta* (established in 1948), he blamed the author for having incited young men to join the IRA. See Ó hUid, *Faoi Ghlas*, 11.

17. Douglas, *Architects of the Resurrection*, 168.
18. Quoted (without reference) by Ní hUigín, "Craobh na hAiséirí," 83.
19. AJHL, Papers of Proinsias Mac an Bheatha, G40/219. A letter to Mac an Bheatha of 17 October 1983 shows that she contributed at least one of these articles, and she arranged for editor Ó hUid to meet a visiting Salzburg corporation member at the Austrian Embassy in Dublin (ibid., G40/218).
20. James [as Ní Mheara], "Comórfar Feragal N.[aofa] in Salzburg," 6; "Comóradh 1200 Fheargail Naofa," 3; and *Inniu*, 6 April 1984, 5.
21. *Inniu* ran a column entitled "Dialann Eorpach" by Máirtín Davy until July 1973 (see issue 6 July 1973, 15), maybe the only other regular newsletter from Europe.
22. James [as Ní Mheara], "Litir ón Eoraip" (Letter from Europe), *Inniu*, 11 November 1977. She proceeds to tell the story of Captain Benno Ruffer who picked up 36 Vietnamese refugees adrift in the Chinese Sea, and a German camp set up for them.
23. For example, see James [as Ní Mheara], "Letter from Europe," *Inniu*, 24 February, 10 March 1978, 5 May 1978, 4 January 1980.
24. James [as Ní Mheara], "Letter from Europe," *Inniu*, 21 July 1978, 15 December 1978, 23 November 1979. On 18 April 1980 she conceded that the Irish traditional musicians, The Dubliners, unfortunately confirmed some of the propaganda about the drunken Irish.
25. James [as Ní Mheara], "Letter from Europe," *Inniu*, 3 November 1978.
26. James [as Ní Mheara], "Letter from Europe," *Inniu*, 30 December 1977, 11 January 1980, 9 May 1980, 11 July 1980—and on 9 May 1980 she also writes about the Katyn massacre.
27. James [as Ní Mheara], "Letter from Europe," *Inniu*, 14 July 1978, and 2 December 1977, 16 December 1977, 23 March 1978, 14 April 1978, 26 May 1978, 28 July 1978, 12 January 1979, 2 February 1979, 17 August 1979.
28. James [as Ní Mheara], "Letter from Europe," *Inniu*, 30 December 1977.
29. James [as Ní Mheara], "Letter from Europe," *Inniu*, 9 December 1977, 21 April 1978, 2 November 1979.
30. James [as Ní Mheara], "Letter from Europe," *Inniu*, 11 November 1977 (Strauss), 7 April 1978, 29 February 1980.
31. In the order listed here: James [as Ní Mheara], "Letter from Europe," *Inniu*, 17 February 1978; 28 September 1979; 25 April 1980; 9 June 1978; 26 May 1978; 16 December 1977. In Hess's case, she goes so far as to say that on the day of his death, Germany will gain a martyr. She does not go into her theory, as in *Cé hÍ Seo Amuigh?* that Hess's choice of Scotland for his flight in 1941 derived from a conversation with her guardian, Sir Ian Hamilton, nor that she herself visited Hess's wife Ilse "some years after the war." *ChÍSA*, 180–81.
32. See Uehling, *Karajan: Eine Biographie*.
33. As opposed to some early women aviation pioneers (e.g., Earhart) who were keen for publicity, Reitsch was first and foremost a flyer who test-piloted some of the most demanding aircraft—including experimental models and jets—that Germany produced. She also crashed fewer planes than Amelia

Earhart (or Elly Beinhorn, another publicity-friendly aviatrix from the same period). See Reitsch, *Fliegen, mein Leben*.

34. Ron Laytner, "The First Astronaut," *Deseret News*, 19 February 1981, 12C. Reitsch died in 1979.

35. James [as Ní Mheara], "Letter from Europe," *Inniu*, 24 February 1978; 9 June 1978, and 13 January 1978; 22 December 1978 ("devilish act"); 27 September 1978.

36. James [as Ní Mheara], "Letter from Europe," *Inniu*, 13 January 1978, 9.

37. Ibid.

38. "B'éasca dó teacht as an ghaiste mar sin," *Inniu*, 13 January 1978, 9.

39. This must refer to the International Tracing Service in Arolsen, Germany. Her "citation" is incomplete and, as such, without value.

40. The Royal Warrant under which the British court was constituted did not permit charges pertaining to acts against civilians (Jews, gypsies, etc.), although plentiful evidence of these criminal acts was admitted at trial.

41. United Nations War Crimes Commission, Law-Reports of Trials of War Criminals, vol. 2, London, HMSO, 1947, Case No. 10, Trial of Josef Kramer and 44 Others, British Military Court, Luneburg, 17 September–17 November 1945, 111. The Crown Prosecutor summed up the evidence as follows: "The evidence made it clear that Belsen was intended to be a new Auschwitz removed from the threat of the Russian advance. Dr. Klein [camp doctor at both Auschwitz and Belsen] said there was some talk of the camp being some kind of exchange camp for prisoners, but that later he realized that it was not a camp for sick people, but a death camp, a torture camp."

42. International Tracing Services (ITS), accessed 1 August 2016, https://www.facebook.com/itsarolsen/.

43. Quoted in Douglas, *Architects of the Resurrection*, 268.

44. Wills, *That Neutral Island*, 398–401.

45. There is one exception: James Clegg from Ontario, Canada, sent an ironic reply to a "Letter" of hers which dealt with the goodness of Mother Theresa and with the dubiousness of Hans Küng, the latter "a paragon of this age without ideals," according to James (*Inniu*, 11 July 1980). The reply was printed in the issue of 8 August 1980.

46. Personal email communication, Ní hUigin to author, 12 October 2010.

47. Institutsbibliothek des ehemaligen Sprachwissenschaftlichen Instituts, Abteilung für Keltologie (Institut für Anglistik, Amerikanistik und Keltologie), Universität Bonn.

48. There are endnotes, again without references to her sources. The work may have been pitched at the interested lay reader, but must present frustrations for the student of Celtic Studies.

49. In German, "Inspektoren des Landesdenkmalamtes" is both impressive and unclear. James [as O'Mara], *König der Bäume*, 125.

50. James [as O'Mara], *König der Bäume*. For example: "Mit freundlicher Genehmigung der Ir[ischen] Akademie, Dublin," 8.

51. Ibid., 11–12.
52. This was a much-enlarged reissue of *Gaelscrínte i gCéin* (1961). See acknowledgements, *Gaelscrínte san Eoraip*, vii; and *I gCéin*, 125.
53. Published in Dublin by Four Courts Press, 1994; quotation from same, ix.
54. *I gCéin*, 106.
55. Seán Ó Riada was an Irish composer (d. 1971) who married the various strands of Irish music (Gaelic old style and classical) in a new way, composing the music for the documentary film *Mise Éire* (I Am Ireland, 1959), as well as two masses in Irish. See "Ó Riada, Seán," in Diarmaid Breathnach and Máire Ní Mhurchú, *Beathaisnéis*, now available on *Ainm.ie: An Bunachar Náisiúnta Beathaisnéisí Gaeilge*, http://ainm.ie.
56. Quinn, "Salzburg Commemorates Irish Monk."
57. Personal email communication, Peter F. Kramml, City Archives Salzburg, to author, 25 July 2013; see *I gCéin*, 114–15 and 111.
58. For James's and other allocations, see "Dáil Éireann Debate," vol. 377, 2 February 1988, and vol. 380, 24 May 1988. "Current Debates," *House of the Oireachtas*, accessed 24 June 2016, http://debates.oireachtas.ie/dail/1988/05/24/00040.asp. The Minister for Foreign Affairs Brian Lenihan explained that the allocations were "for the promotion of cultural relations with other countries" and awarded on the advice of the Cultural Relations Committee.
59. De Bréadún, "Cumann Merriman."
60. Cardinal Tomás Ó Fiaich Memorial Library and Archive (CÓFLA), Papers of Cardinal Tomás Ó Fiaich, 17 December 1988.
61. Ó Muirí, "1300-Jahrfeier des Martyriums."
62. AJHL, Papers of Proinsias Mac an Bheatha, G40/248; CÓFLA, Papers of Cardinal Tomás Ó Fiaich, Box 4/10; *I gCéin*, 125–30.
63. *I gCéin*, 129.
64. Ó Coigligh, "Réamhrá" (foreword), in *Cé hÍ Seo Amuigh?*, vii: "She organized some of the most notable symposiums that celebrated and fostered Irish scholarship all over the continent for the last years."
65. AJHL, Papers of Proinsias Mac an Bheatha, G40/231.
66. AJHL, Papers of Proinsias Mac an Bheatha, G40/272, draft press item. He sums her up as a woman of Irish extraction who has spent her life in Germany.
67. AJHL, Papers of Proinsias Mac an Bheatha, G40/248.
68. AJHL, Papers of Proinsias Mac an Bheatha, especially G40/68, G40/185, and G40/235; and "Cardinal Urges *Inniu* Support," *Irish Times*, 6 December 1983, 3.
69. CÓFLA, Papers of Cardinal Tomás Ó Fiaich, preliminary inventory compiled by Róisín Ní Mheara, 1998. Her own research notes for *Early Irish Saints in Europe* are also deposited there.
70. CÓFLA, *The Ó Fiaich Treasures*, 4.

Chapter 14

1. "Irving v. Penguin Books Ltd.," England and Wales High Court of Justice, Queens Bench Division [2000] 115; "Irving v. Lipstadt," transcripts,"*Holocaust Denial on Trial*, http://www.hdot.org/en/trial/transcripts/.
2. James [as Ní Mheara], "Letter from Europe," *Inniu*, 13 January 1978, 9. She gives no source for the unlikely Hannah Arendt citation, and we cannot locate it.
3. James [as Ní Mheara], "The Racket over Oberammergau," *Inniu*, 28 April 1978, 11, 14. This article is not entitled "Litir ón Eoraip" and is unsigned, but the content and its placement make her authorship very likely.
4. AJHL, Papers of Proinsias Mac an Bheatha, G40/231. FNT (Foilseachán Náisiúnta Teoranta) was a publisher.
5. A small, well-regarded publishing house, Coiscéim was founded in 1980 with a broad range of publications, including fiction, essays, popular history, and the odd academic work such as Declan Kiberd's *Idir dhá chultúr* (1993). Together with Cló Iar-Chonnachta it is one of the most prolific houses for Irish language publications.
6. AJHL, Papers of Proinsias Mac an Bheatha, G40/158.
7. AJHL, Papers of Proinsias Mac an Bheatha, G40/248.
8. Mac Aonghusa, "Ar an tSaoil," 11.
9. AJHL, Papers of Proinsias Mac an Bheatha, G40/234.
10. On both father and daughter, see Breathnach and Ní Mhurchú, *Beathaisnéis*.
11. *ChÍSA*, v. One draft is extant in Proinsias Mac an Bheatha's papers (AJHL, G40/947).
12. *ChÍSA*, vi.
13. See interview with James by Desmond Fennell, in Fennell, "Agallamh le Róisín Ní Mheara," 14–15.
14. Personal email communication with the author, 5 January 2009: "Is fiú a lua gurbh é a thuairim ar deireadh nár chóir an leabhar *Cé hÍ Seo Amuigh* a fhoilsiú mar go dtarrangeodh sí an iomarca raice. B'fhior dó."
15. Proinsias Ó Drisceoil pointed to Ó Coigligh's "enthusiastic" preface that celebrates James's perspective as Gaelic Irish in a false distinction rejected by Geoffrey Keating in the seventeenth century: "[He] holds, in a way deeply insulting both to speakers of Irish and to Irish Jews (two groups which are not mutually exclusive), that Muir saw her experience in a true Gaelic perspective." Ó Drisceoil, Proinsias, "A Monarchial Republican," A9.
16. See O'Sullivan, *Songs of the Irish*, 150–52. The title figure is said to be Edmund Ryan, County Tipperary, who went on the run after the Battle of Aughrim, 1691.
17. Nic Dhiarmada, "Cé hÍ Seo Amuigh?: "Pé hí seo amuigh, ní deas an radharc í" (Whoever she is outside, she is not nice to behold).
18. *ChÍSA*, 265–68.

19. *ChÍSA*, 267.

20. *ChÍSA*, 267. James adds to the drama: The Flemish woman in whose house they heard this testimony quickly closed the shutters, saying, "You are back in France now, love, and this is a new era. We had a change of guards. With all that information you have, it would be in your interest to keep quiet."

21. She calls others of his type "ex-soldiers," but this GI she claims was on leave and found it easy to share military and personal insights with a complete stranger after a few beers in the Café de l'Opera. *ChÍSA*, 271 and 267.

22. Mac Coille, "Lessons Not Yet Learned."

23. Ibid.

24. The Gaeltachtaí are the Irish-speaking regions largely in the west and south of Ireland.

25. Government records from this period will not be available until 2023. The *Sunday Tribune* reported that a grant of this type was normally for around £1,000 and was given to "all Irish-language books if they meet basic standards of production quality." Doyle, "Taylor Says."

26. Doyle, "Taylor Says."

27. Ibid.

28. According to the *Irish Times*, twelve people took part in an hour-long protest outside the Bord na Gaeilge offices, until people inside informed them that the Bord na Leabhar Gaeilge had nothing to do with them: Mac Dhubhghaill, "Tuarascáil."

29. *I gCéin*, copyright page with reference to Bord na Leabhar Gaeilge's grant aid, 3.

30. Mac Aonghusa, "Ar an tSaoil." His article in the Irish weekly *Anois* was a preview of the book, and is a plea for not diluting the collective memory of the holocaust.

31. Mac Aonghusa, "Ar an tSaoil." A little innocently, he doubts whether the people who published it knew what it purported.

32. Titley, "Politically Incorrect."

33. Monthly editorial *Eadrainn*, "Nua-Chinsirí na Gaeilge-Linn!"

34. Article 31 of the Irish Constitution.

35. Ó Snodaigh: "Bímid ag súil le go mbeidh an Ghaeilge squeaky-clean . . . Cinsireacht fheidhmiúil í a rá nár chóir go mbeadh airgead caite ar leabhair den tsaghas seo." See Ní Chonchubhair, "Faighimís réidh leis an mBac seo ar Shaoirse Cainte!," *Comhar* 52, no. 5 (June 1993), 10–12.

36. Signed "our correspondent in Teheran, Fatwa Brown," (Leabhar Naitsíoch ina chnámh spairne). "Nua-Chinsirí na Gaeilge-Linn!"

37. Ó Drisceoil, "A Monarchial Republican," *Irish Times*, A9.

38. Nic Dhiarmada, "*Cé hÍ Seo Amuigh?*" (review).

39. The article is in both James's [as Ní Mheara] and Ó Súilleabháin's names, but a single perspective commenting on James as a third person is

adopted throughout. James [as Ní Mheara] and Ó Súilleabháin, "Faobhar ar a nGuth."

40. Mac Aonghusa's article, in fact, says only that the Allies saved the world that time, "no matter what they did before or afterwards." Mac Aonghusa, "Ar an tSaoil."

41. *ChÍSA*, 112: "ní raibh call leis an triopall treapall daonlathais pharlaimintigh seo a brúdh orainn."

42. James [as Ní Mheara] and Ó Súilleabháin, "Faobhar ar a nguth," 17.

43. Ibid., 15. He shows that her statements about the Jews and the holocaust, about the Jews in the Rundfunkhaus, and about Marx, and the League of Nations were steeped in exaggerations and generalizations.

44. He claims she spent twelve years "faoi anáil Ghoebbels" (under Goebbels's influence), but her year in the finishing school, a year in Vienna, and the war years hardly amount to this much. James [as Ní Mheara] and Ó Súilleabháin, "Faobhar ar a nGuth," 14.

45. Ibid., 15.
46. Ó Drisceoil "A Monarchial Republican," A9.
47. Titley, "Politically Incorrect."
48. Fennell, "Agallamh le Róisín Ní Mheara," 15.
49. James [as Ní Mheara], "Letter from Europe," *Inniu*, 9 June 1978, 28 September 1979, 25 April 1980. It should be noted that both Reitsch and Wagner remained fawning admirers of Hitler until their deaths in 1979 (Reitsch) and 1980 (Wagner). See, for example, *I gCéin*, 75, 93.
50. Nic Dhiarmada, "Cé hÍ Seo Amuigh?"
51. James [as Ní Mheara] and Ó Súilleabháin, "Faobhar ar a nGuth," 13.
52. Fennell, "Agallamh le Róisín Ní Mheara."
53. Ibid., 15.
54. Ibid., "Crann taca uainn. Cailliúint i gcúrsaí gnó, ealaíne agus éigse. Oibreacha fealsúnachta spioradálta agus fionnachtain de dhíth."
55. "... níl ach bealach aingiallta an ábharachais agus an níhileachais romhainn. Ach ... tá Dia ann agus tá Sé láidir." Fennell, "Agallamh le Róisín Ní Mheara," 15.
56. This was one of the allegorical names of Ireland: there is a patriotic song of that name which, according to collector P. W. Joyce, "could be sung with safety in the time of the Penal Laws, as it was in the guise of a love song." Joyce, *Old Irish Folk Music*, 367.
57. Fischer, "... 'thar lear' chomh hiomlán ...," 393.
58. The Irish public service broadcaster for Irish speakers.
59. Mac Murchaidh, "How I Discovered Irish," 92.
60. James, *I gCéin agus i gCóngar*.
61. Ó Muirí, "Review," 293.
62. Ibid., 255. The "generous donation" is that of her own research papers and drafts.

63. *ChISA*, 77. This was yet another in a series of legal anti-Semitic measures which the Nazi state enacted against the Jews. The Law for the Restoration of the Professional Civil Service of 1933 set the tone: removal of all non-Aryans (Jews) from the government positions, to include education, judiciary, and academic appointments. This was soon followed by other legislation excluding Jews from the legal, medical, and accounting professions.

64. *ChISA*, 78.

65. *ChISA*, 79. Not surprisingly, James is wrong. "The Madagascar Plan" was mooted among some aspects of the SS and SD throughout the late 1930s, but by 1941—as documented in the Wannsee Conference protocols—the leadership had already reached the decision to solve the "Jewish Question" through biological extermination, which matured into the Aktion Reinhard extermination camps established in 1942. The British took control of Madagascar in November 1942, well after the orders were issued for genocide.

66. *ChISA*, 80.

67. *ChISA*, 80. James's reference: See the headline of the *Daily Express*, "Judea Declares War on Germany," 24 March 1933. There was no such entity called the World Organization of Jews.

68. *ChISA*, 81.

69. Evans, *Lying about Hitler*, 59. In general, Holocaust denial consists of four central points: minimization of numbers killed, denial of use of gassing, denial of the systematic nature of the genocide, and claims that the evidence was fabricated, above all after the war.

70. Richard Evans, *Irving vs. (1) Lipstadt and (2) Penguin Books: Expert Witness Report*, 66, http://www.phdn.org/negation/irving/EvansReport.pdf: "In conclusion, therefore, it is clear that Irving has consistently and grossly underestimated the number of Jews deliberately killed by the Nazis, usually by quoting a total figure, or figures for individual killing centres such as Auschwitz, of a completely different, lower order of magnitude than those generally accepted by reputable professional historians, frequently by attributing such deaths as he does concede occurred to 'natural' causes such as epidemics and malnutrition, and occasionally even by blaming British bombing raids and the British persistence in prosecuting the war throughout the period 1940–1945. All of this puts him into the same camp as the well-known Holocaust deniers who regularly give a negative answer to the question 'did six million really die?'"

71. Evans, *Irving vs. Lipstadt*, 85.

72. Seidel, *Holocaust Denial*, 39.

73. "Holocaust Denier Irving Is Jailed," *BBC News*, 20 February 2006, http://news.bbc.co.uk/2/hi/europe/4733820.stm. The law, in part, reads:

> Article 3h: 'A person shall also be liable to a penalty under Art. 3g if, in print or in broadcast or in some other medium, or otherwise publicly in any manner accessible to a large number of people, if he denies

the National Social genocide or the National Socialist crimes against humanity, or seeks to minimize them in a coarse manner or consents thereto to justify them.'

Sentences according to the law:

A criminal offence: one to twenty years in prison (the maximum under Austrian law).

An administrative offence: a fine of between 3000–30,000 Schillings (about $180–1,800 or 218 to 2,180 Euro) Osterreich, StGBl 13/1945, amended version BGBl 148/1992.

Conclusion

1. *ChíSA*, 107.
2. See chapter 13, note 58.
3. *I gCéin*, 3.
4. Pryce-Jones, *Unity Mitford*, 281.
5. Personal letter from Pádraig Ó Snodaigh to the author, April 2011.
6. AJHL, Papers of Proinsias Mac an Bheatha, G40/218.
7. Christabel Bielenberg and Charlotte O'Connor, "Aosdána and Francis Stuart."
8. Ball, *Prosecuting War Crimes*, 58.
9. Weirdly, the cover photograph shows a Marine M4A3 Sherman flamethrower tank on Iwo Jima during World War II (she did not credit *Life* magazine's Mark Kauffman or the United States Marine Corps), and the uncredited author's image is the one I sent her (not for publication) from her wartime MI5 "renegades" file at the U.K. National Archives. As with her previous publications, she gives her name as Róisín Ní Mheara.
10. *ChíSA*, 297–98.
11. In Jeremiah 13:23, the line concludes, "Neither can you do good who are accustomed to doing evil."

Bibliography

Archives

Archives of the James Hardiman Library, National University of Galway
    Papers of Proinsias Mac an Bheatha: G40/68 (1984); G40/158 (31 Dec 1987–17 Oct 1988); G40/185 (24 May 1954); G40/218 (17 October 1983); G40/219 (11 November 1983); G40/231 (3 June 1985); G40/234 (23 June 1985); G40/235 (17 October 1985–9 December 1985); G40/248 (12 September 1988); G40/272 (undated); G40/947 (1990)

BBC People's War Archive
    "WW2 People's War: An Archive of World War Two Memories—written by the public, gathered by the BBC." http://www.bbc.co.uk/history/ww2peopleswar/.

Bundesarchiv, Berlin
    I 28044   Abteilung R

Bundesarchiv-Militärarchiv, Freiburg im Breisgau
    RW5/v. 497   Kriegstagebuch der Abwehr II

Cardinal Ó Fiaich Memorial Library and Archive, Armagh
    Papers of Cardinal Ó Fiaich (1939–1990)

City of Westminster Archives Centre, Westminster City Hall, London

Conradh na Gaeilge, Galway
    Papers of An Durlas (1969–1973)

Deutsches Rundfunkarchiv, Frankfurt am Main
    DRA RRG2/002/1942   Telephone directory of the Reichs-Rundfunkgesellschaft 1942

Irish Military Archives, Dublin
    G2/0214   Francis and Iseult Stuart
    G2/0257   Frank Ryan
    G2/1722   Hermann Görtz
    G2/3824   John O'Reilly

Bibliography

G2/4949	John Codd
G2/4953	Patrick O'Brien
G2/X/0154	Irish in Germany (civilians)
G2/X/1091	Misc Inquiries
G2/X/1164	Irish in Germany (suspect)
G2/X/1320	Ailtirí na hAiséirghe

King's College London, Basil Liddell Hart Centre for Military Archives, London
Hamilton Papers
Lady Hamilton Diary
Lady Hamilton Papers

National Archives of Ireland, Dublin
DFA A72
DFA SOF P.14

National Archives, Kew

FO 188/649	Reports on renegade British subjects
FO 369/3171–75	British renegades
FO 369/3547–52	British civilian renegades and collaborators
FO 688/32/21	Renegade British subjects
GFM 24/11	German war documents, Series I (Irland)
HO 45/29512	List of Renegades
HO 45/25793	Arthur Perry, broadcaster
HO 45/25833	Charles Patrick Gilbert
HO 45/25866	Suzanne Prevost-Booth, broadcaster
HO 144/22855	Susan Hilton, treason case
KV 2/119	John O'Reilly
KV 2/256	Pearl Vardon, broadcaster
KV 2/423	Susan Hilton
KV 2/428	Roderick Dietze, broadcaster
KV 2/430	British subjects as broadcasters
KV 2/431	Renegades and Suspected Renegades
KV 2/434–5	Patrick Dillon
KV 2/769	Dr. K. Haller
KV 2/2961	Erich Hetzler, British section, Ribbentrop Buro
KV 4/9	Liddell Report
KV 4/118	Policy on compilation of renegades list
KV 5/6	Dienststelle Ribbentrop
LCO 53/27	Arrangements for detaining renegades

National Library of Ireland, Dublin
MS 37,067/9; MS 37,512 Brian Friel Papers

Politisches Archiv des Auswärtigenen Amts, Berlin
I 28044   Nora O'Mara

University College Dublin, Archives

P261/ 2252	RTÉ Radio Drama
P261/ 3734	RTÉ Radio Drama

Bibliography

Interviews

Ó hAonghusa, Aongus, interview by Vera Moynes, Dublin, Ireland, 11 August 2012.
Uí Ghoill, Nóirín, telephone interview by Vera Moynes, Dublin, Ireland, 14 July 2012.
Uí Mhael Chiaráin, Máire Phaidín, interview by Vera Moynes, Inishmaan, County Galway, Ireland, 4 June 2011.

Books and Articles

Aldous, Richard. *Great Irish Speeches*. London: Quercus, 2007.
Andermann, W. Th. [alias Walter Thomas]. *Bis der Vorhang fiel*. Dortmund: Schwalvenberg, 1947.
Andrew, Christopher. *Defend the Realm: The Authorized History of MI5*. New York: Knopf, 2009.
Balfour, Michael. *Propaganda in War 1939–1945: Organizations, Policies and Publics in Britain and Germany*. London: Routledge & Kegan Paul, 1979.
Ball, Howard. *Prosecuting War Crimes and Genocide*. Lawrence: University Press of Kansas, 1999.
Barrington, Brendan. The *Wartime Broadcasts of Francis Stuart, 1942–1944*. Dublin: Lilliput, 2000.
Bewley, Charles. *Memoirs of a Wild Goose*. Dublin: Lilliput Press, 1989.
Bielenberg, Christabel. *The Past Is Myself*. London: Corgi, 1984.
de Bhulbh, Seán. *Sloinnte uile Éireann*. Limerick: Comhar-Chumann Íde Naofa, 2002.
Black, Edwin. *The Transfer Agreement: The Untold Story of the Secret Pact Between the Third Reich and Jewish Palestine*. New York: Macmillan 1984.
Black, George F. *The Surnames of Scotland*. New York: New York Public Library, 1946, repr. 1993.
Blanke, Richard. "Modern Europe." *The American Historical Review* 97, no. 2 (April 1992): 580–82.
Boelcke, Willi A. *Die Macht des Radios-Weltpolitik und Auslandsrundfunk 1924–1976*. Frankfurt am Main: Ullstein, 1977.
Böll, Heinrich. *Irisches Tagebuch*. Munich: Deutscher Taschenbuch Verlag, 1997.
Broderick, George. "Under the 'Three-Legged Swastika': Celtic Studies and Celtic Revival in the Isle of Man in the Context of the 'National Socialist Idea.'" In *Symbole der Kelten*, edited by Sabine Heinz. Berlin: Schirner Verlag, 1997.
Browning, Christopher R. *The Origins of the Final Solution: The Evolution of Nazi Jewish Policy*. Lincoln: University of Nebraska Press, 2004.
Burleigh, Michael, and Wolfgang Wippermann. *The Racial State: German 1933–1945*. Cambridge: Cambridge University Press, 1991.

Bibliography

Cardinal Tomás Ó Fiaich Memorial Library and Archive. *The Ó Fiaich Treasures: Cardinal Tomás Ó Fiaich Memorial Library and Archive*. Armagh: Cardinal Tomás Ó Fiaich Memorial Library and Archive, 2010.

Carter, C. *The Shamrock and the Swastika: German Espionage in Ireland in World War II*. Palo Alto: Pacific Book Publishers, 1977.

Cassar, George H. "Hamilton, Sir Ian Standish Monteith (1853–1947), army officer." In *Oxford Dictionary of National Biography*. New York: Oxford University Press, 2004–2010. Accessed 20 August 2010 at http://www.oxforddnb.com/index/33/101033668.

Cawley, Mary. "Trends in Population and Settlement in County Galway, 1971–1991." In *Galway: History and Society*, edited by Gerard Moran, 681–702. Dublin: Geography Publications, 1996.

Corcoran, Timothy. "How the Irish Language Can Be Revived." *Irish Monthly* 51 (1923): 26–30.

Cronin, Seán. *Frank Ryan, The Search for the Republic*. Dublin: Respol, 1980.

Delmer, Sefton. *Black Boomerang*. New York: Viking Press, 1962.

Deutsches Bühnen-Jahrbuch (Theatergeschichtliches Jahr-und Adressenbuch gegründet 1889), nos. 52–63. Berlin: Genossenschaft Deutscher Bühnen-Angehörige, 1941–1955.

Diller, Ansagar. *Rundfunkpolitik im Dritten Reich*. Vol. 2 of *Rundfunk in Deutschland*, edited by Hans Bausch. Munich: DTV, 1980.

Doerries, Reinhard R. *Prelude to the Easter Rising: Sir Roger Casement in Imperial Germany*. London: Routledge, 2000.

Douglas, R. M. "Ailtirí na hAiséirghe: Ireland's Fascist New Order." *History Ireland* 17, no. 5 (September/October 2009), 40–44.

———. *Architects of the Resurrection—Ailtirí na hAiséirgthe and the Fascist 'New Order' in Ireland*. Manchester: Manchester University Press, 2009.

Edwards, John Carter. *Berlin Calling*. New York: Praeger, 1991.

Ehrenreich, Eric. *The Nazi Ancestral Proof: Genealogy, Racial Science, and the Final Solution*. Bloomington: Indiana University Press, 2007.

Eicher, Thomas, Henning Rischbieter and Barbara Panse. *Theater im "Dritten Reich"—Theaterpolitik, Spielplanstruktur, NS-Dramatik*. Seelze-Velber: Kallmeyer, 2000.

Elborn, Geoffrey. *Francis Stuart: A Life*. Dublin: Raven Arts Press, 1990.

Evans, Richard. *Lying about Hitler*. New York: Basic Books, 2001.

———. *Irving vs. (1) Lipstadt and (2) Penguin Books: Expert Witness Report*. Available at http://www.phdn.org/negation/irving/EvansReport.pdf

Favre, Muriel. "Goebbels' 'phantastische Vorstellung'—Sinn und Zweck des O-Tons im Nationalsozialismus." In *Original/Ton. Zur Medien-Geschichte des O-Tons*, edited by Harun Maye, Cornelius Reiber, and Nikolaus Wegmann, 91–100. Constance: UVK, 2007.

Fennell, Deasún. "Agallamh le Róisín Ní Mheara" (interview). *Comhar 11* (November 1993), 14–15.

Bibliography

Fennell, Desmond. *Cutting to the Point.* Dublin: Liffey Press, 2003.
Festenberg, Nikolaus von. "Ein Mozart des Plaudertons." *Der Spiegel* 35 (24 August 1998), http://www.spiegel.de/spiegel/print/d-7968955.html.
Fischer, Joachim. *Das Deutschlandbild der Iren 1890–1939.* Heidelberg: Universitätsverlag, 2000.
———. "'. . . "thar lear" chomh hiomlán is chomh haoibhinn . . .' Aspekte des Deutschlandbildes in der zeitgenössischen irischsprachigen Literatur Irlands." In *Philologica et linguistica: Historia, luralitas, universitas: Festschrift für Helmut Humbach,* edited by Walter Bisang and Maria G. Schmidt, 385–411. Trier: Wissenschaftlicher Verlag, 2001.
Fisk, Robert. *In Time of War: Ireland, Ulster and the Price of Neutrality, 1939–45.* Dublin: Gill & MacMillan, 1996.
Freeden, Herbert. *Jüdisches Theater in Nazideuschland.* Frankfurt am Main: Ullstein, 1985.
Fromme, Franz. "Zwei verwandte Freiheitsbewegungen." In *Deutscher Aufstand: Die Revolution des Nachkrieges.* Stuttgart: Karl Hotzel, 1934.
Garfield, Brian. *The Meinertzhagen Mystery.* Washington, D.C.: Potomac Books, 2007.
Grimm, Jürgen, ed. *Französische Literaturgeschichte.* Stuttgart: Metzler, 1991.
Hamilton, Hugo. *The Speckled People.* London: Fourth Estate, 2003.
Hamilton, Ian B. *The Happy Warrior: A Life of Sir Ian Hamilton.* London: Cassell, London, 1966.
Heinz, Sabine, ed. *Symbole der Kelten.* Berlin: Schirner Verlag, 1997.
Hill, Bridget. *English Domestics in the Eighteenth Century.* Oxford: Oxford University Press, 1996.
Hinsley, F. H., and C. A. G. Simkins. *British Intelligence in the Second World War,* vol. 4. Cambridge: Cambridge University Press, 1990.
Hull, Mark M. *Irish Secrets: German Espionage in Wartime Ireland, 1939–1945.* Dublin: Irish Academic Press, 2003.
James, Rosaleen [as Ní Mheara, Róisín]. *Cé hÍ Seo Amuigh?* (Who Is She Outside?). Dublin: Coiscéim, 1992.
———. "The Cult of Patricius in Europe." *Seanchas Ard Mhacha* 16, no. 2 (1995): 83–92.
———. *Early Irish Saints in Europe: Their Sites and Their Stories.* Armagh: Cumann Seanchais Bhreifne, 2001.
———. "Franz Maulbertsch's Portrait of St. Patrick." *Seanchas Ard Mhacha* 20, no. 1 (2004): 24–26.
———. "Die heilige Brigid und ihr Kult im Salzburger Land." In *Virgil von Salzburg—Missionar und Gelehrter. Beiträge des Internationalen Symposiums vom 21–24. September 1984 in der Salzburger Residenz,* edited by Heinz Dopsch and Roswitha Juffinger, 381–83. Salzburg: Landesregierung, 1985.
———. *I gCéin is I gCóngar* (At Home and Abroad). Armagh: Seanchas Ard Mhacha, 2006.

———. *In Search of Irish Saints: The Peregrination in Christo.* Dublin: Four Courts Press, 1994.

———. "Saint Rónán of Brittany: A Path of Penitence Recalled." *Seanchas Ard Mhacha* 20, no. 1 (2004): 26–39.

———. "Sancta Brigida Abroad: A Tale of Two Cities." *Seanchas Ard Mhacha* 18, no. 1 (1999/2000): 49–65.

———. "The Wild Geese in Austria." *Seanchas Ard Mhacha* 16, no. 1 (1994): 76–92.

———, and Ó Súilleabháin, Eoghan. "Faobhar ar a nguth." *Comhar* 52, no. 6 (June 1993), 12–19.

James, Rosaleen [as O'Mara, Nora], ed. *Der König der Bäume. Das altirische Epos von der Ekstase des Suibhne (Buile Shuibhne).* München: Dianus-Trikont, 1985.

———. "Pádraig Pearse." In *Irische Freiheitskämpfer,* edited by Ruth Weiland, 80–95. Berlin: August Scherl Nachfolger, 1940.

James, Rosaleen [as O'Mara, Róisín]. "Chú Chullain of Muirthemne." *Dublin Magazine* 31, no.3 (July–September) 1955, 7.

Joyce, P. W. *Old Irish Folk Music and Songs: A Collection of 842 Irish Airs and Songs Hitherto Unpublished.* Dublin: Hodges, Figgis & Co., 1909.

Kamm, Walter. "Die Deutschen Europasender." *Welt-Rundfunk,* no. 3–4 (April/June 1944): 75–80.

Keogh, Niall. *Con Cremin, Ireland's Wartime Diplomat.* Dublin: Mercier Press, 2006.

Kershaw, Ian. *Making Friends with Hitler.* New York: Penguin, 2004.

Kiely, Kevin. *Francis Stuart: Artist and Outcast.* Dublin: Liffey Press, 2007.

Lee, Celia. *A Soldier's Wife: Jean, Lady Hamilton 1861–1941.* Chatham, Kent: Privately published, 2001.

Lee, John. *A Soldier's Life: General Sir Ian Hamilton, 1853–1947.* London: Macmillan, 2000.

Loringhoven, Bernd Freytag von. *In the Bunker with Hitler.* New York: Pegasus Books, 2007.

Lovell, Mary S. *The Sisters: The Saga of the Mitford Family.* New York: W. W. Norton, 2001.

Lucas, Richard. *Axis Sally: The American Voice of Nazi Germany.* Philadelphia: Casemate, 2010.

Lynam, Shevawn. "A Change of Outlook." In *An Aran Reader,* edited by Breandán Ó hEithir and Ruairí Ó hEithir, 273–279. Dublin: Lilliput Press, 1991.

Mac an Bheatha, Proinsias. *I Dtreo na Gréine.* Westport: Foilseacháin Naisiúnta Teoranta, 1988.

———. *Téann Buille le Cnámh.* Westport: Foilseacháin Naisiúnta Teoranta, 1983.

———. *Téid Focal le Gaoith.* Dublin: Foilseacháin Naisiúnta Teoranta, 1967.

Bibliography

Mac Aodha, Breandán S. *An tSuirbhéireacht ar Ghaeltacht na Gaillimhe / The Galway Gaeltacht Survey.* Galway: Social Sciences Research Centre, University College, 1969.

Marks, Lara. *Metropolitan Maternity: Material and Infant Welfare Services in Early Twentieth Century London.* Amsterdam: Rodopi, 1996.

McBride, Maud Gonne. *Im Dienste einer Königin: Eine Frau kämpft für Irland*, edited by Ruth Weiland, transl. Ruth Weiland. Bremen: Schünemann, 1939.

MacDonogh, Giles. *1938: Hitler's Gamble.* New York: Basic Books, 2009.

Mac Eoin, Uinseann. *The IRA in the Twilight Years: 1923–1948.* Dublin: Argenta, 1997.

Mac Liammóir, Micheál. *Ceo Meala Lá Seaca.* Dublin: Sáirséal agus Dill, 1952.

Mac Murchaidh, Ciarán. "How I Discovered Irish or How Irish Discovered Me." In *"Who Needs Irish?" Reflections on the Importance of the Irish Language Today.* Dublin: Veritas, 2004.

Materialien zu Becketts Endspiel. Frankfurt: Suhrkamp, 1968.

Maume, Patrick. "Ó Cuinneagáin, Gearóid Seán Caoimhín." In *Dictionary of Irish Biography*, edited by James McGuire and James Quinn. Cambridge: Cambridge University Press, 2009. Online edition, http://dib.cambridge.org/.

Misch, Rochus. *Hitler's Last Witness: The Memoirs of Hitler's Bodyguard.* South Yorkshire: Frontline Books, 2014.

Mühlhausen, Ludwig. *Die kornische Geschichte von den drei guten Ratschlägen.* Berlin: Deutsche Gesellschaft für keltische Studien, 1938.

Nic Dhiarmada, Bríona. "*Cé hí Seo Amuigh?* Cuimhní Cinn ag Róisín Ní Mheara." *Comhar* 52, no. 2 (February 1993), 18.

Ní Chonchubhair, Marie. "Faighimís réidh leis an mbac seo ar shaoirse cainte!" *Comhar* 52, no. 5 (June 1993), 10–12.

Ní hAirmhí, Mairéad. "Pilgrimage to Germany, 29 June–8 July." *Seanchas Ard Mhacha* 13, no. 2 (1989): 298–301.

Ní hUigín, Dorothy. "Craobh na hAiséirí, Glún na Buaidhe agus bunú *Inniú*." *Irisleabhar Mhá Nuad* (1995): 74–110.

Ní Mhunghaile, Lesa. "Tarlach Ó hUid." In *Dictionary of Irish Biography*, edited by James McGuire and James Quinn. Cambridge: Cambridge University Press, 2009.

"Nua-Chinsirí na Gaeilge-Linn!" *Comhar* 52, no. 3 (March 1993), 7.

Odenwald, Florian. *Der nazistische Kampf gegen das "Undeutsche" in Theater und Film 1920–1945.* Munich: Herbert Utz, 2006.

O'Donnell, James P. *The Bunker.* New York: Da Capo Press, 2001.

O'Donoghue, David. *The Devil's Deal: The IRA, Nazi Germany and the Double Life of Jim O'Donovan.* Dublin: New Island, 2010.

———. *Hitler's Irish Voices.* Belfast: Beyond the Pale, 1998.

Ó Fiaich, Tomás. *Gaelscrínte san Eorap.* Dublin: Foilseacháin Ábhair Spioradálta, 1986.

Ó hEithir, Breandán and Ruairí, eds. *An Aran Reader*. Dublin: Liliput Press, 1991.
Ó hUid, Tarlach. *Faoi ghlas*. Westport: Foilseacháin Naisiúnta Teoranta, 1985.
Olusoga, David, and Casper W. Erichsen. *The Kaiser's Holocaust: Germany's Forgotten Genocide and the Colonial Roots of Nazism*. London: Faber and Faber, 2010.
Ó Muirí, Réamonn. "1300-Jahrfeier des Martyriums der Frankenapostel." *Seanchas Ard Mhacha* 13, no. 2 (1989), 293–96.
———. "*In Search of Irish Saints* by Róisín Ní Mheara." *Seanchas Ardmhacha* 16, no. 1 (1994): 292–94.
———."Review [of Ní Mheara's *Early Irish Saints in Europe*]." *Seanchas Ard Mhacha* 19, no. 1 (2002): 255–56.
———. "Tomás Ó Fiaich." In *Dictionary of Irish Biography*, edited by James McGuire and James Quinn. Cambridge: Cambridge University Press, 2009. Online edition, http://dib.cambridge.org/quicksearch.do#.
Ó Siadhail, Pádraig. *Stair Drámaíocht na Gaeilge 1900–1970*. Inverin: Cló Iar-Chonnachta, 1993.
O'Sullivan, Donal. *Songs of the Irish*. Dublin: Brown & Nolan, 1960.
Pryce-Jones, David. *Unity Mitford: An Enquiry into Her Life and the Frivolity of Evil*. New York: Dial Press, 1977.
Reitsch, Hannah. *Fliegen, mein Leben*. Munich: Herbig Verlag, 1998.
Rosenbaum, Ron. *Explaining Hitler: The Search for the Origins of His Evil*. New York: Random House, 1998.
Roth, Andreas. "Francis Stuart's Broadcasts from Germany, 1942–44: Some New Evidence." *Irish Historical Studies* 32, no. 127 (May, 2001), 408–22.
Schroeder, Herbert. *Ein Sender erobert die Herzen der Welt: Das Buch vom deutschen Kurzwellenrundfunk*. Essen: Essener Verlagsanstalt, 1940.
———."Wir rufen Europa!" *Reichs-Rundfunk* 1943/44, H. 7 (October 1943), 139–42.
Seidel, Gill. *Holocaust Denial: Antisemitism, Racism and the New Right*. Dublin: Beyond the Pale Publications, 1986.
Sereny, Gitta. *The Healing Wound: Experiences and Reflections, Germany, 1938–2001*. New York: W. W. Norton.
Sherratt, Yvonne. *Hitler's Philosophers*. New Haven, Conn.: Yale University Press, 2014.
Steinweis, Alan E. *Art, Ideology, and Economics in Nazi Germany: The Reich Chambers of Music, Theater, and the Visual Arts*. Chapel Hill: University of North Carolina Press, 1996.
Stephan, Enno. "Die Vergessene Episode: Deutsche Agenten im irischen Untergrundkampf" (unpublished manuscript, used with the author's permission).
———. *Geheimauftrag Irland*. Hamburg: Gerhard Stalling Verlag, 1961.
Stuart, Francis. *Black List, Section H*. Penguin, London, 1997.

Bibliography

———. "Einleitung." In *Irische Freiheitskämpfer*, edited by Ruth Weiland, 7–16. Berlin: August Scherl Nachfolger, 1940.
Synge, John Millington. *The Aran Islands,* edited by Robin Skelton. Oxford: Oxford University Press, 1979.
Thompson, Dorothy. "Who Goes Nazi?" *Harper's Magazine*, August 1941. http://harpers.org/archive/1941/08/0020122.
Thurlow, Richard. *Fascism in Modern Britain*. Sutton: Stroud, 2001.
Uehling, Peter. *Karajan: Eine Biographie*. Hamburg: Rowohlt Verlag, 2008.
United States Holocaust Memorial Museum. "Vienna," *Holocaust Encyclopedia*. Last updated January 29, 2016. http://www.ushmm.org/wlc/en/article.php?ModuleId=10005452.
Vaessen, Kurt. "Aus der Arbeit der Deutschen Europasender." In *Reichs-Rundfunk* 1941/42, H. 13 (14 September 1941), 254–55.
Walsh, John. *Contests and Contexts: The Irish Language and Ireland's Socio-Economic Development*. Bern: Peter Lang, 2011.
Weiland, Ruth, ed. *Irische Freiheitskämpfer*. Berlin: August Scherl Nachfolger, 1940.
West, Nigel, ed. *The Guy Liddell Diaries*. Vol. 1, *1939–1942*. London: Routledge, 2005.
Wills, Clair, *That Neutral Island: A Cultural History of Ireland during the Second World War*. London: Harvard University Press, 2007.

Newspapers and Films

"An Durlas and Its Place in Galway." *Galway Advertiser*, 7 January 1971, 3.
"An lá ar osclaíodh Musaem na nOileán." *Inniu*, 10 August 1973, 1.
"Appointments in Diocese of Tuam." *Irish Times*, 19 July 1973, 4.
Bielenberg, Christabel, and Charlotte O'Connor. "Aosdána and Francis Stuart." *Irish Times*, 10 December 1997, 15.
Burroughs, George. "Home-Spun White Power Is Taking over in Two Aran Islands." *Irish Times*, 13 September 1973, 1.
Candida. "An Irishwoman's Diary." *Irish Times*, 21 July 1975, 9.
"Cardinal Urges *Inniu* Support." *Irish Times*, 6 December 1983, 3.
"Corrections and Clarifications." *Irish Times*, 17 February 1993, 10.
de Bhréadún, Deaglán. "Cumann Merriman Takes to the Road." *Irish Times*, 26 August 1988, 7.
Downing, Eugene. "Frank Ryan." *Irish Times*, 4 March 1993, 13.
Doyle, Diarmuid. "Taylor Says It Would Be 'Scandalous' If Irish Language Book Gets Grant-Aid." *Sunday Tribune*, 31 January 1993, A9.
Doyle, Leonard. "Dublin Gave Subsidy to Anti-Semitic Publication." *The Independent*, 8 February 1993, 3.

Bibliography

Finlan, Michael. "Durlas an Dochais." *Irish Times*, 13 March 1973, 6.
———. "Minister Calls on Aran Islanders." *Irish Times*, 3 August 1973, 8.
Gillespie, Elgy. "This Ireland: Inishmaan Museum." *Irish Times*, 2 September 1975, 8.
———. "What's Happening Out West in the Arts." *Irish Times*, 29 July 1975, A7.
Glaoch ón Tríú Reich (Call from the Third Reich). Mind the Gap Films, 2013 (broadcast by TG4, Winter 2012). Available on YouTube with subtitles, https://www.youtube.com/watch?v=MILibMEWu_Q, retrieved 29 June 2016.
Hayes, Kieran. "Ahead of Her Time." *Galway Advertiser*, 29 January 2004, 33.
"Hitler Lent Me a Tooth-Brush." *Sunday Referee*, 7 August 1938.
"Iarsmalann do Inis Meáin." *Inniu*, 6 July 1973, 1.
James, Rosaleen [as Ní Mheara, Róisín]. "Litir ón Eoraip" (Letter from Europe). *Inniu*, (first and last articles) 11 November 1977, 9; 8 August 1980, 6.
———. "Comóradh 1200 Fheargail Naofa." *Inniu*, 4 November 1983, 3.
———. "Comórfar Feragal N.[aofa] in Salzburg i 1984." *Inniu*, 28 October 1983, 6.
———. "Gaeil Ghorma." *Inniu*, 12 March 1982, 6, 12.
Laytner, Ron. "The First Astronaut." *Deseret News*, 19 February 1981.
"The Kindergarten through Welsh." *Rosc*, 20 November 1972, 2.
Mac an Bheatha, Proinsias. "Athchuairt ar Inis Meáin." *Inniu*, 3 August 1973, 5.
Mac Aonghusa, Proinsias. "Ar an tSaoil." *Anois*, 19–20, December 1992, 11.
Mac Coille, Cathal. "Lessons Not Yet Learned." *Sunday Tribune*, 24 January 1993, B6.
Mac Dhubhghaill, Uinseann. "Tuarascáil-Agóid in aisce." *Irish Times*, 3 February 1993, 9.
Mac Síomóin, Tomás. "Beocheist: Seans nua do na leabhair Ghaeilge." *Irish Times*, 29 August 1988, 12.
"Marriages." *The Times*, 8 December 1947, 7.
"Minister Denies he let down Inishmaan." *Irish Times*, 18 August 1973, 13.
"Minister Rejects Aran Criticism." *Connacht Tribune*, 24 August 1973, 1.
"Museum for Aran." *Connacht Tribune*, 27 July 1973, 1.
"Museum on Inishmaan." *Connacht Tribune*, 3 August 1973, 29.
Ó Conghaola, Seán. "Gan 'ghníomh miorúilteach' beidh Inis Meáin féin ina Musaem." *Inniu*, 10 August 1973, 8.
Ó Drisceoil, Proinsias. "A Monarchial Republican." *Irish Times*, 13 February, 1993, A9.
O'Nolan, Brian [Myles na gCopaleen]. "Cruiskeen Lawn." *Irish Times*, 13 December 1943, 3.
Ó Nualláin, Ciarán, ed. "Eagarthóir." *Inniu*, 10 August 1973, 8.
O'Reilly, John. "I Was a Spy in Ireland." *Sunday Dispatch*, 17 August 1952, 9.
"Oscailt Mhusaem Árann." *Connacht Tribune*, 10 August 1973, 46.

Bibliography

Ó Snodaigh, Pádraig. "Dublin Gave Subsidy to Anti-Semitic Publication." *Irish Independent*, 8 February 1993.
"Publisher Receives Grant Aid from the Arts Council." *Irish Times*, 17 February 1993, 10.
Quinn, Bob. "Salzburg Commemorates Irish Monk." *Irish Times*, 18 October 1984, 8.
"300 People Visit Aran Museum." *Connacht Sentinel*, 23 October 1973, 12.
Titley, Alan. "Politically Incorrect." *Books Ireland*, March 1993, 57.
"Tuairim." *Irish Times*, 24 November 1993, 11.
"Viennese Treasures Have a Strong Irish Legacy." *Irish Times*, 16 August 2005.
White, Declan. "Minister Is 'Blacked' by Newsmen." *Irish Independent*, 3 August 1973, 1.

Online Sources

Breathnach, Diarmaid, and Máire Ní Mhurchú. "Ó Domhnalláin, Pádraig/Ní Dhomhnalláin, Máire." *Beathaisnéis*. Accessed 24 June 2016. http://www.ainm.ie/Bio.aspx?ID=196.
———."Ó Nualláin, Ciarán." *Beathaisnéis*. Accessed 24 June 2016. http://www.ainm.ie/Bio.aspx?ID=1748.
———."Ó Riada, Seán." *Beathaisnéis*. Accessed 24 June 2016. http://www.ainm.ie/Bio.aspx?ID=779.
"Finding Aids for Schools Programmes (1947–2007)." *Bayerischer Rundfunk*. Accessed 4 July 2013. http://www.br.de/unternehmen/inhalt/geschichte-des-br/uebersicht-findbuecher-hoerfunk100.html.
Galsworthy, John. "Windows." *Project Gutenberg*. Accessed 29 June 2016. http://www.gutenberg.org/files/4766/4766-h/4766-h.htm.
"Geschichte der Universitätsbibliothek." Humboldt Universität, Berlin. 2013. Accessed 20 June 2016. http://www.ub.hu-berlin.de/ueber-uns/geschichte.
Irish Parliamentary Debates, with Information on the Allocation of 1987 Lottery Funds. Accessed 24 June 2016. http://oireachtasdebates.oireachtas.ie/debates%20authoring/debateswebpack.nsf/takes/dail1988052400040?opendocument.
"Irving v. Lipstadt, transcripts." *Holocaust Denial on Trial*. Emory University. Accessed 20 July 2016. http://www.hdot.org/en/trial/transcripts/.
Mende, Martin. "Die Geschichte Berlins." Accessed 21 April 2006. http://www.diegeschichteberlins.de/forum/download_thread.php?site=vfdgb&bn=vfdgb_forumzurgeschichteberlins&thread=1145554681.
Reichgesetzblatt, Pt. 1, 661, 22 September 1933. Accessed 24 June 2016. http://avalon.law.yale.edu/imt/2082-ps.asp.
Reichgesetzblatt, Pt. 1, 247, 15 March 1938. Accessed 24 June 2016. http://avalon.law.yale.edu/imt/11-29-45.asp.

Bibliography

"Róisín Ní Mheara-Vinard." *Dáil Éireann* 38 (24 May 1988). http://debates.oireachtas.ie/dail/1988/05/24/00040.asp.

"Verordnung über die Aufgaben des Reichsministeriums für Volksaufklärung und Propaganda vom 30. Juni 1933." Accessed 24 June 2016. http://www.documentarchiv.de/ns/propaganda_vo.html.

"Vincent Coyle." *BBC People's War Archive*. Accessed 19 March 2011. http://www.bbc.co.uk/history/ww2peopleswar/stories/51/a3954251.shtml.

Index

Abbey of St. Moling, 123
Abwehr (German military intelligence), 41–57, 72, 77, 82, 109, 151, 162n7, 163n10; Abwehr II, 42–46, 53, 56, 162n3, 165n21; Abwehr III, 46
Achill Island, 173n30
Aktion Reinhard, 160n37, 181n65
Allied War Crimes Commission, 96
Amery, John, 97
Andersen, Lale, 138
An Durlas (The Fortress), 106–7
Anglo-German Fellowship, 32–33
Anschluss, 27, 29, 30, 148, 160n37
Aosdána, 151
Argonne Offensive, 50
Armagh Historical Society (Seanchas Ard Mhacha), 134
Atlantis (German raider), 99
Aud (German freighter), 55
Auschwitz-Birkenau, 128, 144, 164n4
Auswärtiges Amt (AA; German Foreign Office), 55, 77

Bad Arolsen, 121–22, 129, 176n39
Bad Godesberg, 36
Bailey, Daniel, 55
Baur, Hans, 93
Beneš, Edvard, 36

Berchtesgaden, 34, 36
Bergen-Belsen, 121, 123, 129, 132, 139, 144
Bewley, Charles, 97
Bielenberg, Christabel, 151–52
Black List, Section H (Francis Stuart), 48, 131
Blair, James, 78
Blomberg, Werner von, 161n48
Blut und Boden, 110
Bord na Leabhar Gaeilge, 133–36, 179nn28–29
Brandenburg Regiment, 50–51
British Free Corps, 95–96, 165n20
British Legion, 12–14, 32–34, 36
British Security Service (MI5), 4
British Union of Fascists (BUF), 25, 80, 99
Bromberg (Bydgoszcz), 39
Buchenwald, 122, 131–32, 139, 148
BUF. *See* British Union of Fascists
Buí, Seán, 35
Buile Shuibhne (Mad Sweeney), 112, 124
Bund der Österreichischen Bühnenkünstler (Association of Austrian Stage Artists), 30
Burgos prison, 50
Burgtheater, 30

195

Index

Canaris, William, 46, 50, 52–53, 82, 163n17
Carraroe, 126
Casement, Sir Roger, 55, 81, 170n4
Cé hÍ Seo Amuigh? (Who Is She Outside?), 5, 7, 18, 49, 70, 103, 109–10, 113, 121–22, 130, 132–34, 140, 142, 149, 152–53, 156n9, 175n31, 178n14
Chamberlain, Sir Neville, 27, 36
"Chú Chullain of Muirthemne" (poem), 104
Clann na Gael, 164n3
Clissmann, Helmut, 47, 50, 56
Codd, John, 57, 165n18
Coiscéim (pubisher), 130, 134, 150, 178n5
Comhar, 135–37
Comiskey (a maid of Lady Hamilton), 17, 158n26
CROWCASS (Central Registry of War Criminals and Security Suspects) Consolidated Wanted Lists, 96
Cumann Seanchais Ard Mhacha, 127
Custume Barracks, Athlone, 47

Dáil Éireann, 155n10
Daladier, Édouard, 27, 36
Daly, Helen, 24–25
de Fréine, Seán, 134
de Valera, Eamon, 50, 72, 165n16
denazification, 88, 96, 171n6
Der Fuchs von Glenarvon (film), 90
Der König der Bäume, 123
Der Stürmer, 142
Deutsch-Englische Gesellschaft (German counterpart of Anglo-German Fellowship), 33
Deutscher Akademischer Austauchdienst (German Academic Exchange Service), 47

Deutscher Bühnenverein, 30
Deutscher Kurzwellensender (German shortwave transmitter), 78
Deutsches Bühnen-Jahrbuch, 160n43, 162n13
Deutschlandsender, 170n5
Devers, Jacob, 96
Dowling, Robert, 55
Doyle, Leonard, 134–36
Drahtloser Dienst (wireless service), 54
Dublin Magazine, 104

"Éamonn an Chnoic" (Ned of the Hill; ballad), 132, 156n9
Early Irish Saints in Europe (Rosaleen James), 125, 127, 141, 149
Eichmann, Adolf, 29
Eidlitz, Karl, 25, 160n21
Einsatzgruppe A, 29
Éire, 4, 71
Emergency Powers (Defence) Regulations Act, 1939, 98
Emig, Marianne, 45
Entnazifizierung, 88
Evans, Richard, 145

Fegelein, Hermann, 92–93, 146, 170n1
Fennell, Desmond, 138–40
Filmprüfstelle (film review board), 89
Fischer, Joachim, 105, 140
"Florian Geyer," 8th SS Cavalry Division, 92
Foilseachán Náisiúnta Teoranta (FNT; publishing house), 131, 178n4
Foreign Office (German Auswärtiges Amt), 55–56, 77
Fragebogen (questionnaire), 86
Franco, Francisco, 50
Fremdenpass, 42, 100

Index

French, Sir John, 11
Friesack (village), 56; and Camp, 99
Fritz Rémond Theater (Frankfurt), 104
Fromme, Franz, 43–45, 53, 72
Frowein, Lieutenant, 88
Führerbunker, 92, 170n3

Gaeilgeoir (Irish speaker and Irish language enthusiast), 131
Gaelic League, 107, 114, 116, 131, 135–36, 172n19
Gaelscrínte san Eoraip (Irish Shrines in Europe), 124–25
Gaeltacht (Irish-speaking regions of Ireland), 8, 72, 76, 107, 116, 133, 179n24
Galsworthy, John, 104
Gärtner, Dieter, 52
Geisler, SS-Obersturmführer, 83
Gelöbnis treuester Gefolgschaft (Vow of Faithful Obedience), 158n3
General Post Office (GPO), 73
Gerbalke, Frau, 19, 21
German Military Intelligence (IIIb), 55
Germanentum, 110
Gillars, Mildred "Axis Sally", 79–81, 100, 168nn7–8
Glaoch ón Tríú Reich, 108, 174n12
Goebbels, Josef, 28, 39, 88, 93, 119, 160n27, 180n44
Görtz, Hermann, 4, 44, 48, 52–54, 99, 109, 162n6
Gottbegnadeten-Liste (God-gifted list), 88
Gottschalk, Joachim, 88
Großdeutscher Rundfunk, 169n15
GRU (Soviet military intelligence), 166n9
Günsche, Otto, 93

Haller, Kurt, 4, 41, 48, 56, 82, 109
Hamilton, Christian (Ian Hamilton's father), 10
Hamilton, Corinna (Ian Hamilton's mother), 10
Hamilton, Sir Ian Standish Montieth, 10–12, 14–16, 31–36, 49, 83, 90, 96, 156n8, 157n2, 157n15, 166n1
Hamilton, Jean (Muir) (Ian Hamilton's wife), 11, 13–19, 21–22, 24–27, 34, 58–59, 104, 146, 157n11, 157n15, 158n18, 166n1
Hartmann, Hans, 73, 76–78, 81–82, 86
Harwich, 45
Higgins, Joe, 134
Hilton, Susan (aliases: Susan Sweney and Ann Tower), 78, 99–100
Högl, Obersturmbannführer, 92
Holman, Phyllis, 13–14, 157n4
Horney, Brigitte, 59, 88

I gCéin is i gCóngar (At Home and Abroad), 7, 103, 141, 149–50
In Search of Irish Saints (Rosaleen James), 125, 149
Inis Meáin, 106, 139–41
Inishmaan, 107–8, 110–11
Inniu (Today), 106, 112–16, 123, 126, 129, 131–34, 138–40, 148, 175n21
Intimes Theater Munich, 105
Irische Freiheitskämpfer (Ruth Weiland), 74, 102
Irisches Tagebuch (Heinrich Böll), 108
Irish Republican Army (IRA), 45, 52
Irland-Redaktion, 76, 78, 81–82, 86–87, 89, 93, 100, 104
Irlandreferat, 73
Irlands Kampf um die Freiheit (Franz Fromme), 44
Irving, David, 128, 133, 145

Index

Jacobi, Nadejda (Rosaleen James's daughter), 54, 105
Jakobi, Roderich (Rosaleen James's son), 7
Joyce, William "Lord Haw-Haw", 79, 98, 100

Kerney, Leopold, 50
Kershaw, Sir Ian, 34
Khan, Ali, 95
Kitchener, Lord Horatio, 11
Kleines Theater am Zoo, 105
Klöpfer, Eugen, 88
Knight, Harry (Rosaleen James's adopted brother), 15–16, 22, 27, 58, 157n15, 158n22
Kraft durch Freude (KdF), 22
Kramer, Joseph, 121, 129
Kristallnacht, 28

Laragh Castle, 48
Legion of St. George, 95, 97
Lichnowsky, Prince Karl Max, 18
Liebenau, 100
Lipstadt, Deborah, 128, 145
Litir ón Eoraip (Letter from Europe), 148
Loyson, Susan (character in Francis Stuart's *Black List*), 48, 59
Lullenden, 15, 157n17

Mac an Bheatha, Proinsias, 8, 114–15, 131
Mac an tSaoi, Máire, 151
Mac Aonghusa, Proinsias, 131, 135–37
Mac Coille, Cathal, 133, 135
Mac Eoin, Gearóid, 108
Mac Liammóir, Micheál (né Alfred Willmore), 105
Mac Síomóin, Tomás, 135
Mangan, James, 14, 104
Marwede, Friedrich, 41
Mein Leben für Irland (film), 89–90

Meinertzhagen, Richard, 32
Meissner, Gertrud, 59, 86, 101
MI5 (British intelligence/British Security Service), 4, 14, 16, 95, 97, 100
Ministry of Propaganda and Public Enlightenment (Reichsministerium für Volksaufklärung und Propaganda; RMVP), 30
Mitford, Diana, 19, 23–25
Mitford, Unity, 19, 23–25
Monteith, Robert, 55
Mosley, Sir Oswald, 25, 80
Moyse, Paul, 53
Muir, Nadejda (Rosaleen James's aunt), 17, 58
Muir, Sir Kay, 58
Mulkerrin, Maura Paudeen, 108
Mullally, Liam, 73, 78, 91
Munthe, Axel, 138
Mussolini, Benito, 36

Nic Dhiarmada, Bríona, 132
Ní Chonchubhair, Marie, 135
Ní Dhomhnalláin, Máirín, 130–31
Ní hUallacháin, Caitlín, 49
Ní hUigin, Dr. Dorothy, 123
Ní Mheara-Vinard, Róisín, 103, 125, 127
Nostitz, Frau, 21
Nostitz, Helene von, 158n3
Nuremberg Trials, 33, 148
Nürnberg Laws, 28, 30, 32, 143

Obed, Henry, 52
Obersalzberg, 34
Ó Coigligh, Ciarán, 132
Ó Cuig, Micheál, 131
Ó Dochartaigh, Seán, 18
Ó Domhnalláin, Gaeilgeoir Pádraig, 131
O'Donovan, Jim, 53
Ó Drisceoil, Proinsias, 136

Index

Ó Duilearga, Séamus, 167n10
Ó Fiaich, Tomás, 112, 123, 127, 148
Ó hAonghusa, Traolach, 106
Old Bailey (Central Criminal Court of England and Wales), 45
Ó Muircheartaigh, Aogán, 132
O'Neill, Sean, 86
Operation Dove (Unternehmen Taube), 53
Operation Innkeeper (Unternehmen Gastwirt), 57
Operation Lobster (Unternehmen Hummer), 51
Operation Sea Lion, 42–43, 47, 51
Ó Raghailligh, T., 137
O'Reilly, John, 4; John Francis O'Reilly, 81
Ó Riada, Seán, 176n55
Ó Sé, Seán, 126
Ó Snodaigh, Pádraig, 132, 134, 150, 155n5
Osteria Bavaria (restaurant, Munich), 25
Ó Súilleabháin, Eoghan, 137–39
O'Sullivan, Séamus, 104

Parnell Square, 26
Pearse, Pádraig, 72–73
Peto, Rosemary, 24
Phaidí, Máire, 108, 138
Pillar of Cloud (Francis Stuart), 48
Pryce-Jones, David, 150
Pyper, Gerhard, 84–85

Quinn, Bob, 126

Radió Éireann, 104
Reading, Lord, 31–32
Redesdale, Lady Sydney, 24
Redesdale, Lord, 23
Reichsdeutsch, 56
Reichskulturkammer (Cultural Chamber), 30, 37
Reichsministerium für Volksaufklärung und Propaganda (RMVP), 77
Reichs-Rundfunk-Gesellschaft (Broadcasting Corporation), 79, 168n15
Reichssicherheitshauptamt (RSHA; Security Main Office), 166n8
Reichstheaterkammer (RTK; Theater Chamber), 30–31, 37, 41, 89, 163n13
Reinhard, SS-Gruppenführer, 33
Reitsch, Hanna, 118, 138
Rekowski, Carl, 52
Republican Congress (within IRA), 49
Ribbentrop, Joachim von, 33
Robinson, President Mary, 135
Rosenstock, Gabriel, 140
Rossa, O'Donovan, 74
Rote Kapelle (Soviet spy network), 59, 166n8
Rothermere, Lord, 33
Royal Munster Fusiliers, 55
Royal Welsh Fusiliers, 57
RSHA. *See* Reichssicherheitshauptamt
Rundfunkarchiv, 40
Rundfunkhaus (broadcasting center), 40, 59, 76, 78–79, 84–85, 179n43. *See also* Reichs-Rundfunk-Gesellschaft; Großdeutscher Rundfunk
Russell, Seán, 52, 56, 82, 138
Russo-Japanese War, 11
Ryan, Frank, 49, 51, 53, 56, 59, 138

Scarden, W. J., 95
Schulze-Boysen, Harro, 59, 166n9
Schulze-Boysen, Libertas, 59, 166n9
Seanchas Ard Mhacha, 127, 134
Seidel, Gill, 145
Sereny, Gitta, 28
Sicherheitsdienst (SD; SS intelligence service), 57, 83, 118

Sinn Féin, 55
SLB3 (special section within MI5), 95
Soldatensender Calais, 93
Spende Künstlerdank, 88
Spooner, R. W. (Major), 95
SS Kemendine, 99
Stahlecker, Walter, 29
Stalag III B, Lannesdorf, 57, 165n19
Stalag XX A (301), 56, 165n15
St. Audeons, 26
Stephenson, John (later Sir John), 95, 170n4
St. Kilian, 125–26
St. Moling, Abbey, 123
Stringer, Frank, 57, 165n20, 166n23
Stuart, Francis, 44, 47–49, 54, 56–57, 59, 70, 73, 75–76, 86, 97, 101–2, 114, 135, 151, 156n7, 169n25
Stuart, Iseult Gonne (daughter of Maude Gonne; Francis Stuart's wife), 47, 86, 101, 163n19

Taibhdhearc Theater, Galway, 131
Taylor, Mervyn, 134
Theaterabteilung (Theater Department), 30
Theresienstadt, 88
Thomas, Michele, 97
Thompson, Dorothy, 20
Tirah Campaign, 10–11
Tirranna, 99
Titley, Alan, 135, 137

Tomás Ó Fiaich Memorial Library and Archive, 127
Treachery Act of 1940, 98
Treason Act of 1351, 98
Tributh, Herbert, 52
Türmer, Dr., 40

U-65 (German submarine), 53
UFA Studios, 27, 89
Uí Ghoill, Nóirín, 140
Unternehmen Gastwirt (Operation Innkeeper), 57
Unternehmen Hummer (Operation Lobster), 51
Unternehmen Taube (Operation Dove), 53

Vansittart, Robert, 23
Veesenmayer, Edmund, 52, 56, 82, 164n4
Volksdeutsch, 56

Wagner, Winifred, 118–20, 138
Wandsworth Prison, 98, 157n10
Wannsee Conference, 160n37, 181n65
Warner, Colonel, 22
Warnock, William, 82, 90, 147
Weber-Drohl, Ernst, 52
Weiland, Ruth, 70, 102, 138
Wilhelmi, Dr., 85, 169n17

Zucca, Rita, 168n7

www.ingramcontent.com/pod-product-compliance
Lightning Source LLC
Chambersburg PA
CBHW020838160426
43192CB00007B/705